BILL AND HIS BROTHERS

ADDICTIONS,
from the Stigma of Vice
to Scientific Truths
With a critical perspective
on the Hidden Realities
that have fueled a slow
tragedy, claiming
more lives than war

MARIA FRANCESCA BENE

DEDICATION

"Stop it! Where there's a will, there's a way."
"It's all about self-control."
"You're just weak."
"If you really loved me, you'd quit…"
"You just need to grow up and take responsibility."
"Why don't you think about the people around you?"
"You don't have enough willpower."
"It's not that hard, just say no!"
"You chose to start; now stop!"
"You should be ashamed—you're selfish and only think about yourself."
"You have a problem because you want to have it."
"With all the help you've been given, there's no excuse for not stopping."

If you've ever heard or said one of these phrases, this book is for you.

This work is dedicated to everyone who has faced, or is still facing, the struggle against addiction—and the ignorance, still all too common, about the true nature of this disease.

To their families, to those who didn't make it, and to those who are still fighting.

May this book help open minds and light the way forward.

INTRODUCTION

This book was born out of a desire to challenge the stigma that still surrounds addiction in the first quarter of the 21st century. Too often, even among professionals, addiction is viewed as a vice, a moral failing, or a lack of willpower.

Addictions to substances—like alcohol, illegal drugs, prescription medications, and nicotine—or behaviors—like gambling, internet and technology use, compulsive shopping, and sex or relationship dependency—are fully recognized as diseases. Globally, organizations dedicated to classifying illnesses that affect both individuals and society acknowledge them as such.

These include the World Health Organization (WHO), which lists addiction in its *International Classification of Diseases (ICD)*; the American Psychiatric Association (APA); the *Diagnostic and Statistical Manual of Mental Disorders (DSM)*; the National Institute on Drug Abuse (NIDA); the World Psychiatric Association (WPA); the European Monitoring Centre for Drugs and Drug Addiction (EMCDDA); the International Society of Addiction Medicine (ISAM); the American Society of Addiction Medicine (ASAM); and the World Federation of Neurology (WFN), among others.

I know this list might seem dull, but it's important to make one thing clear: these are not amateurs.

Yet, even today, people struggling with addiction still hear phrases like:

"Stop it! Where there's a will, there's a way."
"It's just a matter of self-control."
"You're simply weak."
"You just need to grow up and take responsibility."
"Why don't you think about the people around you?"
"You don't have enough willpower."
"It's not that hard; just say no."
"You chose to start; now stop!"

"You should be ashamed—you're selfish and only think about yourself."
"You have a problem because you want it."
"With all the help you've been given, you have no excuse for not quitting."

And so on.

It's not just the burden of addiction, but also the sting of blame and shame. No one would dream of telling a cancer patient, "Shame on you!" Or saying to someone with pneumonia, "Stop coughing, and show some willpower!" **Illness is not a choice.** You can choose to follow treatment, but you can't choose to simply erase the disease. Even the decision to seek help begins with recognizing the problem as real and worth fighting against.

Many people who have successfully escaped the grip of addiction (and I've spoken to plenty!) say that realizing addiction is a disease changed everything. It allowed them to redirect the energy wasted on guilt into something constructive.

This book isn't meant to be a scientific manual. Instead, it's a tool—designed for anyone, whether directly affected by addiction or not, as well as their families and friends—to help understand the problem and tackle it effectively.

Addiction is a democratic disease: it affects people everywhere, at every level of society. That's why I've chosen to use simple, direct language, without sacrificing accuracy. I want this message to reach as many people as possible. For those who wish to explore the subject further, I've included precise references to specialized literature.

The book is structured to allow for different levels of reading. The first part examines addiction from historical, sociocultural, anthropological, and scientific perspectives. The second part focuses on one of the most effective and widely available recovery methods: the 12-Step program. This approach is both free and accessible across the globe. My hope is that this book will serve as a light in the darkness—a guide toward escaping the tunnel of addiction.

That most painful suffering, the kind that is not recognized as such and is instead stigmatized.

Enjoy the journey.

M. Francesca Bene

Part 1

FROM THE STIGMA OF VICE **TO THE CONCEPT OF DISEASE**

What is addiction?

It's the compulsion to repeat actions or behaviors you wish you could stop—because instead of bringing joy or relief, they lead you straight into a personal hell.

Alcohol, drugs, medication, cigarettes, gambling, binge eating, toxic relationships, compulsive shopping, and excessive internet use can all become harsh prison wardens for those trapped in this struggle—a disease still too often dismissed as mere vice.

But science tells a different story...

CHAPTER 0

WHY "BILL AND HIS BROTHERS"

In the introduction, I didn't mention anything about the title of this book: *Bill and His Brothers.* Many have told me it wouldn't work, claiming it sounded more like the title of a children's story than of a serious book on a grim reality.

They may have a point—perhaps a more impactful, American-style title would have been better, something like *How to Quit Drinking in 15 Steps, Turning Defeat into Victory,* or *Breaking Free from Addiction: A Guide.* But I'm Italian, and a bit of a romantic. That's why I chose to dedicate the title of this work to Bill Wilson, the New York stockbroker and chronic alcoholic who, in the 1930s, not only recognized his alcoholism as a disease rather than a moral failing, but also developed a method to halt its progression.

Before Bill, one doctor had already understood that alcoholism was a disease, but his discovery led nowhere. That doctor was Benjamin Rush, a physician and a signer of the United States Declaration of Independence. In 1784, he published a treatise titled *An Inquiry into the Effects of Ardent Spirits on the Human Body and Mind,* where he described alcoholism not as a vice or moral weakness but as a medical condition requiring treatment.

Rush believed that:

- Alcoholism was a chronic disease, where behavior became compulsive and uncontrollable once dependence developed.
- Alcoholism had devastating effects on both the body and the mind.
- Alcohol, especially "ardent spirits," acted as a poison that damaged the body.

- Total abstinence from alcohol was the only effective treatment, and he advocated for the creation of support communities—foreshadowing today's self-help groups.

Rush was a true pioneer in viewing alcoholism as a disease and proposing abstinence as treatment, but his insight failed to spark tangible change.

Historically, medical treatments for alcoholism were not only inadequate but often brutal and inhumane. Those suffering from addiction were seen not as patients but as sinners or morally inferior beings. Treatments mirrored this distorted view: people were locked in dark cells, deprived of human contact and warmth. Sensory deprivation could last days, weeks, or months, driving them to despair, madness, or even suicide.

Forced detoxification was another cruel method, abruptly depriving patients of alcohol and food without medical support. Seizures were common, and those who tried to escape were restrained with leather straps. Some were even chained to walls, treated more like dangerous animals than human beings.

Violent gastric lavages, often performed without anaesthesia, caused internal injuries and excruciating pain without addressing the addiction itself. Emetics, laxatives, and extreme purges were standard practice under the misguided belief that "cleansing" the body would cure the patient. In reality, these were barbaric methods, more akin to torture than medicine.

The 20th century didn't bring much improvement. Psychiatry introduced electroshock therapy, hoping to "reset" the brain, but it often left patients physically and mentally devastated. Many never fully recovered, spending their remaining years in psychiatric institutions.

Alcoholism was still seen as divine punishment, and treatments were designed to inflict penance rather than find solutions. Patients were subjected to forced fasting, deprived of food and water to "starve the demon" of alcohol. Psychiatric hospitals administered heavy sedatives, turning patients into near-vegetative states and pushing recovery further out of reach.

Pseudo-scientific practices, such as the use of opiates, often swapped one addiction for another. Even more extreme was insulin shock therapy, which induced comas in a misguided attempt to cure addiction, leaving patients broken in the process.

In this bleak landscape, Bill Wilson began his work, revolutionizing the way alcoholism was understood. Like Rush, Bill alone could not change history.

This is where his "brothers" come in. Together with other alcoholics, and later with people battling other forms of addiction, Bill achieved what no one could have done alone.

Bill Wilson hypothesized that his affliction was a kind of "allergy" to alcohol—an idea now outdated but revolutionary at the time. He recognized that the disease affected not just the body but also the mind, emotions, and spirit, and he understood that medication alone wasn't enough.

Helping other alcoholics became a way for Bill to better manage his own recovery. Along with Dr. Robert Holbrook Smith and others, he founded Alcoholics Anonymous and developed the 12-Step program, later adopted by various addiction recovery groups. The second part of this book is dedicated to these organizations, which remain active worldwide today.

Bill and his brothers not only identified the nature of the problem but also took decisive action, grounded in the belief that no alcoholic could recover alone. The well-known phrase from 12-Step groups, *"I can't, but we can,"* perfectly encapsulates this idea.

Thanks to Bill and his brothers, alcoholism was no longer seen as a vice but as a disease, paving the way for more effective treatments. While their understanding was imperfect, their impact was undeniable. Today, millions of Bill's "brothers" are part of Alcoholics Anonymous and other self-help groups around the world, saving lives and restoring dignity to those battling addiction.

Bill and his brothers truly made a difference, standing at the crossroads of darkness and light, despair and hope. For this reason, I believe *Bill and His Brothers* is a title they more than deserve.

OUR BRAIN AND PATHOLOGICAL ADDICTIONS

The final chapter of this first section is devoted to examining how science currently understands addiction. This placement is deliberate, as today's scientific awareness has been achieved only after a long and difficult journey. However, to make the earlier chapters leading up to this "destination" easier to follow, I've chosen to introduce a few key concepts here. These ideas will be explored in greater detail in the following chapters and revisited in the final chapter dedicated to science.

Addiction does not stem solely from physical or physiological mechanisms. It is a far more intricate reality, and the goal of this book is to explain that complexity as comprehensively as possible.

While the physical aspect isn't the only factor, it remains critically important.

Before we proceed, it's crucial to understand how the brain functions and what happens on a physiological level when alcohol, drugs, psychoactive substances, and certain behaviors trigger the mechanisms of addiction.

Addiction is not confined to chemical substances. Behavioral addictions, which do not necessarily involve consuming drugs or alcohol, can activate the same dysfunctional mechanisms in the brain.

Examples of behavioral addictions include gambling, compulsive internet use, impulsive shopping, uncontrolled debt, overwork, and even pathological emotional or sexual dependencies.

As with substance addiction, these behaviors stimulate the

same brain mechanisms, providing fleeting feelings of pleasure but ultimately feeding a cycle of dependency over time.

Throughout this book, terms like neurotransmitters, dopamine, endorphins, synapses, and receptors will come up often. To make these ideas easier to grasp, I'll introduce them here, laying the groundwork for understanding how these mechanisms make addiction a disease rather than a mere weakness or vice.

The human body is an extraordinary machine, designed through evolution to ensure survival and well-being, both individually and collectively.

At the center of this system is the brain, our "control center," which regulates our needs and, in a sense, teaches us to do what's best for us using a sophisticated system of chemical and electrical signals.

For instance, to survive, we need food. When we're hungry, an empty stomach sends signals to the brain, which activates processes to alert the body to seek nourishment. These signals travel through neurons, the cells that make up the brain. Neurons have three main parts:

- **The cell body**, which contains the nucleus and controls the neuron's vital functions.
- **Dendrites**, branching structures that receive signals from other neurons.
- **The axon**, a long filament that carries signals to other neurons or cells.

Communication between neurons occurs through electrical impulses that travel along the axon. When the impulse reaches the axon's end, it triggers the release of a chemical substance—a neurotransmitter—into the gap between two neurons, called the synapse. The neurotransmitter crosses the synapse and binds to receptors on the receiving neuron, allowing the signal to continue. After delivering its message, the neurotransmitter is reabsorbed or broken down, ending the transmission.

You can think of neurotransmitters as "messengers" that carry information between neurons, and receptors as "mailboxes" where these messages are received. Each messenger has a specific type of mailbox—or, to use another metaphor, neurotransmitters are keys that fit into specific locks on receptors.

Let's explore the main neurotransmitters involved in addiction.

One we'll discuss frequently is **dopamine**, often called the "reward neurotransmitter." Others that contribute to positive feelings and reward include **serotonin**, known as the "happiness molecule," and **anandamide**, whose name comes from the Sanskrit word *ananda*, meaning "bliss."

Then there's **norepinephrine**, the "stress hormone," and **GABA**, often referred to as the "chamomile neurotransmitter" for its calming effects. Finally, we have **glutamate**, an excitatory neurotransmitter that acts like a spark, giving the brain a "boost," and **acetylcholine**, which plays a key role in memory and learning.

We'll also discuss **endorphins**, the body's natural painkillers. While not technically neurotransmitters, endorphins are neuromodulators that influence how the brain perceives pain and pleasure rather than directly transmitting signals between neurons.

This introduction aims to provide a foundation for understanding how addiction alters brain function, why it is considered a disease, and how scientific advances are helping us move beyond outdated notions of addiction as simply a lack of willpower.

HOW DRUGS DECEIVE THE BRAIN

Drugs or compulsive behaviors interfere with the brain by either replacing or flooding it with excessive amounts of substances that our bodies naturally produce in balanced doses to guide us in taking care of ourselves.

Let's now explore some parallels between neurotransmitters, endorphins, and the most common drugs or pathological behaviors.

DOPAMINE: THE REWARD MOLECULE

All addictions, whether related to substances or behaviors, center around one key player: dopamine. This neurotransmitter is the brain's "engine" for pleasure and reward.

Many substances influence the dopaminergic system, creating euphoria and pleasure through similar mechanisms. Cocaine blocks the reabsorption of dopamine, causing it to accumulate in the synaptic space and resulting in an intense euphoric high. Opioids like heroin, morphine, and oxycodone primarily act on their own receptors but also increase dopamine levels, producing profound feelings of pleasure.

Other substances, such as amphetamines, MDMA, methamphetamines, nicotine, and caffeine, stimulate dopamine release, sparking energy, alertness, and satisfaction. Alcohol, by contrast, modulates the dopaminergic system, inducing relaxation and pleasure. Cannabis, through THC, indirectly boosts dopamine release via the endocannabinoid system.

It's not just substances, though—behavioral addictions are just as effective at hijacking the dopaminergic system. Gambling is a clear example: the tension and anticipation of a possible win light up dopamine pathways, driving people to keep playing again and again. Food, particularly when loaded with sugar and fat, is another potent dopamine stimulator, making the craving to eat compulsive.

Compulsive shopping? Dopamine plays a central role there too, as the anticipation and gratification of buying something new create a powerful loop. The same is true for sex and pornography, where dopamine stimulation during sexual activity establishes an addictive cycle.

Internet and social media work in much the same way: every "like" or new notification triggers dopamine, making it hard to step away from the screen. Video games are no different—offering instant rewards and quick gratification, they stimulate dopamine release and encourage compulsive play.

Even exercise, when taken to extremes, can turn into an addiction. The dopamine "rush" that accompanies physical activity becomes an essential fix for those who overdo it.

In all its forms, addiction revolves around this intricate brain mechanism, highlighting how easily the brain's chemistry can be dangerously manipulated, regardless of the type of stimulus.

ENDORPHINS: NATURE'S PAINKILLERS

Endorphins are the body's natural painkillers, produced by the brain to relieve pain and create pleasure. They play a vital role in survival. Imagine a prehistoric human, hungry and in pain—his body would release endorphins to endure the discomfort and stress, allowing him to keep hunting for food.

These chemicals bind to the brain's opioid receptors, blocking pain signals and enabling survival. In addition to relieving pain, endorphins trigger the release of dopamine, boosting feelings of pleasure and well-being once a goal, such as securing food, is achieved. Endorphin production is carefully regulated to avoid overloading the brain's reward system.

Certain substances and behaviors, however, can interfere with this natural system. Opiates and opioids, such as morphine, heroin, codeine, and oxycodone, mimic endorphins by binding to the same receptors. They block pain and produce euphoria, effectively "tricking" the brain.

Other substances, like alcohol, temporarily increase endorphin levels, promoting relaxation. However, chronic alcohol use can disrupt the system, making it harder for the body to regulate mood on its own. Nicotine and cannabis also indirectly affect endorphin levels, creating temporary pleasure that contributes to behavioral addiction.

SEROTONIN: THE HAPPINESS MOLECULE

Serotonin is a vital neurotransmitter responsible for regulating mood, sleep, appetite, and other essential functions.

Various substances can influence its levels in the brain, significantly impacting our emotional state.
MDMA (Ecstasy) triggers an intense release of serotonin already stored in the brain, producing feelings of euphoria and emotional connection. However, this surge quickly depletes serotonin reserves, leading to an emotional "crash" in the following days, characterized by depression, anxiety, and irritability.
Alcohol temporarily boosts serotonin levels, promoting relaxation and an uplifted mood. Yet, prolonged use disrupts the brain's ability to produce serotonin naturally, increasing the risk of mood disorders like anxiety and depression.
SSRIs (Selective Serotonin Reuptake Inhibitors), a common class of antidepressants, work by preventing serotonin reabsorption, allowing it to remain active in the synaptic space longer and enhancing its effects. This helps stabilize mood and reduce symptoms of depression and anxiety. While highly effective, these medications should always be taken under strict medical supervision.

NOREPINEPHRINE: THE SPARK PLUG

Norepinephrine, also known as noradrenaline, is both a neurotransmitter and a hormone essential for attention, alertness, and the "fight or flight" response during stressful situations. It enables us to react with clarity and strength in emergencies, increasing heart rate and blood pressure to prepare the body for action.
Certain substances can artificially influence norepinephrine, leading to pronounced effects on behavior and mood. Amphetamines, for instance, stimulate the release of norepinephrine, dopamine, and serotonin, boosting energy and alertness. However, chronic use depletes norepinephrine reserves, diminishing the body's ability to cope with stress. Cocaine works by blocking the reabsorption of norepinephrine, amplifying excitement and vigilance. Yet, prolonged use similarly drains reserves, resulting in fatigue and anxiety during withdrawal.

Alcohol has a more complex effect: in low doses, it temporarily increases norepinephrine, causing euphoria and reduced inhibitions. However, chronic abuse disrupts the natural regulation of this neurotransmitter, leading to anxiety and hyperactivity during withdrawal.
Certain antidepressants, such as tricyclics and SNRIs (Serotonin-Norepinephrine Reuptake Inhibitors), also increase norepinephrine and serotonin levels, improving mood and energy in patients with depression. However, they can cause side effects, including elevated blood pressure and restlessness. As such, medical supervision is essential when using these medications.

GABA: The "Chamomile" Neurotransmitter

GABA, or gamma-aminobutyric acid, is the brain's primary inhibitory neurotransmitter. Its main role is to calm the nervous system by reducing neuronal activity, helping to manage anxiety, relax muscles, and promote sleep. Various substances can enhance GABA's effects, leading to sedative and anxiolytic outcomes.
Alcohol, for instance, binds to GABA-A receptors, amplifying GABA's inhibitory action and inducing relaxation and sedation. However, prolonged alcohol use forces the brain to adapt by reducing receptor sensitivity. During sudden withdrawal, this reduced sensitivity can trigger symptoms of neuronal hyperactivity, such as anxiety, tremors, and seizures.
Benzodiazepines also work by enhancing GABA's effects and are widely used to treat anxiety, insomnia, and seizures. They promote calmness and reduce excessive neuronal activity. However, long-term use often results in tolerance and dependence, and abrupt withdrawal can lead to severe symptoms such as agitation, intense anxiety, and seizures.
Barbiturates, another class of drugs that interact with the GABA system, are now used less frequently due to their high risks of addiction, overdose, and withdrawal complications.

GLUTAMATE: THE BRAIN'S "TURBO"

Glutamate is the brain's primary excitatory neurotransmitter, playing a crucial role in learning, memory, and synaptic plasticity.

By stimulating neuronal activity, glutamate facilitates communication between neurons. However, excessive glutamate can lead to excitotoxicity, causing damage to nerve cells. Certain substances, such as alcohol, disrupt this delicate balance: alcohol inhibits glutamate's NMDA receptors, reducing neurotransmitter activity and producing sedative effects. However, sudden withdrawal after prolonged alcohol use triggers a "glutamate rebound," leading to hyperactivity, anxiety, and, in severe cases, seizures.

Ketamine and PCP, along with other dissociative drugs, also block glutamate's NMDA receptors, altering perception and causing mental dissociation. While ketamine is sometimes used to treat treatment-resistant depression, prolonged NMDA receptor blockage can impair memory and cognitive function.

ACETYLCHOLINE: THE SPARK OF MIND AND BODY

Acetylcholine is a key neurotransmitter involved in memory, attention, learning, and muscle control. It is essential for the proper functioning of both the central and peripheral nervous systems, ensuring coordination between brain and body.

One substance that influences acetylcholine is nicotine. When tobacco is consumed, nicotine binds to acetylcholine's nicotinic receptors in the brain, temporarily improving attention and memory. However, with chronic use, these receptors become desensitized, requiring larger doses to achieve the same effect, leading to dependence. Over time, the brain reduces its sensitivity to natural acetylcholine, relying instead on nicotine to sustain focus.

Certain medications used to treat Parkinson's and Alzheimer's diseases also modulate acetylcholine, as this neurotransmitter plays a critical role in managing the cognitive and motor functions affected by these conditions.

ANANDAMIDE: THE BLISS MOLECULE

Anandamide, often referred to as the "bliss molecule" (from *ananda*, Sanskrit for joy), is an endocannabinoid crucial for regulating mood, memory, appetite, pain, and overall well-being. It binds to cannabinoid receptors in the brain, influencing both cognitive and physiological functions.

Cannabis, through THC (tetrahydrocannabinol), is the most well-known substance that interacts with anandamide. THC binds to cannabinoid receptors, mimicking anandamide but with more potent and longer-lasting effects, producing euphoria, relaxation, and altered perceptions. However, regular THC use can disrupt the endocannabinoid system, reducing the natural production of anandamide and desensitizing receptors. This imbalance can undermine emotional stability, overall well-being, and increase the risk of dependence.

HEALTHY HABITS THAT BALANCE BRAIN CHEMISTRY

The positive effects of certain behaviors on our neurochemical system are remarkable, extending far beyond simple well-being. These actions regulate various neurotransmitters, creating lasting benefits for both body and mind.

Among all healthy habits, physical exercise stands out as the undisputed champion. Activities like running, swimming, cycling, and other forms of aerobic exercise trigger a cascade of neurotransmitters. Endorphins, responsible for the famous "runner's high," bring euphoria and pain relief; serotonin boosts mood and combats anxiety; norepinephrine increases energy and focus. Exercise also supports GABA, calming neuronal activity and promoting mental relaxation, while regulating glutamate, which helps maintain synaptic balance and protects neurons from oxidative stress. Additionally, it stimulates acetylcholine, improving memory and coordination, and anandamide, the "bliss molecule," for an overall sense of well-being.

Nutrition also plays a vital role. A diet rich in tryptophan—a precursor to serotonin found in foods like nuts, seeds, turkey, and dairy—is essential for maintaining stable levels of this "happiness neurotransmitter." To protect the glutamatergic system and the brain, a diet high in antioxidants, abundantly found in fruits and vegetables, is crucial. Certain foods, like dark chocolate, offer unique benefits by prolonging the effects of anandamide, enhancing mood and well-being.

Exposure to sunlight, especially during winter months, is another ally in regulating serotonin, helping to counteract conditions such as Seasonal Affective Disorder (SAD).

Sleep, in turn, is indispensable for restoring the balance of norepinephrine and GABA—two neurotransmitters critical for focus, stress management, and anxiety control.

Meditation and mindfulness practices also provide significant neurochemical benefits, increasing levels of endorphins and GABA, reducing stress, and stimulating the endocannabinoid system. These techniques further contribute to glutamate stability, helping to regulate stress responses and prevent neuronal damage.

Positive social interactions and laughter complete the picture. Both are powerful generators of endorphins and anandamide, fostering emotional bonds and promoting a sense of shared well-being and connection.

In essence, adopting a daily routine of exercise, balanced nutrition, sunlight exposure, adequate sleep, and mindfulness practices not only enhances mental health but also optimizes the entire nervous system's functioning, creating a virtuous cycle of well-being and emotional stability.

DRUGS AND BRAIN SYSTEMS

Addictions—whether substance-related or behavioral—involve various brain systems that regulate pleasure, reward, and behavioral control. These circuits not only drive the desire to repeat pleasurable behaviors but also contribute to the loss of control and the challenges of overcoming addiction. The primary brain systems involved in addiction encompass several interconnected circuits.

THE REWARD SYSTEM (MESOLIMBIC PATHWAY)

As previously mentioned, the issue with pathological addictions—whether behavioral or substance-based—lies in the external interference with our delicate system for regulating pleasure and pain. Substances or compulsive behaviors overload the reward system, creating a vicious cycle in which individuals become reliant on external sources to experience well-being, ultimately disrupting the brain's natural functioning.

Understanding how this system works is crucial, as we will frequently encounter its role throughout our exploration of addiction.

The reward system is the primary brain circuit involved in addiction. It encompasses various structures, including the ventral tegmental area (VTA) and the nucleus accumbens, which work together to process pleasure and reward.

When a person consumes a substance like cocaine or engages in gratifying behaviors such as gambling, dopamine is released into the nucleus accumbens, generating feelings of euphoria. This reinforces the behavior, motivating the individual to repeat the action in pursuit of pleasure. Over time, this system becomes hypersensitive, driving compulsive seeking of the substance or activity.

THE PREFRONTAL CORTEX

Drug and alcohol use can have a devastating impact on the development of the prefrontal cortex, one of the most critical areas of the brain. Located at the front of the brain, this region is essential for impulse control, planning, decision-making, and emotion regulation.

During adolescence and early adulthood, the prefrontal cortex is still developing and does not fully mature until around the age of 25. Substance abuse during this critical period can severely disrupt its development, impairing these cognitive functions.

Drugs such as cannabis, cocaine, opioids, and others directly affect how neurotransmitters like dopamine and serotonin are released and reabsorbed in the brain. Dopamine, which plays a key role in the reward system, is often overstimulated by substance use, leading to impulsive behavior and the development of compulsive habits.

These chemical changes can alter synaptic connections, interfering with brain plasticity—the ability of the brain to form new neural pathways and adapt to experiences.

Alcohol, for example, can reduce the prefrontal cortex's ability to function properly, negatively impacting memory and emotional regulation. Substances like methamphetamines, on the other hand, massively stimulate dopamine release, creating euphoria but also causing severe, and sometimes irreversible, damage to brain circuits.

Over time, chronic use of these substances impairs the brain's ability to develop normally, leading to difficulties in impulse control, problem-solving, and taking responsibility.

In summary, drug and alcohol abuse during the brain's developmental phase not only disrupts the natural maturation process of the prefrontal cortex but can also leave permanent scars on cognitive functions and emotional well-being.

THE AMYGDALA

The amygdala, a brain structure associated with emotions and stress, plays a significant role in reinforcing addictions.

It is involved in processing fear and emotional responses. During moments of stress or anxiety, individuals with addictions often turn to substances or problematic behaviors, such as gambling or compulsive eating, to alleviate discomfort.

The amygdala helps sustain this cycle by reinforcing the association between stress relief and the addictive behavior, making it harder to break free.

THE HIPPOCAMPUS

The hippocampus is essential for memory formation and learning. In the context of addiction, it plays a key role in creating associations between addictive behaviors and environmental cues.

These "reward memories" make it difficult for individuals with addictions to ignore triggers associated with the substance or behavior. These cues can evoke powerful memories, intensifying cravings even after long periods of abstinence.

THE THALAMUS

The thalamus acts as the brain's "control center," routing sensory information to other brain regions.

In addiction, the thalamus can amplify stimuli associated with substances or addictive behaviors. For instance, in individuals with addictions, visual or olfactory cues related to drug use may become more intense and harder to ignore, contributing to compulsive seeking behavior.

THE STRESS SYSTEM

The stress system plays a significant role in addiction, particularly during withdrawal phases.

The hypothalamic-pituitary-adrenal (HPA) axis regulates the stress response by releasing hormones like cortisol. In individuals with addictions, this system is often hyperactive, leading to an exaggerated stress response and increased cravings for substances or addictive behaviors as a way to relieve discomfort.

THE ENDOCANNABINOID SYSTEM

The endocannabinoid system is essential for regulating various brain processes, including mood, appetite, and pain. It consists of endogenous neurotransmitters (such as anandamide) and cannabinoid receptors (CB1 and CB2).

This system is also influenced by substances like THC, the main active compound in cannabis. THC binds to cannabinoid receptors in the brain, mimicking the effects of anandamide but with a much more potent impact. This produces euphoria, altered perception, and relaxation.

However, prolonged cannabis use can disrupt the endocannabinoid system, leading to dependence and impairments in mood and memory. The endocannabinoid system also interacts with the brain's reward system by enhancing dopamine release in the nucleus accumbens, further reinforcing substance-seeking behavior.

IN SUMMARY

Addictions involve a complex interplay of brain systems. The reward system drives repetitive behavior through dopamine release, while the prefrontal cortex becomes weakened, impairing control and the ability to assess consequences.

The amygdala and hippocampus reinforce emotional, and memory responses tied to the substance or behavior, while the thalamus amplifies sensory signals associated with them. The stress system exacerbates the addiction cycle, and the endocannabinoid system interacts with these processes, affecting mood, memory, and reward, ultimately contributing to the development and maintenance of addiction.

THE VULNERABILITY FACTOR

To better understand the concept of pathological addictions, it's important to recognize that not everyone is equally predisposed to develop them. Some people can enjoy a glass of wine without becoming alcoholics, gamble for fun without ruining their lives, savor good food without obsessing over it, or love without losing themselves in their relationships.

This difference stems from a combination of genetic and environmental factors, which will be explored in detail in the final chapter of this section.

CHAPTER 1

REVERED AND FEARED SINCE THE DAWN OF TIME: DRUGS AND RELIGIONS

In the previous chapter, we marked a historic milestone: 1935, the year Bill Wilson, also known as Bill W., and Robert Holbrook Smith, better known as Dr. Bob, founded Alcoholics Anonymous. This was the first organization to recognize and treat pathological alcohol dependence as a physical, mental, and spiritual illness.

While the concept of addiction is well-defined today—though not fully embraced by everyone—the issue of compulsive behaviors and the use of psychoactive substances has been part of humanity's story since ancient times.

The use of substances to alter consciousness is documented in countless cultures, serving religious, medicinal, or recreational purposes.

In ancient civilizations, substances like alcohol, opium, and hallucinogenic plants were either revered or feared, depending on the context.

Sacred texts from many religions include warnings about the dangers of overuse, though the approach to this issue varied. Even in those early times, excess was observed and condemned, as it disrupted both individual well-being and societal harmony.

However, the ways in which substances and compulsive behaviors were regulated differed across cultures, often reflecting a delicate balance of respect for their power and fear of the consequences they could unleash.

ADDICTION IN SACRED TEXTS

The world's major religions, long-standing guardians of values and wisdom, have always recognized the dangers of addiction—particularly to alcohol—and have warned followers against the misuse of mind-altering substances. Sacred texts, the foundation of religious traditions, reflect a deep history of moral and social concerns tied to excessive substance use. These timeless admonitions offer guidance that has resonated through the ages.

In Christianity, the Bible addresses the issue of excessive alcohol consumption, emphasizing moderation. Its stance on wine is complex: while it is central to rituals like the Eucharist, it also warns against drunkenness. Proverbs states: *"Wine is a mocker, strong drink a brawler, and whoever is led astray by it is not wise"* (Proverbs 20:1). This highlights how alcohol can lead to destructive behavior and a loss of wisdom. Similarly, in Ephesians, we find: *"Do not get drunk on wine, which leads to debauchery. Instead, be filled with the Spirit"* (Ephesians 5:18). Here, alcohol is seen not just as a mental risk but as a spiritual obstacle, preventing closeness to the Holy Spirit.

In Islam, the stance on alcohol is unequivocal: it is strictly forbidden. The Quran explicitly prohibits alcohol in several verses, emphasizing its harmful effects on both the mind and spiritual practice. *"They ask you about wine and gambling. Say, 'In them is great sin and [some] benefit for people. But their sin is greater than their benefit'"* (Surah Al-Baqarah 2:219). While acknowledging potential benefits, the Quran emphasizes that the harms of alcohol far outweigh its advantages. Another verse declares: *"O you who have believed, indeed, intoxicants, gambling, [sacrificing on] stone alters [to other than Allah], and divining arrows are but defilement from the work of Satan, so avoid it that you may be successful"* (Surah Al-Ma'idah 5:90). Here, alcohol is equated with sinful practices and condemned as an instrument of evil.

In Judaism, wine is embraced but always with moderation. It plays a significant role in sacred rituals like Kiddush (the blessing of wine during Shabbat), yet the faith warns against excess. The Torah and other sacred texts vividly caution against drunkenness: *"Who has woe? Who has sorrow? Who has strife? Who has complaints? Who has needless bruises? Who has bloodshot eyes? Those who linger over wine, who go to sample bowls of mixed wine. Do not gaze at wine when it is red, when it sparkles in the cup, when it goes down smoothly! In the end, it bites like a snake and poisons like a viper"* (Proverbs 23:29–32). This passage vividly illustrates the allure of wine while warning of its deceptive dangers.

Hinduism, one of the world's oldest spiritual traditions, contains numerous sacred texts guiding moral and spiritual conduct. The *Laws of Manu* (*Manusmriti*), an ancient code of ethics, explicitly prohibits alcohol consumption for those seeking spiritual elevation. A particularly striking passage reads: *"By drinking alcohol, committing theft, associating with women of lower caste, and killing a Brahmin, a man becomes immediately outcast"* (Manusmriti 11.55). Alcohol consumption is considered as degrading as theft or murder, underscoring its perceived moral and spiritual harm.

Buddhism, emphasizing mindfulness and inner purity, views abstention from intoxicants as essential for maintaining mental clarity. The Five Precepts, the ethical foundation of Buddhism, include the direct admonition: *"Refrain from intoxicating substances that cloud the mind."* This precept is not merely a moral guideline but a cornerstone of spiritual practice. Intoxication dulls the mind, interferes with meditation, and obstructs the path to enlightenment, which demands complete control over one's thoughts and actions.

The *Guru Granth Sahib*, Sikhism's holy scripture, explicitly condemns intoxicants. Alcohol is seen as a barrier to purity and inner peace, undermining spiritual growth. It warns: *"People drink wine for pleasure, but the pleasure is deceptive. Drinking wine, they lose self-control, argue, and fall into sin"* (*Guru Granth Sahib* 554). Sikhism places a premium on mental clarity and righteous behavior, with alcohol viewed as an enemy to these principles.

Jainism, one of India's most ancient religions, promotes non-violence (*ahimsa*) and self-control, extending these principles to strict abstinence from intoxicants. Jain texts teach that such substances distort the mind and lead to violence or destructive behavior, violating the core tenets of the faith. The *Dasavaikalika Sutra* advises: *"He who desires his own good and happiness should never drink wine or other intoxicating substances"* (*Dasavaikalika Sutra* 6:11). Abstinence is not only a form of self-discipline but also a safeguard against moral and spiritual decline, fostering purity of body and mind.

THE RITUAL USE OF SUBSTANCES

The ritual use of psychoactive substances, an ancient practice rooted in various cultures and religions, has accompanied humanity on its journey through the mysteries of existence. These substances, known as entheogens—a term derived from the Greek meaning "to generate the divine within"—have been used for millennia to open the doors to altered states of consciousness, evoke spiritual visions, and facilitate a deeper connection with the divine.

Because of their ability to "open" the boundaries of perception, the use of these substances has traditionally been restricted to ritualistic and religious contexts, forbidden outside of these sacred frameworks.

Now, let us embark on a journey through the cultures and spiritual practices that have embraced these sacred tools.

ANCIENT RITUALS OF WESTERN CULTURE

The use of psychoactive substances for religious and ritual purposes in Western culture, particularly in ancient Greece and the Roman Empire, dates back to the dawn of time.

Mood- and mind-altering substances were often employed to facilitate contact with the divine, enable mystical experiences, and explore the nature of existence and spirituality. Among these, alcohol in its various forms was by far the most prevalent substance used in ancient rituals.

THE EFFECT OF THE "NECTAR OF THE GODS"

Wine, often called the "nectar of the gods," is one of the most widely consumed alcoholic beverages in the world, with its psychoactive effects stemming from its ethanol content. When we drink wine, the alcohol is quickly absorbed and reaches the brain within minutes, activating parts of the reward circuit responsible for our perception of pleasure and gratification.

In the brain, alcohol alters the function of several neurotransmitters—chemical messengers that enable communication between nerve cells. One of the primary neurotransmitters affected is GABA, which acts as a brake on brain activity. Alcohol enhances GABA's effect, making us feel relaxed and less anxious. However, at higher doses, it can cause slurred speech, loss of coordination, and slowed thinking.

Ethanol also impacts glutamate, a neurotransmitter that stimulates brain cells. By inhibiting glutamate, alcohol further slows brain activity, impairing concentration and memory.

The most enticing effects of alcohol, however, come through dopamine, the primary neurotransmitter in the brain's reward circuit. Every time we drink, alcohol triggers the release of this "feel-good" molecule in the nucleus accumbens, creating sensations of pleasure and satisfaction.

Yet, as with other addictions, the brain adapts by reducing its response to pleasure. This drives individuals to consume more alcohol to achieve the same initial

effect, setting off a vicious cycle that can lead to dependence.

THE KYKEON IN THE ELEUSINIAN MYSTERIES

In ancient Greek culture, psychoactive substances were often intertwined with religious rituals, most notably the Eleusinian Mysteries, devoted to Demeter and Persephone. At the heart of these mysteries lies a profound myth of maternal love, nature, and spiritual rebirth. Persephone, daughter of Demeter, the goddess of earth and agriculture, is abducted by Hades, god of the underworld, to become his queen. In her anguish, Demeter halts the fertility of the earth, causing famine and widespread suffering. Zeus intervenes, decreeing that Persephone will spend part of the year with Hades and part with her mother. This arrangement came to symbolize the changing seasons: when Persephone is with Demeter, the earth blossoms in spring and summer; when she resides in the underworld, autumn and winter descend.

Beyond the natural cycle of the seasons, this myth also embodies themes of death and spiritual renewal. Persephone's journey to the underworld and back represents a transformative passage through life, death, and rebirth, mirroring the soul's perpetual cycle of evolution. This narrative was central to the Eleusinian Mysteries—ancient secret rites that guided initiates through a symbolic journey of death and spiritual resurrection. These rituals sought to deepen participants' understanding of life and death, exploring the cyclical nature of existence and humanity's bond with the natural world.

Initiates partook in secret ceremonies that simulated death and rebirth, experiencing ecstatic states and forging a profound connection to the divine and the promise of the soul's immortality. Persephone's descent into the underworld symbolized the confrontation with one's deepest fears, while her return heralded spiritual regeneration.

A central element of these rites was the *Kykeon*, a sacred drink. Some theories suggest it may have contained ergot, a fungus that, when properly processed, could induce mystical visions and altered states of consciousness. This could explain the transformative, ecstatic experiences described by those who participated in the mysteries.

THE BRAIN AND HALLUCINOGENS

Hallucinogens, such as ergot and certain psychoactive plants, have intricate effects on the brain, particularly on neurotransmitters responsible for regulating mood and sensory perception.

Ergot, a fungus containing alkaloids like ergotamine, interacts with serotonin receptors, a neurotransmitter that plays a crucial role in controlling emotions, mood, and perception. This interaction can profoundly alter one's perception of the world, sometimes inducing hallucinogenic experiences.

While serotonin is not as directly tied to the brain's reward circuit as dopamine, changes in sensory perception and mood can still influence feelings of gratification and well-being. These temporary disruptions in normal brain activity can distort reality, and prolonged or uncontrolled use can become dangerous. For example, ergot can also affect blood vessels, causing vasoconstriction—a response that may be medically beneficial in specific contexts but harmful if unchecked, potentially leading to seizures or intense hallucinations.

Other psychoactive plants, such as mandrake, henbane, belladonna, and datura, are well-known for their powerful hallucinogenic effects. These plants contain alkaloids like atropine, scopolamine, and

hyoscyamine, which block the neurotransmitter acetylcholine, further disrupting normal brain function.

Interestingly, the effects of hallucinogens on the brain's reward system differ from substances like alcohol or stimulants. Instead of directly activating the reward circuit, hallucinogens alter sensory experiences in unique ways, often producing vivid visual and sensory phenomena. While these experiences can be captivating, they do not typically create the same compulsive desire for repetition driven by a neurological "reward."

THE DIONYSIAN RITES

The rites of Dionysus, the god of wine, ecstasy, and primal forces, were intense celebrations imbued with mysticism and spirituality.

Dionysus symbolized the connection between humanity and the divine, a force that dissolved the constraints of rationality and pushed individuals beyond ordinary limits. In the Mysteries dedicated to him, a blend of chanting, dancing, and theatrical performances—combined with the ritual use of wine and possibly psychoactive substances—sought to transform participants, allowing them to reconnect with nature's forces and the divine.

A "liminal" deity, Dionysus led his followers into a state of divine madness (*enthousiasmos*), where they were filled with his presence and transcended their individual selves. The Mysteries had a collective essence: participants shed their individual identities to merge in an ecstatic union with the god, transcending societal norms. Wine, as a symbol of Dionysus, broke down the boundaries of ordinary consciousness, transporting initiates to a higher, transcendent dimension. This sacred "nectar of the gods"—possibly accompanied by hallucinogenic plants like henbane, mandrake, or belladonna—was not consumed for mere intoxication but to achieve transcendence. Through

this ecstatic state, participants could surrender to a profound communion with the divine and the natural world.
Beyond sensual liberation, the Dionysian rites had a deeply spiritual purpose. As the god of transformation, Dionysus embodied the cycle of death and rebirth, like a vine that grows back stronger after being pruned. Much like the Eleusinian Mysteries, participating in these rites involved undergoing a symbolic "death," dissolving the rational self to free the soul from its limitations.
During these ceremonies, social conventions melted away—men and women united without distinctions, and individuals broke free from societal norms, returning to a state of primal purity.
Dionysus carried a dual nature: he offered joy and divine communion but could also unleash destruction and madness. The frenzy of his rites, which pushed participants to extreme self-abandonment, symbolized nature's uncontrollable forces—both creative and destructive. For the initiates, however, this ecstatic experience served as a spiritual healing process: losing control allowed them to cast off corruption and be reborn into an original purity, fully united with the primordial forces Dionysus represented.

WHEN SEX BECOMES A DRUG

In the Dionysian rites and Eleusinian Mysteries, sexuality was an integral part of altered states of consciousness and was therefore socially accepted.
Compulsive sexuality, however, is something entirely different from what occurred in those rituals. But what brain mechanisms turn sex into an addiction? Understanding its link to the brain's reward circuit is central to answering this question.
In a healthy individual, the reward circuit functions in a balanced way. During pleasurable experiences like sex, the

brain releases dopamine, creating a sensation of pleasure that encourages repeating the behavior. Simultaneously, serotonin plays a critical role in regulating pleasure and preventing obsessive behaviors. Acting like a "thermostat," serotonin dampens desire once satisfaction has been achieved.

Two key brain areas already encountered—the nucleus accumbens and the amygdala—work together to regulate pleasure and emotions.

Under normal conditions, dopamine and serotonin maintain a balance between desire and satisfaction. However, in individuals who develop sexual addiction, this delicate balance breaks down. Dopamine receptors become less effective, requiring increasingly intense stimuli to achieve the same level of pleasure.

At the same time, the serotonin system becomes impaired, unable to temper desire, leaving the brain in a constant state of craving new stimulation. This creates a vicious cycle: the more sexual pleasure is sought, the less satisfying it becomes.

In this process, the reward circuit becomes hyperactivated, driving compulsive sexual behavior in a relentless pursuit of dopamine surges, without ever achieving true fulfillment.

THE BACCHANALIA IN ANCIENT ROME

In the Roman Empire, the ritual use of psychoactive substances was less widespread than in classical Greece. However, the consumption of alcoholic beverages and other substances did play a role in certain religious celebrations. Even the Roman aristocracy, enchanted by Greek culture, took part in the Eleusinian Mysteries and adopted some of their spiritual practices.

As in Greece, wine held a central place in many Roman religious cults, including the cult of Bacchus, celebrated during the famed Bacchanalia. During these festivities, the "nectar of the gods" was consumed in large quantities and was sometimes mixed with plants or herbs to enhance its effects.

The Bacchanalia were known for their euphoric atmosphere and the altered states of consciousness they induced, where participants sought a mystical union with the deity.

In 186 BCE, the Roman Senate issued the *Senatus Consultum de Bacchanalibus*, a decree that either banned or severely restricted the Bacchanalia. These rites, with their orgiastic and secretive nature, were seen as subversive and a threat to the public order and moral standards of the Roman state. Authorities feared that such celebrations could encourage political conspiracies and unlawful behavior.

Despite the prohibition, it is believed that the Bacchanalia continued clandestinely in some regions, albeit in a reduced form.

While the Romans did not develop a ritual system involving psychoactive substances akin to the Eleusinian Mysteries, they were aware of the mind-altering effects of certain plants and beverages. Priestesses of the Apollo cult and the Cumaean Sibyl, for instance, reportedly used vapors or fumes from plants such as datura, laurel, myrrh, or incense to enter trances and receive prophetic visions.

However, the use of hallucinogenic substances in Roman rituals remains speculative and is not supported by concrete evidence.

ROMAN FEASTS: OVERINDULGENCE IN PLEASURE

Ancient Rome provides some of the earliest examples of feasting behaviors reminiscent of what we now call binge eating, though motivated by different cultural values.

During the Empire, eating to the point of exhaustion served as a form of escapism, with food representing both a source of pleasure and a symbol of abundance. At banquets, especially among the elite, dining was an all-encompassing sensory experience.

These Roman feasts were not simply meals but lavish celebrations of extravagance, featuring elaborate dishes and copious amounts of wine. It was not uncommon for attendees to induce vomiting in order to continue eating—a cycle of excess that was not only socially accepted but often encouraged.

For the Romans, these banquets symbolized status and power, serving as an opportunity to display wealth and mastery over resources. Historical accounts describe how the wealthiest individuals would eat to the point of discomfort, a behavior that, by modern standards, might seem both excessive and peculiar.

THE BRAIN AND BINGE EATING

Binge eating is characterized by excessive food consumption in a short period, often accompanied by a sense of losing control. This behavior isn't just about the quantity of food; it directly involves the brain's reward circuit—the same system that governs pleasure and gratification and is implicated in substance addiction. The primary neurotransmitter in this process is dopamine, which is released when we engage in activities the body associates with pleasure. Eating, aside from being a physiological necessity, is also a gratifying experience. In binge eating, dopamine is released in large amounts, creating temporary pleasure that compels the repetition of the behavior.

Over time, the brain becomes less sensitive to dopamine, requiring increasingly larger quantities of food to achieve the same level of gratification. This cycle

closely mirrors substance addiction: the behavior repeats, but satisfaction diminishes, creating a vicious loop.

Binge eating is often triggered by stress or difficult emotions, with food becoming a dysfunctional coping mechanism for emotional pressure. External factors, such as hormonal imbalances or the easy availability of high-sugar and high-fat foods, exacerbate the issue.

Individuals with binge eating disorder lose control over their eating impulses, which can lead to severe physical problems like obesity, diabetes, and heart disease, along with psychological consequences such as guilt, low self-esteem, and depression.

As with other forms of addiction, binge eating becomes a way to cope with stress but ultimately worsens both mental and physical well-being. This behavior can also lead to social isolation and sleep disturbances. Early intervention and adequate psychological support are crucial to preventing long-term complications.

Dysfunctional eating behaviors as a whole will be explored further in the final chapter.

CHRISTIANITY AND THE DEMONIZATION OF RITUAL "HIGHS"

The rise of Christianity in the West marked a dramatic decline in the use of psychoactive substances in pagan religious rituals, which had been widespread in many spiritual practices.

As Christianity gradually established itself as the dominant religion, ceremonies dedicated to pagan deities—often involving altered states of consciousness through the use of plants or substances—were increasingly suppressed or reinterpreted. These ecstatic states or visions, central to pagan worship as a means of connecting with the divine, were demonized by the Church and associated with witchcraft, idolatry, or demonic possession.

Christianity promoted a spirituality no longer direct and ecstatic but mediated by prayer and faith, with the clergy serving as the sole legitimate conduit to God. Pagan rites were frequently replaced by Christian festivities that emphasized purity of body and spirit, free from the influence of mind-altering substances.

For example, while wine, a key element in Dionysian cults, retained a ritual role in the Christian Eucharist, its consumption became symbolic and measured, devoid of the intoxicating effects associated with pagan practices.

With the Edict of Thessalonica in 380 CE, which declared Christianity the official religion of the Roman Empire, many pagan practices, including rites involving psychoactive substances, were outlawed.

Nevertheless, in rural areas and among marginalized communities, the use of psychoactive plants persisted, often hidden or reinterpreted, particularly in connection with folk medicine and witchcraft.

During the Middle Ages and the Renaissance, women and herbalists continued to use plants such as datura, mandrake, belladonna, henbane, and fungi like ergot to induce trance states or treat illnesses.

PSYCHOACTIVE HERBS AND COLLECTIVE HYSTERIA

During the Middle Ages, **ergotism** caused numerous outbreaks of collective hysteria, triggerd by poisoning from grains—primarily rye—contaminated with the fungus *Claviceps purpurea* (ergot).

This fungus, rich in alkaloids like ergotamine, produces symptoms ranging from hallucinations and convulsions to burning sensations in the limbs and, in severe cases, gangrene caused by reduced blood flow.

One of ergotism's most devastating effects was its ability to deeply distort sensory perception and human behavior. Entire communities, during these outbreaks, fell prey to

hallucinations and bizarre actions often interpreted as **demonic possession** or **divine intervention**.
These episodes led to phenomena of **collective hysteria**. People entered states of collective ecstasy, dancing uncontrollably for hours, even days, sometimes collapsing or dying from exhaustion. Such events occurred throughout Europe during the Middle Ages and Renaissance.
In regions along the Rhine River and in Germany, from the 14th century onward, individuals affected by ergotism experienced a trance-like state, engaging in frantic, unstoppable dancing—a phenomenon known as **Tanzwut**. While ergotism may not have been the sole cause, its typical symptoms—convulsions, hallucinations, and irrational behavior—match the descriptions of these episodes.
Another example of collective hysteria potentially linked to ergotism is **Tarantism**, which flourished in southern Italy, particularly in Puglia. Popular belief held that the bite of a tarantula triggered agitation, convulsions, and frenzied movements that could only be alleviated by continuous dancing, often accompanied by the hypnotic rhythms of pizzica music.
The ritual "cure" required those "bitten" to dance tirelessly for hours, sometimes days, until the venom was believed to be purged. Scholars suggest that ergotism may have contributed to such behaviors, as ergot-contaminated grains could cause hallucinations and altered states of consciousness similar to those observed in Tarantism. Interestingly, these events peaked during the grain harvest in June, aligning with the feast of **Saint Paul** on June 29, under whose protection these manifestations were eventually placed.
Other traditions across Italy and Europe echo Dionysian and pagan rituals, involving frenzied dances, collective trances, and an intrinsic connection to music and movement.
In Italy's mountainous regions, such as the Alps and Apennines, fertility festivals celebrated seasonal cycles with collective dances and songs honoring nature's abundance.

These celebrations, often tied to agricultural rituals, resemble the **Bacchanalia**, where rhythmic music, alcohol, and communal dancing unleashed collective energy.

An example from Provence is the **Tarasque**, a festival centered on a legendary dragon, marked by excessive drinking, group dances, and vibrant processions.

The Witch Hunts

Ergotism was also indirectly tied to the **witch hunts**, most famously during the Salem trials of 1692. Some researchers argue that ergotism may have fueled the hysteria behind witchcraft accusations, as many reported symptoms—convulsions, hallucinations, erratic behaviors—align with those caused by ergot poisoning. While this theory remains debated, it offers a plausible explanation for certain episodes of mass hysteria.

Despite its ominous history, **ergot** and other psychoactive plants played significant roles in medicine. In small doses, ergot was used to induce uterine contractions during childbirth and treat migraines, thanks to its vasoconstrictive properties.

However, during the Inquisition, the use of such plants was harshly banned, as they became synonymous with heresy and occult practices.

The Church's "Monopoly" on Herbs

While the Church did not hold an official monopoly over the use of herbs, it strictly regulated their application, condemning popular practices involving herbs in magical, heretical, or unauthorized medicinal contexts.

Within Christian monasteries, however, medicinal gardens became centers for cultivating and studying herbs for therapeutic purposes. Herbal medicine was accepted and encouraged within these religious settings, but its practice was forbidden to lay healers.

Religious orders like the Benedictines and Franciscans played a significant role in the use of herbs for healing, preserving and disseminating herbal knowledge, as long as it adhered to Christian doctrine.

Despite these restrictions, the use of psychoactive plants persisted covertly in rural Italian culture and other parts of the West until relatively recent times, especially in contexts linked to folk medicine, magic, and local superstitions.

Plants such as **belladonna**, **mandrake**, **henbane**, and fungi like **ergot** were used to induce visions or altered states of consciousness, often as part of healing rituals or to ward off ailments such as the **evil eye**.

During the Middle Ages, the **evil eye** was believed to be a malevolent power transmitted through the gaze of an envious or malicious person. It was thought to cause illness, misfortune, or both physical and spiritual harm. Symptoms associated with the evil eye ranged from unexplained sickness and loss of property to infertility and relational or familial discord.

Folk medicine of the time sought to offer protection through the use of amulets like the **horn** or the **horseshoe**, as well as specific rituals. Herbs, both medicinal and psychoactive, were commonly employed to break the curse or shield its victims.

Although the Catholic Church did not officially accept these beliefs, they were often tolerated, blending into the cultural practices of the time.

THE CRUSADES AND THE SPREAD OF OPIUM

During the Crusades—those so-called "Holy Wars" waged by Christians in the Middle East, officially to protect the Holy Land but also aimed at maintaining political and commercial control of the region—the cultivation and use of the opium poppy saw significant expansion. This plant, already known in antiquity and utilized by the Greeks and Romans, became increasingly widespread.

Opium extracts were traditionally used in small doses to alleviate pain and induce sleep. This practice persisted in rural communities, including in Italy, until relatively recent times. For instance, children were given poppy decoctions via soaked cloths to help them sleep or ease teething pains.

OPIUM AND THE BRAIN'S CHEMISTRY

The effects of opium on the brain are deeply intertwined with the reward circuit, much like the mechanisms we've previously explored.

Opium, through its active compounds such as morphine, manipulates the reward system deceptively, altering dopamine release and the perception of pain and pleasure. When consumed, the chemical compounds in opium bind to the brain's opioid receptors, acting like keys that unlock a profound sense of relief and euphoria. This dopamine release is excessive, similar to the activation of the reward circuit by food or sex. However, what sets opium apart is the intensity of its effect. The pleasure it generates is far more potent and longer-lasting than what the body could naturally achieve through endorphins, the brain's own chemicals for managing pain and inducing well-being.

Over time, the brain adapts to this chemical deception. While the reward circuit is designed to reinforce behaviors that make us feel good, in the case of opium, the brain becomes "trained" to rely increasingly on these external substances to experience pleasure or relieve pain. The result? Natural endorphin production decreases, leaving the brain unable to manage pain or generate well-being without the drug's assistance. This is the essence of addiction: a hijacked reward circuit

that cannot function properly without external chemical input.
Opium dependency also dangerously distorts the perception of pain. Just as the reward circuit motivates us to eat or socialize for survival, pain is a crucial signal that alerts us when something is wrong in our bodies. With prolonged opioid use, this alarm system is effectively "silenced."
The consequences are devastating: not only does tolerance to the drug increase, driving the user to seek ever higher doses, but there's also a risk of ignoring injuries or illnesses that require immediate attention.
This creates a vicious cycle where addiction exploits and manipulates the natural functioning of the reward circuit, leading to a gradual deterioration of both physical and mental health.

"*SEMEL IN ANNO LICET INSANIRE*", FROM ANCIENT RITUALS TO MODERN CELEBRATIONS

Since ancient times, humans have sought moments of controlled chaos to break free from the constraints of daily life. The Latin phrase *"Semel in anno licet insanire"* (once a year, it is permissible to go mad) captures this enduring need. Unlike the unregulated indulgence we often see today, ancient cultures channeled such desires through structured rituals that balanced the human craving for excess with a societal framework of restraint.
Christian celebrations, many of which absorbed elements from older pagan festivals, illustrate how these traditions evolved. Historically, rituals often incorporated substances like wine or psychoactive plants to induce states of ecstasy or spiritual transcendence.
Take, for example, **Carnival**, which traces its origins to Roman festivals such as the Bacchanalia and Saturnalia. These events, dedicated to Bacchus, the god of wine, and

Saturn, symbolized a temporary suspension of social hierarchies. Drunken revelry and collective euphoria were integral to the rites. With Christianity, Carnival became a pre-Lenten celebration in the liturgical calendar, but its spirit of uninhibited festivity endures, manifesting in costumes, indulgence, and excessive consumption of alcohol.
In the Anglo-Saxon world, **Halloween**, rooted in the Celtic festival of Samhain, marked the transition from summer to winter. Originally a solemn occasion to honor ancestors and connect with the spirit world, it has morphed into a festive event marked by costumes, parties, and—often—excessive drinking.
Similarly, **St. Patrick's Day**, dedicated to the patron saint of Ireland, coincides with the spring equinox. What began as a religious observance has evolved into a global celebration of Irish culture, filled with parades, traditional music, and abundant beer consumption.
The **summer solstice**, or **Midsummer**, remains a cornerstone of Northern European and Anglo-Saxon traditions. Once associated with fertility rites and renewal, it is now celebrated with outdoor gatherings, bonfires, and often, copious amounts of alcohol, maintaining its connection to seasonal cycles and community.
Thanksgiving, though uniquely American, reflects themes of harvest and abundance seen in ancient festivals. Originally a time to give thanks for the season's bounty, it has become synonymous with lavish feasts, often accompanied by wine and other drinks, blending gratitude with indulgence.
New Year's Eve, a secular holiday today, echoes the themes of ancient rituals marking the end of a cycle and the start of a new one. Across the Anglo-Saxon world, the night is celebrated with fireworks, midnight toasts, and exuberant gatherings fueled by alcohol, symbolizing renewal and hope for the future.
The **Bonfire Night** in the UK, held on November 5, commemorates the thwarted Gunpowder Plot of 1605. While

politically rooted, its celebratory elements—bonfires, fireworks, and hearty food—harken back to older fire festivals, blending historical remembrance with indulgence.
Though these modern celebrations have shed much of their original ritualistic structure, they still fulfill a fundamental human desire: to break free from societal norms, revel in collective joy, and reconnect with the rhythms of nature. Alcohol, symbolic inversions of social order, and moments of rule-breaking remain at the heart of these festivities, providing a temporary escape and a shared sense of renewal.
Even in their transformed state, these traditions remind us of the enduring power of communal indulgence and the balance between chaos and order in the human experience.

ACROSS THE AFRICAN CONTINENT

African civilizations have a profound and enduring history of using psychoactive substances, intricately tied to religious, ceremonial, and spiritual practices. In ancient Egypt, the blue lotus was revered for its ability to deepen connections with the afterlife, symbolizing transformation and renewal. In Central and West Africa, traditional societies such as the Bantu and the San embraced plants like **iboga**, renowned for its potent visionary effects, often used to foster spiritual enlightenment and communion with ancestors.
In the Horn of Africa, the stimulant plant **khat** has long been woven into social and spiritual rituals, serving as both a communal tradition and a means of achieving heightened focus and introspection.
While these practices have evolved over the centuries, the ritualistic and cultural use of psychoactive substances continues to thrive in parts of Africa, reflecting a profound harmony between spirituality, community, and the natural world.

THE BLUE LOTUS IN ANCIENT EGYPT

The blue lotus (*Nymphaea caerulea*) was revered in ancient Egypt as a plant of profound symbolic and spiritual significance, deeply embedded in rituals, particularly those associated with the journey to the afterlife.

Its delicate blossoms were central to religious ceremonies, believed to hold mild psychoactive properties capable of inducing states of tranquility, introspection, and spiritual connection. In funerary rites, the blue lotus became a symbol of spiritual rebirth, often depicted in hieroglyphs and artistic motifs as a powerful emblem of regeneration, guiding the departed on their path to the next world.

The flower's connection to the sun god Ra and the cycle of resurrection underscored its importance. Its daily rhythm of opening at sunrise and closing at sunset mirrored the eternal cycle of life, death, and rebirth. During funerary rituals, the blue lotus was frequently offered to the gods or placed near the deceased to support their spiritual transition.

Other psychoactive substances also featured in ancient Egyptian rituals. Wine, often infused with herbs to enhance its effects, was commonly used, and some of these additives likely had mind-altering properties, though precise records remain scarce.

Crucially, these altered states of consciousness were not sought casually but were deeply integrated into a structured and sacred framework of rituals, reflecting the Egyptians' disciplined approach to spirituality and the divine.

CENTRAL AFRICA

The use of psychoactive substances in African religious rituals has a deep and ancient history that spans from antiquity to the present day. Plants such as iboga and cannabis have traditionally been used to foster spiritual connection, induce visions, and promote healing.

The Tabernanthe iboga, a perennial shrub native to the tropical regions of Gabon, Congo, and Cameroon, plays a pivotal role in these practices. Its root contains the alkaloid ibogaine, renowned for inducing altered states of consciousness, vivid visions, and a profound sense of spiritual cleansing. This plant is central to the Bwiti religion, where it is used to facilitate contact with ancestors and promote emotional and spiritual healing.

In the Bwiti tradition, spiritual purification is understood as a process through which individuals cleanse themselves of impurities, negativity, or harmful influences, achieving a state of inner harmony and deeper connection to the divine. Ibogaine-induced visions are believed to provide wisdom and deep healing, purging the body and mind of negative energies.

The rituals involving iboga often evoke a sense of "rebirth," enabling participants to confront and transcend past traumas, fears, or inner conflicts. These experiences often bring suppressed memories and emotions to the surface, enabling individuals to achieve a form of emotional cleansing and clarity.

Cannabis, too, holds a place in both ritualistic and medicinal contexts. While initially used primarily in spiritual practices, cannabis has also become part of social and recreational traditions in some African cultures. However, traditional use typically includes safeguards to prevent misuse, ensuring a balance between its spiritual benefits and the risks of dependency.

Unlike cannabis, ibogaine has not become a recreational drug in Western cultures due to its intense and potentially hazardous effects. The profound and often demanding experiences it induces require a controlled setting and precise administration. As a result, its use remains largely confined to ritualistic and medical contexts, where it is administered under careful supervision.

THE HORN OF AFRICA: LAND OF KHAT

In the Horn of Africa, particularly in Ethiopia, Somalia, and Yemen, the chewing of khat (*Catha edulis*) has been a centuries-old tradition. This plant, known for its stimulating effects similar to caffeine, has long been used in social and ritual contexts to enhance mood, combat fatigue, and boost alertness. However, habitual consumption can lead to compulsive dependency, as regular use often results in tolerance and psychological addiction.

Khat contains two active compounds, cathinone and cathine, which impact brain chemistry by stimulating the central nervous system. Cathinone, in particular, functions similarly to amphetamines, increasing the release of dopamine and norepinephrine—neurotransmitters associated with euphoria, heightened focus, and pleasure. While this stimulation can temporarily elevate mood and energy levels, excessive or prolonged use can result in restlessness, insomnia, and psychological dependency.

THE ARAB WORLD AND THE MIDDLE EAST

In the lands of *One Thousand and One Nights*, certain psychoactive substances were traditionally used in Sufi and shamanic contexts, often as part of religious rituals aimed at fostering mystical experiences.

One of the most emblematic substances associated with these practices is hashish, a resin derived from cannabis with a high concentration of THC. Some sources even suggest that hashish gave its name to the sect of the Assassins (*Hashshashin*), although many historians dispute this claim. There is no concrete evidence that the Assassins systematically used hashish to alter the consciousness of their followers. This narrative may have been propagated by their Sunni adversaries to discredit them and later amplified by Western travelers and chroniclers such as Marco Polo.

The Assassins were renowned for employing political assassination as a strategy against their enemies, particularly Sunni leaders and Crusaders.

In contrast, the Sufis represent a mystical branch of Islam focused on achieving a personal and direct connection with God through spiritual practices such as meditation, prayer, and, in some traditions, ecstatic dance (as exemplified by the whirling dervishes). While some Sufi groups have used psychoactive substances to facilitate divine communion, such practices were often condemned by orthodox Islam.

Beyond hashish, opium (*Papaver somniferum*) has also been used in some Middle Eastern and Arab cultures for both medicinal and spiritual purposes. In religious rituals, the poppy capsule was sometimes employed to induce states of contemplation or trance. However, its severe side effects, including addiction and physical harm, led many to denounce its ritual use.

As is well-known, opium has analgesic properties and has been used extensively in medicine. However, the risk of dependency and overdose far outweighs its benefits if not administered under strict medical supervision.

In addition to Sufi traditions, other communities in the Arab and Middle Eastern worlds have also used psychoactive plants and substances for ritual purposes. In Iran, for example, there is evidence of the ritual use of wine (despite its prohibition under Islam), often associated with mystical rites of certain pre-Islamic Gnostic traditions. In ancient Persian culture, *haoma* (known as *soma* in Indo-European contexts) was a sacred, intoxicating drink used in Zoroastrian religious ceremonies to facilitate communication with the divine.

Although many of these practices were lost or transformed with the advent of Islam, traces of them persist in later mystical traditions.

Soma, a sacred beverage mentioned in ancient Indian texts like the Vedas and Persian Zoroastrian scriptures, is believed to have been derived from an unknown plant. Scholars have long debated the identity of this plant, speculating it could have been a mushroom, an herb, or a blend of various plants. However, no consensus has been reached on its exact origins.

CANNABIS, HASHISH, AND MARIJUANA

Let's explore the effects of cannabis and its derivatives—marijuana (dried leaves and flowers) and hashish (resin).

The active ingredient, THC, acts on complex brain circuits, significantly influencing both the Endocannabinoid System and the Reward Circuitry. The former is a cellular communication network spread throughout the body, essential for maintaining internal balance. It consists of three key components: CB1 and CB2 cannabinoid receptors, endocannabinoids naturally produced by the body (molecules similar to THC), and enzymes that regulate their synthesis and breakdown.

CB1 receptors, primarily found in the brain and central nervous system, play a crucial role in regulating mood, memory, pain perception, and appetite. CB2 receptors, mainly located in the immune system and peripheral tissues, modulate inflammatory responses and pain. When cannabis-derived THC binds to these receptors, it disrupts normal functions like sleep, appetite, memory, and stress response, causing temporary effects such as euphoria, relaxation, and sensory alterations.

This interaction with CB1 receptors triggers a cascade of effects that directly influence the Reward Circuitry. THC stimulation prompts the release of dopamine, the key neurotransmitter responsible for feelings of pleasure.

Thus, cannabis doesn't simply induce "relaxation" or "euphoria"; it activates the mechanism that can lead to tolerance and dependency.

This has sparked a still-heated debate. For some, cannabis remains a "soft drug," lacking the devastating effects of substances like cocaine or heroin, and many argue for its legalization. However, its action on the Reward Circuitry suggests

that habitual use of marijuana or hashish could pave the way to more potent substances. The risk lies in the increased tolerance to cannabis, potentially driving users to seek the effects they can no longer achieve, leading them to experiment with stronger drugs.
Additionally, one must consider that cannabis on the illicit market is often laced with harder drugs, intentionally designed to accelerate and deepen dependency.

THE ARABIAN PENINSULA: COFFEE AND THE ART OF SACRED WAKEFULNESS

The ancient use of coffee as a stimulant—and occasionally in ritual contexts—originated in Ethiopia and spread to the Arabian Peninsula. The coffee plant (**Coffea arabica**) is native to Ethiopia's highlands, where local tribes such as the Oromo chewed raw coffee beans or mixed them with animal fat to form energy-packed "balls." These were consumed to enhance stamina and endurance during long journeys or hunting expeditions.
Although not classified as a psychoactive substance in the traditional sense, coffee was valued for its invigorating properties, which boosted both physical and mental resilience.
Later, coffee found its way to the Arabian Peninsula, where it was embraced as a beverage. In Yemen, it became a cornerstone of **Sufi religious practices**, consumed during nocturnal vigils to maintain alertness during prayers and meditation.
Over time, these traditions evolved, and coffee emerged as an essential part of both social and spiritual gatherings throughout the Islamic world. Rather than being seen as a psychoactive drug, coffee was regarded as a tool to enhance focus and endurance.

While it may not be labeled as a traditional psychoactive substance, coffee undeniably possesses addictive qualities, further solidifying its unique place in cultural and social history.

COFFEE ADDICTION: THE STIMULATING TRAP

Coffee, with its active compound caffeine, exerts a notable influence on the brain. It impacts energy levels, focus, and even mood by activating the infamous Reward Circuit, stimulating the release of dopamine, the neurotransmitter that generates pleasure and drives us to repeat gratifying behaviors. This effect leaves us feeling more alert, motivated, and occasionally euphoric.

However, regular and prolonged consumption can lead to caffeine tolerance, as the brain adjusts to its presence. Over time, larger amounts of coffee are needed to achieve the same stimulating effect. This mirrors a fundamental mechanism observed in addictions to other substances: the Reward System becomes manipulated, and the brain begins to demand higher doses to maintain the same sense of satisfaction.

When caffeine intake is suddenly stopped, withdrawal symptoms can set in, including headaches, excessive fatigue, irritability, trouble concentrating, and a general feeling of discomfort. Some individuals may also experience nausea, muscle aches, or an overwhelming urge to sleep. These withdrawal effects can begin within 12 to 24 hours after the last cup and may last up to a week, especially for heavy or habitual coffee drinkers.

The allure of coffee lies not only in its taste but in its ability to invigorate, making it easy to underestimate how quickly reliance on caffeine can develop.

FAR EAST: ALCHEMY AND POISONS

In ancient China and Japan, as in other parts of Asia, **psychoactive substances** played a significant role in religious and spiritual practices, intertwining deeply with traditions that spanned medicine, philosophy, and mysticism. These substances were used to **connect with the spiritual realm**, induce visions, and promote states of trance or enlightenment.

In **China**, one of the most widely used substances was **tea**, considered a powerful tool to stimulate both body and mind, clear thoughts, and elevate spiritual awareness. Though not hallucinogenic by modern definitions, tea was integral to **Taoist** and **Buddhist** practices, as it enhanced focus during extended sessions of meditation and prayer.

Taoist practices also involved the creation of alchemical compounds, often referred to as **"elixirs of immortality,"** which frequently contained **minerals and metals**. While believed to extend life, these concoctions often resulted in severe poisoning and even death. A well-known case is that of **Qin Shi Huang**, China's first emperor, who died from mercury poisoning in his quest for eternal life.

In Taoist philosophy, these substances held symbolic meaning: **mercury**, with its fluid and reflective qualities, symbolized life energy. However, ingesting mercury caused **convulsions, nervous system damage**, and death.

To counteract the toxicity of these ingredients, **ginseng** and other herbs were often added to the mixtures to **restore balance** and enhance vitality. Although ginseng offers genuine health benefits, it fell far short of granting the immortality many sought. Ultimately, these elixirs were aimed at facilitating spiritual transformation, with physical immortality seen as a secondary manifestation of **cosmic harmony**.

Opium, while less associated with ancient spiritual rituals, was significant in **traditional Chinese medicine**, serving as both an analgesic and sedative. Another prominent substance was **cannabis**, known as "má" (麻), used in both medicinal and spiritual contexts. Historical accounts suggest cannabis was employed to **induce trance states**, enabling shamans to communicate with spirits. It was seen as a gateway to the unseen world, offering access to higher planes of existence.

In **Japan**, the documented use of psychoactives in religious rituals is less extensive than in China. However, it is believed that **shamanistic practices** tied to **animistic beliefs** and **Shintoism** were present in ancient times. **Japanese shamans**, including "kannushi" and "miko" (priestesses), may have used **fermented rice beverages**, like **sake**, to reach altered states of consciousness and commune with the **kami**, the spirits of nature.

Today, the use of psychoactive substances in Asian religious rituals has **significantly declined** and is largely confined to specific, localized traditions. In **modern China**, consumerism and external influences have distanced the population from ancient shamanistic practices. However, in remote regions of **Mongolia** and **Siberia**, the use of cannabis and other herbs persists, albeit on a smaller scale. In **Japan**, sake remains an important element of Shinto ceremonies, but its use is primarily **symbolic** rather than **psychedelic**.

THE SAINT OF ADDICTS IS CHINESE

The patron saint of those struggling with addiction hails from China—**Saint Mark Ji Tianxiang**.

Born in the 19th century, Saint Mark Ji Tianxiang battled a lifelong addiction to opium. Despite his repeated efforts to overcome his dependence on the substance, he struggled to break free. Due to his addiction, he was denied communion for many years. However, he never abandoned his faith or his hope in God's grace.

In 1900, during the anti-Christian Boxer Rebellion, Saint Mark was imprisoned along with his family for their religious beliefs. Despite the threat of death, they all refused to renounce Christianity and were executed as martyrs.
Saint Mark Ji Tianxiang was canonized by Pope John Paul II in 2000 as one of the 120 Chinese Martyrs. Today, he serves as a beacon of hope and perseverance for those grappling with addiction, embodying unwavering faith even in the face of adversity.

RELIGIONS OF INDIA

India, a land of ancient sages and timeless rituals, holds a sacred view of cannabis. During festivals like **Holi** and **Shivaratri**, believers consume **bhang**, a drink made from the cannabis plant, to honor the god **Shiva**, who is often depicted as a user of this sacred substance.
For devotees, the ritual use of bhang serves as a means to commune with the divine, purify the mind and body, and celebrate with renewed spiritual devotion. Bhang is prepared from the leaves and female flowers of the **Cannabis sativa** or **Cannabis indica** plants, which contain **THC**, the psychoactive compound responsible for its mind-altering effects.
In addition to THC, bhang also contains **CBD**, a cannabinoid known for its relaxing and anti-inflammatory properties without significant psychoactive effects. The preparation is rich in **terpenes**, which may enhance mood and relaxation. Traditionally, bhang is mixed with yogurt, milk, almonds, and spices, creating a flavorful and potent drink.
Depending on the dosage and preparation, its effects can range from mild relaxation to intense euphoria and altered perception.
Pros and Cons of Psychoactive Substances in Spiritual Contexts. On the positive side, the use of psychoactive substances in religious and spiritual practices offered a way to reach altered states of consciousness. These states

were believed to enable communion with deities, the acquisition of wisdom, and prophetic visions. For substances like tea and sake, their use could enhance focus, aid meditation, and strengthen the connection to the sacred.

However, the drawbacks were significant, especially with more potent or potentially toxic substances like alchemical compounds or improperly used hallucinogenic plants. The use of such substances, including cannabis and alchemical herbs, carried risks of dependence and harmful side effects, including poisoning or damage to the nervous system.

While these practices offered profound spiritual insights, they also demanded careful regulation to prevent misuse and protect both the body and the spirit.

SIBERIA AND SHAMANISM

In the icy expanses of Siberia, shamans among the Chukchi and Koryak peoples used **Amanita muscaria**, the iconic red-capped mushroom speckled with white, to enter altered states of consciousness and communicate with spirits.

For these communities, the shaman was not merely a healer but a living bridge between the human and spiritual realms. **Amanita muscaria** served as the tool to traverse that bridge, allowing shamans to transcend physical boundaries, gain visions, and access higher wisdom. This knowledge was often used to heal the sick or guide their communities through challenging decisions.

Rituals involving **Amanita muscaria** also reinforced community bonds. Collective experiences during these spiritual journeys fostered cultural identity and a shared sense of belonging.

However, consuming the mushroom came with significant risks. **Amanita muscaria** contains potent toxins such as **ibotenic acid** and **muscimol**, which can cause severe side effects. In high doses, these compounds may lead to nausea, vomiting, delirium, visual and auditory hallucinations, and in extreme cases, seizures or coma.

Some Siberian peoples developed methods to mitigate the mushroom's toxicity, such as having the shaman urinate after ingestion and reusing the urine, which retained the active compounds but was free of the more dangerous toxins. Despite these practices, the risk of overdose remained high. This delicate balance between spiritual power and physical danger made **Amanita muscaria** both revered and feared.

While such practices are less common today, they persist in specific contexts. The expansion of Russia and the Soviet Union contributed to the gradual decline of these rituals, yet they survive in some isolated Siberian and Arctic tundra communities. In these areas, shamanic traditions endure, albeit often blended with Christian or modern influences.

Shamanism, along with the use of psychoactive substances like **Amanita muscaria**, is typically practiced within small, often secretive groups, as a way of preserving ancestral traditions in an increasingly globalized world dominated by Orthodox Christianity and other mainstream religions.

In recent decades, a renewed interest in shamanic traditions has emerged among scholars, anthropologists, and spiritual seekers. This cultural revival has led to a rediscovery and appreciation of these practices beyond Siberia. **Amanita muscaria** has also found its way into contemporary spiritual movements such as neo-shamanism and New Age practices. These groups draw inspiration from ancient shamanic techniques to access altered states of consciousness.

However, modern use of this mushroom carries significant risks due to its toxicity and potential side effects. In traditional societies, the safe preparation and use of **Amanita muscaria** were integral to the shamanic practice. In contemporary neo-shamanic or Western contexts, the use of psychoactive substances is often less disciplined or regulated, increasing the likelihood of misuse or harm from this powerful mushroom.

THE EFFECTS OF THE FAIRY TALE MUSHROOM

Amanita muscaria, often called the "fairy tale mushroom," interacts with the brain in unique ways, impacting the reward circuit, though differently from substances that directly stimulate dopamine release. Its primary psychoactive compound, muscimol, binds to GABA receptors, which play a key role in regulating neuronal activity. By influencing the balance between inhibition and excitation of nerve cells, Amanita muscaria produces profound effects on perception, memory, and coordination.

When muscimol binds to GABA receptors, it mimics the natural inhibitory action of this neurotransmitter, but with significantly intensified effects. This can lead to a general slowing of brain functions, inducing sensations ranging from calm and euphoria to confusion and disorientation.

In some cases, Amanita muscaria can create feelings of pleasure or vivid hallucinations. However, these experiences are not always controllable or enjoyable. At higher doses, the effects may escalate to agitation, muscle spasms, and in extreme cases, seizures.

The disruption of the brain's inhibitory system may also temporarily impair short-term memory and motor coordination, making the use of this mushroom risky without proper supervision or preparation.

Despite its enchanting reputation in folklore, Amanita muscaria demands caution due to its unpredictable and potent impact on the brain.

INDIGENOUS RELIGIONS OF THE AMERICAS

The ancient peoples of the Americas had a profound connection to nature and the spiritual world, with many cultures integrating the use of **psychoactive substances** into their religious and ceremonial practices. Among the most well-known of these civilizations are the **Maya**, **Aztecs**, and **Inca**, alongside numerous indigenous groups in North and South America, including those of the **American Southwest** and the **Amazonian shamans**.

These substances—ranging from hallucinogenic mushrooms to **peyote cactus** and **ayahuasca**—were regarded as sacred tools. They facilitated communication with the spirit realm, provided visions, and imparted divine wisdom. Each culture had its unique traditions surrounding the use of these plants, often reserving them for priests, shamans, or spiritual leaders.

Psychoactive substances were viewed as essential for connecting with the supernatural, helping guide religious and political decisions within the community. Many of these traditions persist in indigenous cultures today, where these substances remain integral to spiritual rituals.

The Maya: Mushrooms and Divine Communication

The Maya widely used **hallucinogenic mushrooms**, known as *teonanácatl*, or "flesh of the gods," which contained **psilocybin**. During ceremonies, priests and shamans consumed these mushrooms to communicate with ancestors and receive messages from the spiritual realm. The induced visions were seen as divine manifestations, offering a higher understanding of the universe.

The Aztecs: A Diverse Arsenal of Psychoactives

The Aztecs employed a broader range of substances, including **psilocybin mushrooms**, **peyote**, and **tlitliltzin**. The latter, derived from the seeds of *Ipomoea violacea* (morning glory), contained **ergine**, an alkaloid with hallucinogenic properties similar to LSD.

The seeds were crushed and consumed to induce altered states of consciousness, facilitating divination rituals and spiritual communication. For Aztec priests and shamans, **tlitliltzin** was a sacred tool, its visions providing divine guidance for both religious and political matters.
The Aztecs also venerated **cacao**, preparing it as a bitter drink known as *xocolatl*. Made from roasted cacao beans, water, and sometimes spiced with vanilla or chili, it was linked to **Quetzalcoatl**, the god of wind and wisdom. The drink was believed to bestow strength and mental clarity, making it a central feature of religious ceremonies.

The Inca: Coca Leaves and Ayahuasca
The **Inca** primarily used **coca leaves**, considered sacred, for both their energizing properties and spiritual significance. Shamans chewed coca during ceremonies to connect with spirits or gain mystical insight. Additionally, **ayahuasca**, a potent Amazonian hallucinogen, was used by Inca and neighboring tribes to journey into the spiritual realm.
Unlike the cacao-rich cultures of Mesoamerica, cacao played a lesser role in Incan traditions. However, the Inca relied on **coca leaves** and other stimulants, including wild varieties of coffee, especially in religious ceremonies or preparations for war.

Sacred Beverages and Spiritual Connection
In all these cultures, drinks like **cacao infusions**, coffee, or other plant-based concoctions were far more than simple nourishment. They were powerful tools for connecting with the spiritual world, acquiring strength and clarity, and preparing for significant events.
Even today, these ancient practices continue to influence the spiritual and cultural identities of many indigenous communities, preserving a rich legacy of respect for the sacred and the transformative power of nature.

CACAO AND THE BRAIN

Cacao, thanks to compounds like theobromine, caffeine, and phenylethylamine, influences the brain's reward circuit in a way that mirrors other substances that stimulate dopamine release, albeit more subtly.

Its ability to activate the dopaminergic system fosters feelings of pleasure and satisfaction. While the effect of phenylethylamine in cacao is not strong enough to induce intense euphoria, it does contribute to an overall sense of well-being, often prompting people to seek out this gratification repeatedly.

However, cacao does not create the kind of strong physical dependence seen with caffeine or other addictive substances.

Beyond its impact on the reward system, cacao contains flavonoids that support cognitive function and protect the brain from oxidative stress. These compounds enhance blood flow to the brain, contributing to improved mental clarity, energy, and long-term wellness.

That said, excessive consumption of cacao-based products—especially those high in sugar and fat—can lead to negative effects such as nervousness or insomnia, particularly in individuals sensitive to caffeine.

Cacao remains a remarkable example of a natural substance that not only delights the senses but also provides tangible cognitive and emotional benefits when enjoyed in moderation.

NATIVE AMERICANS AND PEYOTE

Across the vast deserts of North America, the Huichol people and tribes within the **Native American Church** engage in ancient rituals centered around **peyote**, a cactus containing **mescaline**, a powerful hallucinogen.

Revered as sacred, peyote takes a central role in spiritual ceremonies where it is consumed to facilitate **mystical visions**, healing experiences, and a deeper connection with the spirit world. Its use is treated with profound respect and occurs exclusively within ritualistic settings, safeguarding its sanctity and preventing misuse.

The **Native American Church**, established in 1918, has been instrumental in protecting the ritualistic use of peyote, particularly in the United States, where restrictive laws might otherwise limit its availability. Through the Church, many tribes have preserved their spiritual and medicinal practices involving peyote, viewing it as a means to communicate with the divine and receive sacred revelations considered gifts of spiritual insight.

Scientifically known as **Lophophora williamsii**, peyote is a small, spineless cactus native to Mexico and the southwestern United States. Its active compound, **mescaline**, alters perception, heightening colors, sounds, and physical sensations while inducing visions integral to the ritual. These experiences are often described as profound "journeys" into a higher reality, enabling participants to explore their consciousness and connect with spirits. For the Huichol people, the insights gained through peyote are seen as sacred messages from the spiritual realm.

Ceremonies often take place in traditional **lodges** or **teepees**, led by a spiritual guide known as a **roadman**. Throughout the night, participants pray, sing, and share reflections, fostering a collective connection to ancestral traditions and the divine. These rituals, which frequently extend until dawn, serve as a vital means of preserving cultural identity and spiritual heritage.

While peyote offers significant spiritual benefits, its consumption can cause physical side effects such as **nausea**, **vomiting**, and general discomfort. This underscores the importance of its use within structured ceremonies under the guidance of experienced spiritual leaders.

In Mexico, efforts have been made to safeguard the sacred lands where peyote grows, and in the United States, federal law protects its religious use. However, overharvesting and increased tourism threaten the cactus in certain areas, highlighting the need for sustainable management to ensure it remains integral to indigenous spiritual practices.

Peyote is not merely a powerful hallucinogen; it stands as a **symbol of cultural and spiritual resilience** for Native American communities, embodying their enduring connection to sacred traditions and the natural world.

AMAZON: THE REALM OF AYAHUASCA

Journeying through the Amazon, one steps into the realm of **ayahuasca**, a hallucinogenic brew used by many indigenous tribes, including the **Shipibo** and **Siona**, for profound spiritual purposes.

Central to **shamanic ceremonies**, ayahuasca is consumed to induce altered states of consciousness, enabling participants to connect with the spirit world and receive guiding visions for the community. This sacred concoction is crafted from the **Banisteriopsis caapi vine** and the leaves of **Psychotria viridis**.

For these tribes, the ritual is far more than a hallucinatory experience; it is a deeply sacred practice aimed at healing both body and spirit. The ceremonies are led by **shamans**, who guide participants through intense spiritual journeys, facilitating visions and insights that are often interpreted as messages from the divine.

In recent decades, ayahuasca has transcended its Amazonian origins, becoming a central sacrament in **syncretic religious movements** such as **Santo Daime** and **União do Vegetal** in Brazil. These groups blend elements of Christianity with indigenous practices, viewing ayahuasca as a gateway to profound spiritual connection. During rituals, adherents drink the brew to purify the soul, seek spiritual guidance, and deepen their relationship with the divine.

Despite its sacred applications, ayahuasca's effects demand caution. The experience often involves **nausea, vomiting**, and other intense physical reactions, which are seen as integral to the purification process. Participants are encouraged to embrace these sensations as symbolic of the cleansing of emotional and spiritual impurities.

As ayahuasca gains global attention, it remains deeply rooted in its indigenous origins, representing a bridge between the material and spiritual worlds—a testament to the enduring wisdom of Amazonian cultures.

SACRED PLANTS AND THE BRAIN

Mescaline and ayahuasca are two fascinating and complex psychedelic substances, both capable of profoundly altering consciousness, yet distinct in the mechanisms by which they achieve these effects. While both interact with serotonin receptors, opening doors to visions, reflections, and emotional transformations, their impact on the brain highlights key differences.

Mescaline, derived from the peyote cactus, significantly influences the reward circuit, heightening sensory activity and altering perceptions of space and time. These effects can induce euphoria or, in some cases, disorientation. Conversely, ayahuasca, the ritual beverage of the Amazon, operates through DMT, which expands consciousness but rarely elicits the euphoria typical of mescaline. Instead, ayahuasca emphasizes intense, often spiritually significant internal experiences.

Mescaline modulates serotonin receptors, particularly 5-HT2A, triggering vivid sensory and visual distortions that alter one's perception of time and space. This

sensory expansion often leads to states of euphoria and spiritual connection but can occasionally result in confusion or panic. Although mescaline does not cause physical dependency, its ability to create ecstatic states may lead to psychological dependency, with individuals seeking repeated experiences to escape reality or achieve spiritual transcendence.

Ayahuasca, on the other hand, induces an altered state of consciousness by stimulating serotonin receptors without directly involving dopamine or the reward circuit. The DMT in ayahuasca generates profound visions and deep introspections, often experienced as a journey toward emotional healing or spiritual insight. In its ritualistic context, ayahuasca can help individuals overcome emotional blockages, but its intense effects can also provoke panic or confusion, necessitating the guidance of an experienced shaman or facilitator.

While neither mescaline nor ayahuasca creates physical dependency, the intensity of their effects and the profound sense of "purification" they evoke can lead some individuals to seek repeated use, fostering a form of psychological dependency. These sacred substances, when used responsibly in the proper context, can act as powerful tools for personal transformation, though they also demand respect and careful supervision to mitigate potential risks.

AFRO-AMERICAN RELIGIONS

In **Cuban Santería** and **Haitian Vodou**, two spiritual traditions blending Christianity with ancient African practices, contact with spirits is an intense and transformative experience, often facilitated by rituals where sacred herbs play a crucial role. While these plants are not always psychoactive in the conventional sense, they influence states of consciousness, opening a channel to the spiritual realm under the guidance of skilled priests who carefully avoid misuse, understanding the potential dangers involved.

Santería, also known as **Regla de Ocha**, emerged from the fusion of **Yoruba beliefs** and the Catholicism introduced by Spanish colonizers. The **Orisha**, divine entities in this tradition, communicate with devotees through rituals involving sacrifices, music, and dance. Among sacred plants, **tobacco** holds a place of prominence. Its smoke is offered to the Orisha and aids **Babalawo** (priests) in entering a focused state for divination. Additionally, non-psychoactive herbs like **rosemary** and **basil** are used in spiritual baths, promoting relaxation and spiritual openness. Certain mildly psychoactive plants, such as **ayahuama**, are also employed in rituals, albeit with less intensity than in Amazonian traditions.

A cornerstone of Santería is the **toques de tambor**, ceremonies where rhythmic drumming and dance create an atmosphere that induces trance states, enabling spiritual possession as the Orisha manifest through their followers.

Similarly, **Haitian Vodou**, with origins rooted in the Yoruba, Fon, and Ewe spiritual systems combined with Catholic elements, revolves around invoking the **Loa**, its divine entities. Possession rituals and healing ceremonies often feature sacred plants. One of the most potent and dangerous is **Datura**, also known as the "Devil's Herb." Used to induce deep trance states, it is meticulously dosed, as overuse can lead to extreme hallucinations or even death. The association of Datura with Vodou's **zombie mythology** reflects the belief that the plant can induce a deathlike state, creating an appearance of suspended life.

Like in Santería, **tobacco** is essential in Vodou, used to summon the Loa and purify ritual spaces. In some modern practices, **cannabis**, though not traditional, has been incorporated as a tool to aid meditation and spiritual communication.
In both Santería and Vodou, the use of plants reflects a complex system of meanings and symbolism, where the boundary between the visible and invisible worlds is thin and permeable. While the approaches and rituals differ, both religions harness the power of herbs to facilitate divine connection, relying on profound expertise and respect to maintain the delicate balance between spiritual blessings and potential risks.

THE EFFECTS OF TOBACCO ON THE BRAIN

Tobacco plays a role in the brain's reward circuit similar to other substances that stimulate dopamine. When nicotine, its active ingredient, reaches the brain, it binds to acetylcholine receptors, triggering the release of the neurotransmitter associated with gratification. This creates an immediate, fleeting sense of pleasure.
Here's where the dangerous game begins: this dopamine surge convinces the brain that the experience is worth repeating, setting in motion a cycle that inevitably leads to addiction. Much like caffeine or other drugs, the pursuit of that same pleasurable sensation drives the brain to demand increasingly higher doses. Over time, the body builds a tolerance to nicotine, requiring more tobacco to achieve the same effect. The result? A deep-seated physical and psychological dependency that makes quitting smoking an incredibly challenging task.
The negative health effects of tobacco are no secret: from cancer to cardiovascular issues

such as stroke and hypertension, its dangers are well-documented. However, tobacco's insidious power lies in its ability to manipulate the brain's reward circuit so effectively that breaking free becomes extraordinarily difficult, even in the face of its devastating consequences.

For many, tobacco retains an ambiguous allure. It provides a temporary boost in focus and suppresses appetite. Yet, these benefits are short-lived, and repeated use demands ever-increasing amounts of nicotine to achieve the same effects. What starts as a stimulant soon becomes a trap, draining the body and damaging the dopamine system over time.

RASTAFARIANISM IN JAMAICA

In Jamaica, **Rastafarianism** has elevated cannabis, known as ganja, to a sacred and sacramental symbol. This religious and cultural movement originated in the 1930s, following the coronation of Ras Tafari Makonnen as Emperor of Ethiopia under the name **Haile Selassie I**. For many Jamaicans, influenced by the ideas of Pan-Africanist leader **Marcus Garvey**, Selassie's coronation was interpreted as the arrival of a messiah destined to liberate the descendants of Africans from oppression.

Garvey, revered as a prophet within Rastafarianism, urged Africans in the diaspora to reconnect with their roots and return to Africa, viewed not only as a physical homeland but also as a spiritual symbol of redemption and liberation. Rastafarianism venerates Haile Selassie as a divine incarnation and blends biblical beliefs with a strong African identity, standing in opposition to colonialism and social injustices.

Cannabis plays a central role in Rastafarian spiritual practices. Smoking ganja is seen as a sacred act, used to draw closer to **Jah** (God), purify the mind and body, and aid in meditation. This spiritual use allows followers to connect with a higher dimension of wisdom and inner peace.

However, as previously mentioned, the benefits and risks of cannabis should not be overlooked. While deeply respected within Rastafarian culture as a spiritual tool, cannabis can still carry psychological and physical effects that require careful consideration, particularly outside the sacred and ceremonial context where it is revered.

AUSTRALIA: RITUALS AT THE EDGE

Among Australia's Aboriginal populations, there is little documented evidence of the use of psychoactive substances comparable to the practices observed in other indigenous cultures, such as those in South or North America. Instead, Aboriginal spirituality is deeply rooted in a profound connection to the land and ancestral spirits, expressed through elaborate ceremonies involving **song, dance, and ritual art**, such as the **Dreamtime** or **Tjukurpa** stories.

Aboriginal spiritual practices emphasize the interconnection between humans, nature, and the spirits of their ancestors. Ceremonies like the **corroboree**—which are healing rituals or cultural celebrations—typically do not involve the use of hallucinogenic substances. Instead, altered states of consciousness are achieved through **rhythmic singing, the resonant tones of the didgeridoo, and physical movement**, inducing trance-like states through physical and auditory stimulation rather than chemical intervention.

That said, some sources suggest the limited and specific use of local plants with stimulating or sedative properties. For instance, **Pituri**, a plant containing alkaloids like nicotine, has been traditionally used in some Aboriginal communities. Pituri was often chewed during long journeys or stressful times for its stimulating effects, and while it may have held some ceremonial significance, it is not considered a hallucinogenic substance.

In Aboriginal culture, the focus remains on the harmony between individuals, the natural world, and spiritual ancestors, with altered states often achieved through practices that are inherently physical and rhythmic rather than chemically induced.

DANCING AND THE HORMONES OF HAPPINESS

Intense, prolonged physical activities like ritual dancing or singing affect the brain in ways remarkably similar to drugs, leveraging the reward circuit through the release of dopamine and endorphins. Often referred to as "happiness hormones," these chemicals generate feelings of pleasure and satisfaction, mimicking the effects of psychoactive substances that stimulate the brain's dopaminergic system.

Dopamine, in particular, activates the nucleus accumbens, the brain's "pleasure center," driving us to repeat the activity to relive that same sense of well-being. Meanwhile, endorphins act as natural painkillers, reducing the perception of discomfort and inducing a euphoric sensation. This effect is strikingly similar to that of substances like cannabis or alcohol, which also act on the reward circuit.

These effects are amplified when individuals enter a state of flow, a mental state in which they feel completely absorbed in the activity. In this state, there is often a seamless connection between mind and body, akin to a natural trance or a "psychotropic journey." This sensation mirrors the altered states of consciousness induced by substances like ayahuasca or mescaline, which distort perceptions of time and reality.

Interestingly, the rhythmic movement of dance and the euphoria it generates share

another similarity with psychoactive substances: the potential for behavioral addiction. Just as drugs can create psychological dependency, some individuals may develop an addiction to physical activity or adrenaline, constantly seeking the highs generated by these experiences.
While this might seem harmless, such dependencies can lead to negative consequences, including physical issues like muscle injuries or joint strain, as well as psychological challenges like anxiety or depression when the individual is unable to engage in their preferred activity.
Ritual dancing and rhythmic practices are powerful tools for inducing states of joy and unity, but like all mechanisms that tap into the brain's reward system, they must be approached with awareness and balance to avoid unintended consequences.

IN CONCLUSION

The use of psychoactive substances in ritual contexts has never been a mere act of recreation; it is a sacred practice deeply rooted in the spirituality of countless cultures. These substances, revered and sometimes feared, have long been regarded as tools to connect humans with the divine, heal the soul, and strengthen communal bonds.
However, their profound power comes with inherent risks. Many traditions caution against indiscriminate or out-of-context use, acknowledging the potential for harmful consequences, both physical and psychological. This delicate balance between the sacred and the profane reveals a deep, respectful understanding of the power of psychoactive substances—complex and fascinating spiritual legacies that have accompanied humanity through the ages.

In the next chapter, we will shift our focus to the other side of the coin: exploring how the use of psychoactive substances, initially intended for sacred and spiritual purposes, has evolved over time into a pathway for self-destruction, culminating in pathological addictions.
This transition poses a significant challenge for modern society, which grapples with the consequences of substance abuse in non-ritual contexts.

CHAPTER 2

PATHOLOGICAL ADDICTIONS IN HUMAN HISTORY

The journey of understanding pathological addictions spans centuries, crossing cultures and continents. What was once regarded as a moral failing has gradually been recognized as a complex condition worthy of scientific inquiry.

In earlier times, the misuse of substances such as alcohol or opium was often perceived as an individual flaw, tied to personal weakness or a lack of self-control. This moralistic view dominated much of history up until the 19th century. However, with the advent of modern medicine and social sciences, addiction began to be seen not as a sin or character defect, but as a clinical condition rooted in intricate chemical and psychological processes.

This shift in perception coincided with growing awareness that addictions—be they to alcohol, drugs, gambling, or even relationships and sexual behaviors—are not merely the result of poor choices but manifestations of disorders that impact the brain and nervous system. This evolving understanding paved the way for more scientific treatments and fostered greater societal empathy for individuals suffering from these conditions. Yet, the path to this awareness has been far from linear.

Across different eras, societies have swung between moral condemnation and scientific acceptance, creating a tension that persists even today.

Throughout history, the struggles of prominent figures—artists, politicians, and intellectuals—who succumbed to addiction have revealed not only the fragility of the human spirit but also the insidious power of compulsive behaviors. These personal stories, woven into the fabric of shifting social norms, offer profound insights into humanity's attempts to understand and combat addiction. From the ancient Greek philosophers, who spoke of "intemperance," to the sophisticated scientific approaches of today, our perception of addiction has undergone significant transformation.

Today, addictions are studied as neurological and behavioral disorders, with a particular focus on the brain mechanisms that make breaking the cycle of dependence so extraordinarily challenging. This modern understanding underscores the importance of treating addiction not with judgment, but with compassion and evidence-based care.

ANTIQUITY AND EARLY UNDERSTANDINGS

Even in ancient times, civilizations were aware of the dangers associated with substance abuse.

In classical Greece, alcohol, personified by the god Dionysus, was both celebrated during festivals and rituals and feared for its destructive effects. One of the earliest historical accounts of addiction-related struggles comes from the life of Alexander the Great. His untimely death remains a topic of debate among historians, with some suggesting that excessive drinking during a banquet may have contributed to his illness and premature demise. While more accepted theories attribute his death to typhoid fever or malaria, the symbolism of his struggle with wine—his "inner demon"—illustrates the grip alcohol can exert, even over the most powerful figures.

Another significant historical account revolves around the opium epidemic in China, which began during the Han dynasty and escalated under the Qing dynasty. Opium, derived from the poppy plant, became a major social scourge, leading to widespread addiction and culminating in the Opium Wars between China and Britain. This marked one of the earliest large-scale crises of substance abuse in global history.

Roman society, known for its grandeur and indulgence, was not immune to excesses either. Gambling became so pervasive that Emperor Augustus felt compelled to introduce laws to curb it, recognizing its socially corrosive effects. Despite these efforts, gambling remained a widespread and uncontrollable practice, highlighting how even a superpower like Rome was vulnerable to the grip of pathological addiction.

Interestingly, addiction-related behaviors were not limited to southern civilizations. In Nordic cultures, mead—a fermented honey drink—played a central role in social and ritual contexts. Mead halls were hubs of communal gatherings where warriors and leaders celebrated victories or reinforced social bonds. While mead was an integral part of these societies, its overconsumption often led to impulsive behaviors and violent outbursts, as captured in Norse sagas and poems. These stories frequently depict the dangers of unchecked indulgence and the way alcohol could amplify both courage and recklessness.

The decline of imperial Rome, often attributed to political and military factors, was also fueled by social decay, with substance abuse and compulsive behaviors contributing to its downfall. Similarly, in the Nordic world, excessive drinking and the chaos it could unleash became cautionary tales, emphasizing the need for balance and moderation.

As we delve deeper into history, it becomes clear how addiction has shaped and influenced the course of human civilization, revealing its profound and lasting impact.

MESOPOTAMIA: MYTHS AND OBSESSIVE EGOCENTRISM

The myths of ancient Mesopotamia, cradle of the world's first great civilizations like the Sumerians, Akkadians, and Babylonians, offer profound insights into the dangers of a psychological trait often associated with pathological dependencies: obsessive egocentrism.

This condition, marked by a relentless focus on oneself and an insatiable need for immediate gratification, often stems from a deep emotional void or a sense of inadequacy. Legendary rulers such as Gilgamesh, Sargon of Akkad, and Nebuchadnezzar II embody the consequences of this mindset, revealing how it can lead to personal and societal instability.

Gilgamesh, the king of Uruk, is perhaps the most striking example of obsessive egocentrism. In the epic that bears his name, he initially appears as a tyrannical ruler, consumed by the abuse of power and an obsessive quest for immortality. It is only through the death of his close companion, Enkidu, that Gilgamesh is forced to confront his mortality, embarking on an inner journey of transformation.

Enkidu, a wild man connected to nature, serves as a balancing force. Their encounter leads Gilgamesh to mature, culminating in a realization that life's true value lies in wisdom and legacy, far beyond fleeting glory.

Similarly, **Sargon of Akkad**, who rose from humble beginnings to establish the first Mesopotamian empire, demonstrates how a relentless drive for control often masks inner vulnerabilities. Despite his conquests, Sargon's empire crumbled after his death, revealing the fragility of a legacy built on domination rather than sustainability.

Once again, an obsession with power proves insufficient to address emotional and existential needs.

The extreme consequences of unchecked egocentrism are epitomized by **Nebuchadnezzar II**. According to biblical accounts, he experienced a psychological breakdown when confronted with the realization that his achievements were not solely the product of his own efforts. His fixation on self-glorification led to isolation and a loss of connection with reality.

The moral of these stories is clear: without a path of personal growth and self-awareness, egocentrism inevitably leads to internal collapse.

Overcoming obsessive egocentrism requires both mental and spiritual awareness—a journey toward genuine balance. Modern psychological theories echo this wisdom: the compulsive pursuit of power or immediate gratification often originates from an emotional void. Without meaningful transformation, this dependency erodes mental and physical health, as well as the relationships of those caught in its grip.

ANCIENT EGYPT

Historical sources on Ancient Egypt do not provide detailed accounts of pathological dependencies as we understand them today. However, evidence suggests that behaviors such as excessive alcohol consumption, gambling, and compulsive tendencies were present. Alcohol, in the form of beer or wine, was widely consumed in both social and religious contexts, sometimes leading to negative consequences. Similarly, the use of opium cannot be ruled out. While there is no concrete proof of specific cases of addiction, gambling was a common practice in the land of the Pharaohs. The game of **Senet**, one of the oldest known board games with traces dating back over 5,000 years, stands as a testament to this.

Moreover, it is plausible that compulsive behaviors related to overeating or dysfunctional relationships were prevalent among the upper classes. Nobles and Pharaohs lived lives of excess, and although addiction as a formal concept was not recognized, such practices likely had a significant impact on their lives.

CLEOPATRA: THE ART OF MANIPULATION

If the myths of Mesopotamia teach us about the dangers of obsessive egocentrism, the decline of Egyptian civilization introduces another crucial theme linked to pathological dependencies: **manipulation**.

Cleopatra VII, Egypt's last queen, embodied this dynamic with a mastery that Roman chronicles and later traditions often misrepresented as victimhood or emotional weakness. However, her reign and persona tell a very different story.

A complex and captivating figure, Cleopatra was a brilliant and calculating ruler who wielded charm and diplomacy to maintain her kingdom's independence in a perilous geopolitical landscape. Far from being a victim of her passions, Cleopatra used her allure as a strategic tool. Her relationships with Julius Caesar and Mark Antony were not born out of emotional dependency or naive devotion but were part of a well-orchestrated political plan. Cleopatra's ability to separate emotional ties from political strategy showcased a rare clarity and determination. She understood that safeguarding Egypt required forging alliances with the era's most powerful figures, using seduction as a crucial element of her diplomacy.

Why, then, discuss Cleopatra in a text about addiction? Because the interplay between manipulation and dependency is rooted in the same neurochemical mechanisms of the brain.

Manipulators often experience gratification similar to the compulsive satisfaction sought by those with addictions. Both behaviors activate the brain's **reward circuit**, releasing dopamine and reinforcing the desire to repeat the behavior.

At the same time, those being manipulated fall victim to the same mechanism, driven by the pleasure of perceived connection or influence. Manipulation, therefore, is not merely a control strategy but can become a near-compulsive behavior fueled by the satisfaction of wielding power over others.

Interestingly, it was not Cleopatra but rather **Caesar and Antony** who became victims of "relational dependency." Both men were drawn not only to the queen's charm but also to the prospect of expanding their own power through their alliance with her. Caesar brought her to Rome, breaking social taboos, while Antony sacrificed much of his authority to remain by her side. Their attraction to Cleopatra verged on a form of emotional dependency that compromised their ability to pursue political goals effectively. Cleopatra emerges as a figure who skillfully manipulated her surroundings and the people around her to ensure her kingdom's survival. Similarly, individuals with pathological dependencies employ manipulation to secure what they perceive as vital to their existence: the continuation of their addictive behaviors.

GREECE: HEROISM AND SELF-DESTRUCTION

Pathological addictions, while conceptualized differently in antiquity compared to modern times, find numerous parallels in the mythology and philosophy of ancient Greece. Through symbolic stories and archetypal figures, the Greeks explored the dynamics of obsession and loss of control in areas such as pleasure, power, and self-destruction.

From the unbridled desire for wine and carnal pleasures represented by the god Dionysus to myths that highlight compulsions surrounding gambling, love, and food, Greek culture offers a fascinating and intricate perspective on the fragile boundary between indulgence and pathological addiction.

ADDICTIONS IN MYTHOLOGY

Greek mythology, rich with stories and legends, reflects the complexities of the human condition, including the universal struggle of confronting the inability to have absolute control over life's events.

In the face of this lack of control, humanity—especially in the absence of strong spiritual faith—has often sought to soothe its anxieties through external means, whether through substances, the accumulation of wealth, or destructive behaviors. This unmediated need for control lies at the root of many addictions.

Indeed, many mythological tales feature figures and narratives that highlight the destructive consequences of obsessive and compulsive behaviors, such as substance abuse, gambling, and toxic relationships. While we've already discussed Dionysus in the previous chapter, let's now examine other figures.

Sisyphus and the Endless Task

The myth of Sisyphus, who was condemned to push a boulder up a mountain only to see it roll back down each time he reached the summit, serves as a profound metaphor for compulsions and obsessions.

The cyclical and futile nature of Sisyphus's punishment mirrors the self-destructive cycle of addiction, where behaviors are endlessly repeated without ever achieving lasting satisfaction or resolution. This myth symbolically represents the dysfunctional cycle seen in pathological dependencies, where, despite great effort, individuals remain trapped in destructive patterns.

OBSESSIVE-COMPULSIVE DISORDER AND ADDICTIONS

Obsessive-Compulsive Disorder (OCD) manifests as recurring, intrusive thoughts—known as obsessions—that provoke anxiety, leading to repetitive behaviors, or compulsions, aimed at alleviating that distress.

The exact causes of OCD remain unclear, but it involves specific brain regions, such as the orbitofrontal cortex and the basal ganglia, as well as imbalances in neurotransmitters like serotonin.

An intriguing aspect of OCD is its resemblance to pathological addictions, such as substance abuse or gambling. In both cases, repetitive behavior provides temporary relief from anxiety or a fleeting sense of pleasure, reinforcing a compulsive cycle that becomes difficult to break. Despite the irrationality of these

actions, the brain struggles to properly regulate the circuits controlling them, leading to continuous repetition of the same patterns.

From a neurochemical perspective, OCD and addictions share several overlapping characteristics.

Both conditions involve brain regions critical for regulating repetitive behaviors, pleasure, and reward. The basal ganglia, including the nucleus accumbens, are part of the reward circuit, responsible for releasing dopamine when the brain experiences gratification. In OCD, the basal ganglia are dysfunctional, making it challenging to control compulsive actions and to break repetitive cycles. In addictions, the same circuit becomes overstimulated by substances or behaviors that trigger excessive dopamine release.

The orbitofrontal cortex, another key player, is responsible for decision-making and evaluating the consequences of actions. In OCD, this region sends excessive signals to the basal ganglia, driving individuals to perform compulsive behaviors to reduce anxiety. Similarly, in addictions, the orbitofrontal cortex can become impaired, leading to irrational decision-making and persistent pursuit of substances or behaviors that provide gratification, even in the face of negative outcomes.

Another crucial region is the anterior cingulate cortex, which monitors emotions and behavior. In OCD, this area can become hyperactive, making it difficult to "turn off" obsessions and compulsions. In addictions, however, the anterior cingulate

cortex may become dysfunctional, intensifying the drive for immediate rewards while ignoring long-term consequences. The shared mechanisms between OCD and addictions underline the complex interplay of brain regions and neurochemistry, offering valuable insights into the challenges of breaking free from compulsive behaviors in both conditions.

DESTRUCTIVE RELATIONSHIPS: SEX AND DEPENDENCY

Destructive relationships, particularly those involving sex and love, are a recurring theme in Greek mythology, where gods and heroes often succumb to uncontrollable impulses that push them beyond the limits of reason. Desire, when unchecked, transforms into a powerful force capable of harming not only its victims but also those who wield it. Unlike the monotheistic God, who represents a transcendent and perfect moral guide, the Greek gods were flawed beings, mirroring human experiences in their strengths and weaknesses. Zeus serves as one of the most striking examples of unchecked sexual desire. The king of the gods was unable to control his impulses, often leading to conflict and suffering. His compulsive desire drove him to wield power as a tool for personal gratification, with devastating consequences for those around him.

Love that destroys

Obsessive passion is a theme woven throughout Greek myths, and *The Iliad* offers a quintessential example in the story of Paris and Helen. The Trojan prince and the Spartan queen, consumed by an overwhelming love, elope, igniting the Trojan War. Unable to reign in their passion, they sacrifice everything, succumbing to an emotional dependency that blinds them to the disastrous consequences of their actions. Their tale serves as an archetype of dysfunctional relationships, where obsessive love eclipses reason and leads to ruin.

Another poignant myth is that of Echo and Narcissus, a narrative that reveals the dynamics of relational dependency and self-loss. Echo, cursed by Hera to repeat only the words of others, loses her ability to express herself. When she falls in love with Narcissus, she can only echo his words, unable to communicate her true feelings. Narcissus, obsessed with his reflection, is incapable of loving anyone but himself and coldly rejects her. Heartbroken, Echo withdraws, consumed by despair, until she fades into nothing but a voice among the mountains.

This tragedy illustrates two facets of dysfunctional relationships: Echo loses her identity in her unrequited love, while Narcissus remains trapped in self-obsession. Their doomed connection symbolizes what modern psychology terms a codependent relationship, where partners feed into each other's dysfunctions. Boundaries dissolve, and the relationship's balance hinges on perpetuating harmful behaviors.

Medea: the ultimate destructive passion

The myth of Medea takes the concept of destructive passion to an extreme. After sacrificing everything for Jason—helping him obtain the Golden Fleece and abandoning her family and homeland—Medea is betrayed when he leaves her to marry the daughter of King Creon in a bid to consolidate power.

Devastated and humiliated, Medea enacts a chilling revenge. She kills Jason's new bride and Creon, but her most harrowing act is murdering her own children, depriving Jason of his lineage and severing the last ties of their love. This act of ultimate vengeance reflects the profound depths of her pain, where anguish transforms into an extreme bid for control and retribution, leaving an indelible mark of passion's destructive potential when unchecked.

These myths resonate as timeless explorations of human relationships, underscoring how unbridled emotions and compulsive attachments can spiral into devastation for all involved.

GAMBLING AND DEFYING THE GODS

Gambling in Greek mythology is closely tied to the concepts of fate and fortune, where chance and risk intertwine with the will of the gods. The Greeks believed that much of life's events were influenced by destiny, personified by the **Moirai**, the three goddesses who spun the thread of each person's life. Yet, mortals often sought to challenge this destiny through gambling, a practice that could easily spiral into obsession.

A popular game in ancient Greece was dice, frequently associated with wagers involving money or property. Citizens risked significant sums, sometimes even their lives, in pursuit of fortune.

One myth that highlights the connection between gambling and fate is the division of the universe among **Zeus, Hades, and Poseidon**. After their victory over the Titans, the three brothers decided to divide the cosmos by casting dice: Zeus won the heavens, Hades claimed the Underworld, and Poseidon ruled the seas. Not even the gods themselves could escape the randomness of chance.

Another intriguing story is that of **Pandora** and her infamous jar, often seen as a metaphor for risk. While the myth doesn't directly involve gambling, Pandora's act of opening the jar—releasing all the evils into the world—can be interpreted as a gamble with devastating consequences. Driven by curiosity, Pandora takes an action with uncertain and potentially catastrophic results, much like a gambler risking everything to uncover the outcome of their wager. These myths underscore the timeless tension between human agency, divine will, and the unpredictable forces of chance—a dynamic that continues to resonate in the modern understanding of gambling and its risks.

DRUGS IN THE ODYSSEY

Addiction to substances finds symbolic expression in numerous stories from Greek mythology, where the desire to escape reality through fleeting pleasures often leads to a loss of identity.

One of the most famous episodes is that of the **Island of the Lotus-Eaters**, as described in the *Odyssey*. Odysseus' companions encounter a people who subsist on lotus flowers. These flowers have the effect of erasing all memories of home and duty. Those who consume the lotus fall into a state of oblivion, desiring nothing but to continue eating the fruit.

This tale serves as a powerful metaphor for substance addiction: the lotus becomes a symbol of temporary gratification, drawing individuals away from their goals and true selves. Much like drugs, the temptation to indulge in temporary bliss leads to a neglect of responsibilities and a loss of identity.

Another pivotal figure in the *Odyssey* is the sorceress **Circe**, who embodies the seductive and destructive power of mind-altering substances. Circe offers Odysseus' crew a magical drink that transforms them into animals, reducing them to their primal instincts.

This transformation can be interpreted as a metaphor for the effects of drugs: under the influence of a substance, individuals lose control over themselves, forgetting their humanity and purpose. The shift from human to animal reflects the erosion of awareness and dignity often caused by addiction, where the individual becomes enslaved to their desires and detached from reality.

Even **Odysseus**, though spared the transformation into an animal, succumbs to Circe's allure, remaining on her island for a year. While his stay is consensual, it represents a deviation from his mission—he yields to pleasure and oblivion, risking complete derailment. Circe thus symbolizes the irresistible allure of addiction, which promises pleasure and relief but can ensnare individuals in a life devoid of purpose.

Another example is the story of **Polyphemus**, the Cyclops, whom Odysseus outwits with the help of wine. The one-eyed creature overindulges in wine, rendering himself vulnerable and unable to defend against Odysseus' cunning. This episode, while showcasing Odysseus' resourcefulness, also highlights the power of wine (and by extension, substances) to impair judgment and lower defenses, leading to inevitable defeat.

In all these myths, the use of substances—whether symbolic or literal—is often portrayed as a dangerous temptation: an escape from responsibility or suffering that inevitably leads to destructive consequences.

As in real life, addiction offers a fleeting reprieve but ultimately ensnares individuals in a cycle of pleasure and pain, from which it becomes increasingly difficult to break free.

EATING DISORDERS: THE INSATIABLE HUNGER

The theme of eating, whether driven by an obsession to consume food (compulsive eating and bulimia) or to deny it entirely (anorexia), finds symbolic expression in Greek mythology through figures embodying uncontrollable desire and insatiable hunger.

The myth of **Tantalus** is particularly poignant. Accused of grievous offenses against the gods, the king was condemned to eternal punishment: he stood in a river with delectable fruits hanging above his head, yet each time he tried to drink or eat, the water receded, and the fruits moved out of reach.

This tale can be seen as a reflection on the relentless yearning for gratification through food, where hunger is never satisfied. It mirrors the emotional and psychological torment of compulsive eating, where the pursuit of relief remains elusive.

Another compelling myth is that of **Erysichthon**, a king cursed by the goddess Demeter for cutting down her sacred tree. He was afflicted with an unquenchable hunger; no matter how much he consumed, his appetite could never be sated. Eventually, this uncontrollable desire led to his downfall.

The story of Erysichthon can be interpreted as an allegory for the insatiable need to consume, which spirals into self-destruction. His plight resonates with the cycle of binge eating, where the relentless compulsion to consume often leaves individuals trapped in a destructive loop.
Even the myth of **Cerberus**, the three-headed dog guarding the entrance to the Underworld, offers symbolic insights into uncontainable desires. Constantly poised to devour anyone attempting to cross the boundary between the worlds of the living and the dead, Cerberus represents a primal force perpetually seeking nourishment. While not directly tied to food, Cerberus can be viewed as a metaphor for insuppressible cravings that, when left unchecked, become dangerous.

Through these myths, ancient Greece provides profound insights into the complexities of human desire and the perils of excess. The stories remind us that, without balance and self-awareness, the pursuit of satisfaction—whether through food, power, or pleasure—can lead to ruin.

THE TRAP OF FATS AND SUGARS

The human body is an extraordinary machine, honed by millions of years of evolution to achieve maximum results with minimal effort. This principle of efficiency was vital for our ancestors' survival, as food was not always readily available, and they needed to store energy whenever possible.
In prehistoric environments where hunting and gathering were the primary means of sustenance, foods rich in sugars and fats were particularly valuable. They provided immediate energy and reserves of fat for periods of scarcity. The brain evolved to favor these "energy-dense" foods, which

activate the reward circuit more powerfully than other types of food.
When we consume sugars and fats, our brains release dopamine, the neurotransmitter associated with pleasure and gratification. This neurochemical response encouraged our ancestors to seek out such foods whenever they were available, aiding survival in environments of food scarcity—a fundamental mechanism for staying alive.

Sugar has an immediate impact on the brain. Once consumed, it is rapidly broken down into glucose, which enters the bloodstream and provides instant energy to brain cells. This quick energy supply activates the brain's pleasure centers, creating a positive sensation that drives repeated consumption. Moreover, sugar stimulates the endogenous opioid system, releasing endorphins that amplify feelings of well-being.
This dual activation of the dopaminergic and opioid systems makes sugar feel like a "drug" for the brain, creating a compulsive desire to consume it.

Fats, on the other hand, engage the reward circuit in a slightly different manner.
When we eat fatty foods, the body produces endocannabinoids, chemicals that influence the brain by inducing prolonged feelings of satiety and well-being. Unlike sugar, the pleasurable effects of fats last longer.
Fats also affect the hormone leptin, which regulates hunger and satiety. In an environment abundant with fatty foods, however, this system can become dysfunctional, leading to a compulsive desire to

keep eating even when the body doesn't need more energy.

<u>A perfect system becomes dysfunctional</u>

The problem arises in modern environments, where fats and sugars are widely available with little to no effort. The brain's reward system, designed to respond to rare and precious foods, is now overwhelmed, leading to a system overload.

Regular overconsumption of sugary and fatty foods causes the brain to develop tolerance: dopamine receptors become less sensitive, requiring larger amounts of these foods to achieve the same level of gratification. This creates a compulsive cycle where individuals keep seeking out such foods to stimulate dopamine release.

Stress and emotional triggers further exacerbate this cycle. In times of stress, the brain seeks quick gratification to ease tension, turning to food as a coping mechanism. Sugars and fats provide a temporary surge of pleasure, helping to reduce stress, but this short-term relief often leads to long-term compulsive behaviors and food addictions.

WORK ADDICTION IN MYTHS

The myth of **Heracles (Hercules)** provides a profound reflection on the theme of work addiction through his legendary Twelve Labors. These tasks, imposed as punishment for the murder of his family during a fit of madness caused by the goddess Hera, symbolize not only a quest for redemption but also an insatiable need to prove his worth.

From a modern perspective, Heracles' behavior can be interpreted as a form of workaholism, where the hero subjects himself to relentless and superhuman challenges, pushing his physical and mental limits in pursuit of approval and forgiveness. His labors become a continuous form of penance, a compulsive quest for validation that, while bringing him glory, ultimately drains him emotionally. This unending pursuit of self-worth through constant labor mirrors contemporary notions of work addiction: an excessive dedication to tasks at the expense of personal well-being and relationships.

Each of Heracles' labors—from slaying the Hydra to capturing the Erymanthian Boar—represents a seemingly endless cycle of duties and obligations. Like a modern workaholic, Heracles appears trapped in the need for ever-new challenges, never attaining a lasting sense of fulfillment or satisfaction.

Another myth that resonates with the theme of work addiction is that of **Daedalus**, the brilliant inventor and craftsman. Famous for building the Labyrinth for King Minos, Daedalus ultimately becomes imprisoned within his own creation by the very king he served. This episode encapsulates the paradox of the artisan or professional who, in the relentless pursuit of perfection, becomes ensnared by their own achievements.

The idea of being trapped by one's work is a powerful metaphor for modern forms of professional dependency. Daedalus' attempt to escape his predicament by crafting wax wings for himself and his son, Icarus, reflects the struggle to break free from the consequences of one's labor. Yet the tragic outcome—marked by Icarus' fall—underscores the futility of striving for total control over one's projects or destiny.

When Work Becomes an Addiction

Workaholism can be understood as a behavior that overstimulates the brain's reward circuits, creating a dependency on work

and the sense of gratification it provides.
As with other addictions, this process is primarily driven by dopamine, but it also involves other neurotransmitters such as serotonin and stress hormones like cortisol, which add layers of complexity to the condition. Over time, the brain becomes "desensitized" to the pleasure derived from work, leading to a vicious cycle in which individuals work harder without ever feeling genuinely fulfilled.
Much like substance addictions, workaholism can also result in tolerance. Initially, professional achievements trigger a strong dopaminergic response, but as the brain adapts, it requires increasingly larger "doses" of work to achieve the same level of satisfaction. This compels individuals to push themselves further, often at the expense of other critical aspects of life, such as personal relationships or physical and mental health.

MONEY AND THE ILLUSION OF CONTROL

In Greek mythology, the obsession with wealth and material possessions is vividly portrayed in stories that highlight the dangers of excessive greed.
One of the most iconic tales is that of **King Midas**, the ruler of Phrygia, whose insatiable desire for riches led him to make a fateful choice. When Dionysus offers Midas a wish, he requests the ability to turn everything he touches into gold.
At first, this newfound power seems like a blessing: every object Midas touches transforms into the precious metal, fulfilling his dream of endless wealth. However, the gift soon becomes a curse as Midas realizes that

even **food, water,** and **his beloved daughter** are not spared from his golden touch.
This myth starkly illustrates how an obsession with money and material gain can consume a person's life, stripping away what truly matters and leading to an existence that is empty and devoid of meaning.
Another compelling figure is **Plutus**, the god of wealth. While not a hero of grand adventures, Plutus is often depicted as blind or blindfolded, symbolizing the inability of wealth to discern between the deserving and the undeserving. This imagery suggests that unchecked accumulation of riches can result in a life where true **value and meaning** are obscured. The pursuit of money, much like Midas' golden curse, has the potential to blind those who chase it, making it impossible to see the things that genuinely matter.

EXCESSES IN ANCIENT ROME

Several Roman emperors are known for their lives marked by various excesses, including indulgence in alcohol, gambling, and sexual behavior that often crossed boundaries.
It is important to consider, however, that the moral standards regarding sexuality in Ancient Greece and the Roman Empire were very different from those we hold today. In those societies, sexual behavior was not taboo, and many behaviors that seem excessive by modern standards were often seen as part of everyday life. The emperors discussed here stand out because their personal indulgences affected their ability to rule, leading in some cases to personal and political decline.
Caligula (12-41 AD) is perhaps the most infamous of these emperors, remembered for his erratic behavior and excesses. After ascending to the throne following Tiberius' death, he was initially welcomed with enthusiasm. However, his reign quickly descended into chaos and cruelty.

His obsession with power and self-indulgence became apparent, and his eccentric decisions shocked both the Roman elite and the general population.
One of the most notorious aspects of Caligula's reign was his reportedly inappropriate relationships within his own family and the way he blurred the lines between power and personal gratification. His actions, which included a string of controversial decrees and decisions, made him extremely unpopular. Additionally, his love of gambling led him to spend vast sums of money, even allegedly pilfering from the state treasury and seizing the property of wealthy citizens to cover his losses. His unpredictable rule and increasing cruelty eventually led to his assassination in 41 AD by his own guards.
Vitellius (15-69 AD), although less famous than other emperors, also became notorious for his excessive lifestyle. Rising to power during the chaotic Year of the Four Emperors, he was famous for his lavish feasts and indulgence in food and drink. These banquets were said to last for days, with an overwhelming consumption of food and alcohol. Vitellius' inability to govern effectively and his focus on indulgence rather than leadership contributed to his unpopularity. After less than a year in power, he was deposed and killed by the forces of Vespasian.
Vitellius exemplifies how unchecked indulgence can lead not only to personal downfall but also to the collapse of one's political career.
Nero (37-68 AD), one of the most famous emperors for his extravagant lifestyle, began his reign with promises of moderation and good governance. Over time, however, he became increasingly focused on personal pleasures and artistic pursuits. Nero was known for organizing lavish parties, where wine and entertainment flowed freely. His interest in the arts, particularly music and theatre, became a defining feature of his reign. One of the most scandalous episodes was his reported marriage to a young man, whom he reportedly treated in a manner that shocked many in Roman society. These behaviors, combined with accusa-

tions surrounding the Great Fire of Rome in 64 AD (although there is no conclusive evidence linking him to the event), led to growing resentment toward him from both the populace and the nobility. Ultimately, after being declared a public enemy, Nero took his own life in 68 AD, marking the end of the Julio-Claudian dynasty.

Commodus (161-192 AD), the son of the renowned Marcus Aurelius, represents a stark contrast to his father, known for his wisdom and stoic philosophy. Commodus, by contrast, focused much of his life on personal indulgence and physical prowess. He was known for his participation in gladiatorial games, where he sought to portray himself as a powerful warrior rather than a ruler. His private life was filled with lavish feasts, indulgent pleasures, and reports of inappropriate relationships. Commodus' obsession with his public image and his neglect of state affairs led to the decline of the empire during his reign. His eventual assassination in 192 AD, orchestrated by those closest to him, marked the end of his rule, driven by widespread frustration with his behavior and the state of the empire under his leadership.

PANEM ET CIRCENSES

In Ancient Rome, gambling played a notable role in social life. Although it was not officially a tool of social control like public games, it nevertheless contributed to entertaining the masses and distracting the population from political and social issues.

The concept of *panem et circenses*—famously coined by the poet Juvenal—criticizes the Roman leaders' strategy of maintaining power and pacifying the population. By providing free food (bread) and organizing public spectacles (circuses), such as chariot races at the Circus Maximus and gladiatorial combats, the Roman elite successfully diverted the public's attention from everyday struggles by offering immediate distractions.

In this context, gambling held secondary but still significant importance. While officially prohibited in many circumstances, it was tolerated during specific festivals, such as the *Saturnalia*, when social norms were suspended, and hierarchies temporarily dissolved. During these festivals, social classes mingled, and wealthy patrons sometimes used gambling as part of their client relationships with the common people.

The *ludi*—public games—were the true strategic opportunities for politicians, who could win the favor of the people. During these events, betting and the distribution of money were common practices, reinforcing the bond between the elite and the plebeians. Gladiatorial games and chariot races were crucial moments for demonstrating generosity, consolidating the popularity and power of the aristocracy.

Betting played a key role, especially in chariot races, where a mass phenomenon involved both the rich and the poor. While there is no evidence that gambling improved long-term economic conditions, historical figures like Suetonius and Plutarch mention instances where individuals had temporary winnings. However, these fortunes were often quickly lost due to the unpredictable nature of gambling.

On the other hand, Suetonius mentions cases where wealthy patricians and senators lost fortunes to their passion for betting. Some members of the elite, caught up in the frenzy of gambling, squandered large sums of money at the chariot races in the Circus Maximus. Although specific names are not always cited, Suetonius highlights how gambling was a "vice" that could affect even the wealthiest and most powerful, putting not only their finances at risk but also their social prestige.

However, not everyone favored the excesses associated with gambling. Emperor Augustus, for example, attempted to regulate it, aware of the social risks it posed. His policy reflected the fear that gambling could destabilize social order, despite its potential as a tool of distraction.

The irresistible allure of gambling and betting did not spare even the most prominent figures, including emperors and senators, who found themselves compromising their

reputation and power. One emblematic case is that of Emperor Claudius, known for his passion for gambling. Despite being one of the most educated and intelligent emperors of his time, Claudius developed an obsession with gambling. According to historical records, he always carried a gaming board with him, even during travels and public affairs. While there is no evidence that this habit had a decisive impact on his governance, it damaged his public image and made him appear disengaged from state matters.
Another significant example is that of General Lucius Cornelius Sulla, one of the most powerful leaders of the late Roman Republic. It is said that Sulla actively participated in gambling and used his winnings and losses as tools of political manipulation.

GAMBLING AND THE BRAIN

When someone suffers from compulsive gambling, their brain chemistry undergoes significant changes that affect how the reward system and impulse control function.
Much like drugs, gambling stimulates the release of dopamine, the neurotransmitter that governs feelings of pleasure and reward. Large amounts of dopamine are produced during moments of betting and suspense, triggering an euphoria similar to what's experienced with substances like cocaine or amphetamines.
This overproduction of dopamine creates a vicious cycle where the individual is driven to seek out new opportunities to gamble in order to relive those pleasurable sensations.
However, over time, the brain becomes accustomed to these dopamine spikes, developing a tolerance that pushes the gambler

to bet more or take bigger risks to achieve the same level of gratification.

The reward system, which involves areas of the brain like the nucleus accumbens and the prefrontal cortex, is central to this process. The nucleus accumbens is responsible for pleasure sensations, while the prefrontal cortex manages rational decision-making and inhibits impulses. In people with gambling addiction, the reward system becomes overstimulated, and the prefrontal cortex loses its effectiveness at managing impulsive behavior, leading to risky and often irrational decisions. This is the same mechanism seen in drug addicts: dopamine drives the repetition of pleasurable behaviors, but over time the brain loses its ability to control these behaviors in a healthy way.

One particularly fascinating aspect of gambling is the phenomenon of the "near win."

When someone comes close to winning but doesn't quite make it, the brain still releases dopamine, creating a false sense of success. This mechanism tricks the individual into believing victory is just within reach, even though it isn't. As a result, the gambler is compelled to keep playing, convinced that they're on the verge of winning. This effect makes gambling particularly addictive and hard to quit.

The chemical mechanisms behind compulsive gambling have much in common with drug addiction. Both excessively stimulate the reward system, causing an abnormal release of dopamine. In both cases, tolerance develops, meaning the person needs to escalate their behavior to achieve the same

sensations. This leads to craving—the obsessive desire to repeat the experience—and reduces the ability to make rational decisions. Impulse control weakens, pushing the individual toward impulsive and risky behaviors, often with severe negative consequences.

Unlike drugs, gambling doesn't introduce external substances into the body, but it directly impacts the brain's circuits through the behavior itself. However, the neurochemical effects are so similar that gambling is considered a true behavioral addiction.

THE NORSE AND CELTIC PEOPLES: CONNECTION TO PSYCHOACTIVE SUBSTANCES

When we think of the ancient Norse and Celtic cultures, we often imagine fierce warriors, mystic druids, and gods who commanded the forces of nature. But beyond their legendary sagas and epic battles, these ancient peoples also had a deep connection to psychoactive substances. Whether for spiritual, medicinal, or recreational purposes, substances that altered consciousness played an important role in their societies, shaping their rituals, beliefs, and way of life.

In the cold, rugged landscapes of Scandinavia, the Norse peoples—Vikings, seafarers, and explorers—used plants and fungi with hallucinogenic properties, both in religious ceremonies and as part of their warrior ethos. The most famous of these substances was the *fly agaric* mushroom (*Amanita muscaria*), known for its psychoactive effects. This bright red mushroom, with its white speckles, was consumed by the Norse to induce altered states of consciousness, often used by the *berserkers*—elite Viking warriors who were said to fight with a ferocity akin to wild animals.

The berserkers would reportedly enter a trance-like state, believed to be enhanced by the consumption of these mushrooms. This altered state gave them the strength to fight without fear or pain, a vital trait in battle. It's said that the mushrooms worked by causing hallucinations and confusion, heightening their aggression and enabling them to endure extreme physical stress. This was not just a form of war-induced madness; it had a spiritual dimension as well. The Norse believed that by stepping outside of ordinary consciousness, they could commune with the gods, especially in times of war.

While the use of *Amanita muscaria* was perhaps the most famous, the Norse also made use of other plants like *henbane* (*Hyoscyamus niger*), which has psychoactive properties, often for ritualistic or shamanic purposes. The ancient Norse shamans, known as *völvas*, were believed to use these substances to enter trance states during their prophecies and ceremonies, communicating with spirits or gods for guidance.

Meanwhile, across the sea in the British Isles, the Celts also had their own complex relationship with psychoactive substances. Known for their elaborate religious practices and deep spiritual beliefs, the Celts had a profound respect for nature and its ability to alter the mind and spirit. They too used various plants to induce altered states, especially in their religious rituals and celebrations.

One of the most notable substances in the Celtic world was *mistletoe*, considered sacred and revered by the druids, the priestly class of Celtic society. Mistletoe's use went beyond its role in wintertime festivities; it was seen as a powerful plant that could connect the earthly and spiritual realms. The druids would harvest it with great ceremony, often using it in healing potions and in rituals designed to connect with the gods, especially during the winter solstice.

The Celts also made use of *psychedelic plants* like *belladonna* and *henbane*, both of which contain alkaloids that can cause hallucinations and altered states of consciousness. These substances were likely used during certain ceremonies to induce visions or to help participants transcend ordinary perception and enter the spiritual realms. The use of these plants in rituals allowed the Celts to commune with nature and their gods, offering them insights and guidance from the unseen world.

Like the Norse, the Celts also held deep reverence for the intoxicating power of alcohol, particularly mead, a fermented drink made from honey. Mead was not just a source of pleasure—it was deeply embedded in their myths and rituals. The drink was often associated with the gods, particularly *Odin* in Norse mythology and *Dionysus* in the Celtic world, representing both the intoxicating power of nature and the spirit of divinity itself. Drinking mead in feasts or ceremonies was seen as a way of connecting with the divine, and it was used in a range of rites, from weddings to sacrifices, with the belief that it could offer wisdom, strength, and divine favor.

The connection between the Norse and Celts and psychoactive substances was far from random; it was tied to their deep respect for the mysteries of the natural world and the belief that by altering their states of consciousness, they could gain deeper insight into the universe and their place within it. For both these cultures, the use of substances was as much about spiritual transcendence as it was about personal or societal transformation.

Whether to enter battle without fear, to commune with the gods, or to heal the body and mind, psychoactive substances were deeply woven into the fabric of Norse and Celtic culture. They were not just mind-altering experiences; they were transformative acts of connecting with the unseen forces that shaped their lives, their beliefs, and their understanding of the world around them.

MEDIEVAL TIMES: EXCESSES AND "HOLY ANOREXIA"

In the Middle Ages, many behaviors that today would be recognized as symptoms of pathological addictions were viewed through a different lens, often a moralistic one. The most common issues we know of were related to alcoholism, gambling, and behavioral excesses, frequently connected to relationships and sexuality. While there is little evidence of widespread drug use in the West, such as opium or cannabis, there are traces of their use, primarily in medical or ritualistic contexts.

Alcohol abuse was rampant. The Church attempted to curb these behaviors, often labeling them as grave sins rather than venial ones, redeemable only through penance. Medieval taverns, mostly frequented by the lower classes, were seen as places of damnation where alcohol flowed freely, and debauchery reigned. Even high-ranking figures, like kings and nobles, were not immune to excessive behaviors, proving that power and wealth did not protect against addiction, just as today.

While documentation on excesses is sparse, chronicles do delve into another behavior that would now be considered pathological but was viewed as virtuous at the time: food rejection.

EATING DISORDERS AND SPIRITUALITY

The "holy anorexics" represent a religious and cultural phenomenon that primarily developed during the Middle Ages. Women, often mystics or members of religious orders, practiced extreme fasting as an expression of their devotion to God. This behavior, which today might be interpreted as an eating disorder, was seen at the time as a manifestation of sanctity and spiritual sacrifice.

In the Middle Ages, the idea of mortifying the body as a means of drawing closer to God was deeply ingrained in Christian culture. Extreme fasting was viewed as a form of spiritual purification, a way to deny earthly pleasures and demonstrate one's dedication to faith. Women, in particular, were often encouraged to adopt ascetic practices to highlight their purity and devotion. In this context, fasting was not only tolerated but often celebrated as a sign of divine grace.

The "holy anorexics" were often described as women who, through extreme control of food, sought to establish a direct connection with God, expressing a desire to suffer for the redemption of the world or to atone for sins. Among the most famous figures is *Saint Catherine of Siena* (1347-1380), who practiced such rigorous fasting that, toward the end of her life, she consumed only minimal amounts of food. Her biography tells of her refusal to eat as an act of penance, offering herself as a sacrificial victim for the salvation of others. Her "mystical anorexia" was seen as a sign of sanctity, and the Church regarded her as an example of extreme devotion.

Another example is *Saint Clare of Assisi* (1194-1253), co-founder of the Order of Poor Ladies (the Clarisses), who practiced fasting as a form of penance, though not as extreme as Catherine of Siena's.

With the development of modern psychology and psychiatry, the phenomenon of the "holy anorexics" has piqued the interest of scholars. Many psychologists and psychiatrists have begun to draw parallels between the behaviors of these medieval mystics and modern eating disorders, such as anorexia nervosa. Psychologist *Joan Jacobs Brumberg*, for example, has studied the phenomenon in depth, highlighting how the ascetic fasts of medieval and Renaissance women reflected a desire for control over the body, much like the behaviors seen in modern cases of anorexia. While the manifest motivations were different from today's, the practice was the same.

Other scholars, such as psychologist and historian *Rudolph Bell*, have examined the link between religiosity and anorexia in a more specific way. In his book *Holy Anorexia* (1985), Bell explores how body mortification, particularly through fasting, was a common characteristic

among medieval saints. He suggests that these "holy anorexics" used fasting to exert power in a context where women had little authority. By controlling their own bodies through fasting, these women were able to assert their spiritual and social autonomy in a male-dominated world.
Another interesting aspect highlighted by studies is the role of the social and cultural context. Many of these women, like Catherine of Siena, were venerated by their communities and received special attention and recognition for their fasts and mystical visions. This social reinforcement could have helped sustain and reinforce their ascetic behavior.
In any case, regardless of historical, cultural, and social differences, the repression of a primary drive such as nourishment, both then and now, represents a form of extreme control. Sadly, despite current knowledge and scientific advances in the study of eating disorders, common perceptions still view thinness and control of pleasures as virtues, while excess and "gluttony" are seen as vices.

WHAT HAPPENS IN THE BRAINS OF ANOREXICS

When a person suffers from anorexia, their brain undergoes significant changes in chemistry, which affects the way they perceive food, hunger, and pleasure.
Anorexia is not just about controlling weight or body image; it results from a complex interaction between psychological, biological, and neurochemical factors.
One of the central elements, as is often the case, is the brain's reward system, which becomes altered in individuals suffering from this disorder.
Under normal conditions, food stimulates the release of dopamine, the neurotransmitter that regulates pleasure and motivation. Eat-

ing should therefore produce a feeling of satisfaction and contentment. However, in anorexic individuals, this mechanism is distorted: instead of feeling pleasure, the act of eating can generate anxiety or discomfort. The release of dopamine may be insufficient or associated with negative feelings, driving those affected to avoid food, which is perceived as a source of stress.

This imbalance in the dopaminergic system is somewhat similar to what happens in people with substance addictions, such as cocaine or heroin, which excessively stimulate the reward system, making the brain dependent on those pleasurable experiences.

Similarly, anorexia can be viewed as a form of behavioral addiction. The act of avoiding food or exercising strict control overeating becomes a source of relief or gratification. Control over food activates the same reward circuits in the brains of anorexics that, in individuals dependent on substances, are stimulated by drug use.

In the brains of anorexics, a reduction in serotonin levels is often observed, another important neurotransmitter for regulating mood and eating behavior. This imbalance can exacerbate symptoms like anxiety and depression, creating a vicious cycle where food control becomes a mechanism to manage distress. The parallel with substance abuse is present here as well: serotonin, involved in regulating well-being, undergoes similar changes in both conditions.

Another key aspect is the increase in cortisol levels, known as the "stress hormone." In anorexic individuals, cortisol levels are often elevated, fueling a state of chronic stress. This can push the individual to continue rigidly controlling their diet in an attempt to reduce anxiety. This vicious cycle makes it increasingly difficult to break the behaviors associated with anorexia, as the brain becomes accustomed to finding relief through food control, and rejecting food becomes a defense mechanism.

These neurochemical changes have severe consequences not only for mental health but also for physical health. The lack of nutrition leads to an energy deficit, further compromising brain function. In response to this state of malnutrition, the brain reduces activity in certain areas to conserve resources, exacerbating the ability to make rational decisions and reinforcing the obsession with food control. This behavior is reminiscent of what happens in drug addictions, where the brain, accustomed to the euphoria induced by the substance, loses the ability to self-regulate.

In conclusion, anorexia significantly alters brain chemistry, affecting the reward and emotional control circuits in ways similar to substance addictions. The main difference lies in the fact that, while drugs introduce an external substance that alters neurotransmitters, in anorexia, it is the behavior itself—the control of food—that causes chemical imbalances that deeply impact both mental and physical health.

DURING THE RENAISSANCE

During the Middle Ages, the knowledge and use of medicinal herbs were primarily controlled by the Church and monasteries. Monks, especially Benedictines, preserved and passed down ancient medical wisdom, cultivating herbs in the monastery gardens and compiling herbals that described the healing properties of plants. Caring for the sick was part of their religious mission, and monasteries were often the only source of medical assistance for local communities.

However, with the Renaissance and the rise of science, a significant change occurred. Medicine began to free itself from religious influence, and lay scholars, philosophers, and physicians began to study medicinal plants in a more systematic way, relying on direct observation and experimentation. Universities began to include the study of medicinal herbs in their curricula, progressively detaching medicine from ecclesiastical control.

The loss of the "control" that religious and spiritual authorities had over psychoactive substances had its undeniable pros, but also its terrible cons.

With the Renaissance, humanity rediscovered the ancient "vices," bringing them back to light in a new form—more refined but no less dangerous.

HENRY VIII'S OBSESSIONS

The Renaissance was a period of great cultural and political ferment, but it was also a time when prominent figures, often in the spotlight, displayed behaviors linked to excesses that today might be considered pathological addictions.

Among these stands Henry VIII of England, known for his tumultuous reign and radical political decisions, but also as an example of how personal addictions can have far-reaching consequences.

The king suffered from overeating, which worsened significantly in his later years, leading to severe obesity and debilitating health problems. His diet, rich in meat and fatty foods, combined with a massive consumption of alcohol, contributed to a physical decline that affected both his behavior and his ability to make political decisions.

Henry's relationship with food and alcohol was emblematic of his impulsive personality and lack of self-control, and these excesses had a direct impact on his mental and physical health. In his final years, the king suffered from gout, leg ulcers, and heart problems, conditions that made him increasingly vulnerable. His choices were often driven by growing isolation and deep frustration, partly due to his physical ailments, but also due to a progressive loss of self-regulation.

Alcohol and excesses fueled Henry's tyrannical temperament, intensifying his inclination toward arbitrary and violent decisions. His obsessive desire for a male heir, combined with his decadent lifestyle, led to a series of failed marriages and political choices that changed the course of English history. His divorce from Catherine of Aragon and the resulting schism with the Catholic Church, which led to the creation of the Anglican Church, were partly influenced by a mix of personal and political factors, but the influence of his physical and psychological deterioration on his decisions cannot be overlooked. His impulsive and excess-driven character led him to break with the papacy, causing a religious fracture that would mark England for centuries.

Moreover, his inclination for gambling was not merely a personal pastime but revealed a compulsive side to his personality. Henry often indulged in long gaming tournaments, reflecting his approach to power—risky and challenging, which manifested also in his politics. For him, gambling was a form of control and power, but also a way to escape the pressures of monarchy.

CARAVAGGIO AND CELLINI: GENIUS AND TORMENT

Michelangelo Merisi da Caravaggio, one of the greatest painters of the Italian Renaissance, is the epitome of the tormented genius. His personal life was marked by excesses and self-destructive behavior that, today, might be interpreted as behavioral disorders compatible with pathological dependencies.

Caravaggio is famous not only for his revolutionary painting technique, characterized by a dramatic use of light and shadow, but also for his turbulent life. Born in 1571, he lived a short but intense life, filled with episodes of violence and run-ins with the law.

Although there is no concrete evidence that he was addicted to alcohol, it is plausible that the consumption of alcoholic beverages fueled his impulsive behaviors. The taverns of Rome, where Caravaggio spent much of his time, were often the site of brawls in which the painter was involved. Frequented by people of all social classes, these taverns were environments where tensions could easily escalate into physical altercations, and Caravaggio did not hesitate to take part.

As for his love life, it is known that he had a rather tumultuous romantic life.

The turning point in Caravaggio's life was the murder of Ranuccio Tomassoni in 1606, during a brawl that may have been linked to a dispute over a game or personal issues. This event marked the beginning of a period of wandering between Naples, Malta, and Sicily, during which he continued to paint extraordinary works but repeatedly found himself in conflict with local authorities. In Malta, for example, he was arrested for attacking a knight, an incident that once again reflects his violent and unstable temperament.

Caravaggio's death, which occurred in 1610 in Porto Ercole, remains shrouded in mystery. The most widely accepted theories suggest that he may have died from malaria, a common disease in that area, but the possibility of murder is not excluded, perhaps as revenge for past conflicts.

The painter represents a fascinating and tragic example of how talent and torment can coexist within the same individual. His uncontrollable passions and inclination toward violence not only marked his personal life but also deeply influenced his artistic production, leaving an indelible legacy in the history of art.

The artistic genius of Benvenuto Cellini, the renowned sculptor and goldsmith of the Renaissance, is also often overshadowed by his violent temperament and tendency toward excesses. His *Memoirs* recount a turbulent life, marked by episodes of rage and impulsive behaviors. Cellini was known for his love of wine and parties, but his

exuberant personality often led him to live conflicts that endangered his career.
One of the most well-known episodes was the murder of Pompeo de' Capitaneis, which led the artist to be imprisoned in Castel Sant'Angelo. Cellini's excesses and intemperance are reflected not only in his creations but also in his personal relationships, which dragged him into dangerous situations and often put him at odds with the political and religious powers of his time.
The personalities of the two artists have often been described as turbulent, impulsive, and prone to violence—traits that, in light of current knowledge, could suggest a diagnosis of borderline personality disorder (BPD).
Today, we know that borderline personality disorder is characterized by emotional instability, difficulties in interpersonal relationships, impulsive behaviors, and a tendency toward extreme reactions, such as outbursts of anger or violence.
Exaggerated reactions, such as the use of weapons in public and ongoing conflicts with the law, as well as the apparent inability to manage frustration or conflict, could correspond to the symptoms of this disorder.
The Renaissance figures described above, while great in their artistic, political, and religious achievements, demonstrate how dependency on excess was a constant in the lives of powerful figures. Their personal weaknesses—ranging from alcohol to gambling, from overeating to impulsive violence—not only influenced their personal fates but, in many cases, had repercussions on their works and the political and social choices that marked their time.

BPD: The Link Between Emotional Instability And Pathological Addictions

Borderline Personality Disorder (BPD) is a psychological condition characterized by significant emotional instability, relational difficulties, and an impaired sense of self.

Individuals with BPD experience very intense emotions that change rapidly, alternating between feelings of anger, sadness, anxiety, and even euphoria.

These emotional shifts can significantly impact relationships, often leading to impulsive behaviors and a strong fear of abandonment. From a scientific perspective, BPD is linked to dysfunctions in brain areas that regulate emotions, such as the amygdala, and in the prefrontal cortex, which is responsible for controlling and regulating emotional reactions. Additionally, altered serotonin levels, a key neurotransmitter for mood regulation, play a critical role, contributing to the difficulty in controlling impulses and emotional reactions.

Another important aspect of BPD is its strong connection to pathological addictions. Impulsivity, a defining characteristic of this disorder, often leads people with BPD to engage in risky behaviors, such as substance abuse or compulsive actions. These behaviors provide immediate gratification, which becomes particularly enticing when the person seeks to alleviate emotional pain or escape from stressful situations. However, in the long term, they worsen psychological suffering, creating a vicious cycle.

Emotional regulation in BPD is a central theme. People suffering from it find it difficult to maintain emotional balance. Often, substance use becomes a way to "self-medicate" and temporarily relieve these emotions, but this does not resolve the underlying issue. In fact, comorbidity between BPD and addictions is extremely high: studies show that up to 60% of individuals with BPD may develop an alcohol or drug dependency. Self-harm is another common behavior in BPD, and it is often

accompanied by addictions, as substances are used to alleviate emotional pain or facilitate self-injurious acts.
Ultimately, BPD and pathological addictions are closely linked. Research has shown that the need for immediate gratification, combined with the difficulty in managing intense emotions, makes people with BPD particularly vulnerable to developing addictions.

NEW WORLDS - NEW "FORBIDDEN" PLEASURES

The discovery of new territories brought spices, gold, and unknown lands, but also a revolution in forbidden pleasures. As Europe expanded toward the Americas and the East, new psychoactive substances began to spread across the Old Continent, forever changing European culture and society.
Tobacco, imported from the Americas, quickly became the symbol of a new era of "vices," spreading everywhere, from aristocratic courts to the streets of cities. At the same time, hashish from the Middle East captivated intellectuals and artists, opening the doors to new inner explorations. These substances helped shape entire cultures, leaving an indelible mark on the way pleasure was experienced and perceived.

EUROPE CONQUERED AMERICA, AND SMOKE CONQUERED EUROPE

Tobacco, used by indigenous populations for ritual and recreational purposes for centuries, was introduced to Europe after the discovery of the New World. In 1492, Christopher Columbus and his crew were among the first Europeans to observe its use among Caribbean natives. However, it was the Spanish conquistadors and subsequent explorers who brought this new substance to the Old Continent.

By the mid-16th century, tobacco became popular both as a smoking and chewing product. This rapid spread marked an important turning point in the culture of pleasure, adding a new dimension to the consumption of recreational substances in Europe, which was already familiar with wine and beer.

HASHISH, FROM MYSTERIOUS ORIENT TO FASCINATED WEST

The resin extracted from Cannabis sativa has deep roots in the cultures of the Middle East and South Asia, where it had been cultivated and used for medicinal and ritual purposes for millennia. As we saw in the previous chapter, this substance was often used in religious and spiritual contexts, as well as for therapeutic treatments.

In medieval Islamic societies, its use was known, though not officially approved by religious authorities. It was tolerated in various societies, especially in urban areas and among the lower classes, though it was often the subject of moral debates.

The introduction of hashish to Europe primarily occurred through colonial and mercantile contacts. European explorers and traders brought fascinating stories back home about its properties, and some encouraged its introduction into the Old Continent.

By the 19th century, this plant extract gained popularity in France, becoming part of the bohemian culture. Artists, writers, and intellectuals such as Baudelaire and Gautier experimented with its effects, seeing it as a means to expand the mind and imagination. The *Club des Hashischins* was one of the most famous circles of Parisian intellectuals drawn to the psychedelic effects of the substance.

Despite its spread, the Eastern resin soon became a concern for authorities. By the early 20th century, legislations began regulating drugs more strictly, and hashish became associated with recreational use and crime, leading to harsh laws against its possession and consumption.

Nevertheless, it remained a symbol of cultural rebellion and psychedelic exploration, continuing to influence the modern debate on the legalization of soft drugs.

ENLIGHTENMENT, ROMANTICISM AND THE INDUSTRIAL REVOLUTION

With the dawn of the Enlightenment, the Church's influence over medicine and medicinal herbs began to wane. The rise of rationalism, the cornerstone of Enlightenment thought, led to a profound shift in how psychoactive substances were used, gradually distancing them from the spiritual or divine connections that had shaped their role in ancient cultures.

The Enlightenment, alongside the Scientific Revolution, ushered in a more secular approach to medicine. Physicians and botanists not tied to religious institutions gained growing authority over the use of medicinal plants, paving the way for a more independent medical science, based on empirical observation and clinical practice.

However, this historical shift also had its darker side. Prior to this period, the consumption of mind-altering substances, such as drugs, had been loosely regulated by religious authorities. As medicine gradually detached from the Church's control, the practices surrounding substance abuse spread without the moral checks once imposed by religious institutions.

The social consequences of alcohol use, as well as psychoactive plants like coca, morphine, and heroin, became increasingly visible and concerning. It was during this time that science began to reconsider addiction as a real phenomenon, with some physicians, such as Dr. Benjamin Rush, becoming early advocates for treating alcoholism as a medical condition in need of specialized care.

In the 19th century, the Industrial Revolution sparked an unprecedented growth in the use of "vices." Substances like opium, which had been widely used in the East, found their way into the West, especially following the Opium

Wars. This era marked the beginning of a global addiction crisis that would go on to deeply affect both medicine and society.

GAMBLING AND SOCIAL REDEMPTION

During the Industrial Revolution, the concept of risk became central both to economic life and personal existence. Industrial capitalism offered new opportunities, often accompanied by uncertainty, and fostered a mentality that closely linked risk to the potential for profit. Entrepreneurs and investors operated in an environment marked by speculation and instability, where gambling found a natural place. Betting, lotteries, and card games embodied the spirit of risk and reward that characterized emerging markets.

Even the working classes were drawn into this phenomenon, albeit for different reasons than the industrial bourgeoisie. For many workers, with their low wages and precarious living conditions, gambling represented an escape from reality and a hope for sudden wealth, although this hope was often illusory. In reality, this illusion only served to worsen their already fragile economic situation.

But the industrial bourgeoisie was not immune to the allure of risk either. For these emerging classes, gambling was not merely a pastime, but also a way to express ambition and assert their economic status. Betting and other forms of gambling reflected the desire for wealth and success, perfectly aligned with the competitive spirit of capitalism. Gambling became a symbol of social ascent: a mix of skill, risk, and fortune.

DOSTOEVSKY AND THE GAMBLING ADDICTION

A significant example of the impact of gambling is found in the life of Russian writer Fyodor Dostoevsky, who personally struggled with addiction. During Russia's transition to industrial modernity, the novelist accumulated massive debts through gambling. This experience is reflected in his novel *The Gambler* (1866), written in a state of extreme urgency to pay off his debts.

The book offers a vivid portrayal of the desperation and compulsion that define gambling addiction, showing how it could overwhelm not only the poorest classes but also people of culture and intelligence, reflecting a universal issue.

THE GAMBLING INDUSTRY

Betting quickly evolved into a full-fledged industry in rapidly growing cities. Lotteries, horse races, and gaming halls provided opportunities to try one's luck, creating a vicious cycle of addiction and financial loss.

In response to these problems, authorities attempted to introduce laws and regulations to limit gambling's impact, but enforcing these measures proved difficult. Illegal gambling continued to thrive in urban areas, challenging regulatory efforts.

ROMANTICISM AND EMOTIONAL DEPENDENCIES

The Industrial Revolution, with its profound economic and social changes, significantly impacted human relationships, transforming emotional dynamics. Rapid urbanization and the intensification of labor led many people to a state of alienation, pushing them to seek comfort in complex and often problematic emotional bonds. These relationships, characterized by an extreme need for security and love, often spiraled into emotional dependencies, reflecting the personal and social tensions of the time.

Romanticism, which emerged at the end of the 18th century, was an emotional reaction to these changes. The movement exalted individualism, deep passions, and impulsivity. Artists and intellectuals sought refuge in love and nature, in contrast to the growing rationality imposed by industrial life. However, the exaltation of extreme emotions often led to dysfunctional relationships, where passion degenerated into obsession and unhealthy attachment.

IN NOVELS, A REFLECTION OF THE TIMES

Tormented and dysfunctional relationships were at the center of many Romantic literary works, embodying the eternal conflict between passion and reason, desire and reality. In an era of profound cultural and social changes, writers explored the depths of emotions with intensity, exposing their contradictions and destructive potential.

In *The Sorrows of Young Werther* by Goethe, the protagonist is consumed by an impossible love for a woman already promised to another. His inability to control his passion leads him into a spiral of suffering, culminating tragically in suicide. Similarly, Emily Brontë's *Wuthering Heights* draws us into a fierce and self-destructive relationship between Heathcliff and Catherine Earnshaw, where love is not salvation but a fire that consumes everyone it touches. Their bond defies conventions, but also the very laws of happiness, leading them both to ruin.

The theme of emotional manipulation emerges powerfully in *Les Liaisons Dangereuses* by Choderlos de Laclos, where love is transformed into a tool of power. The protagonists, skilled puppeteers, exploit the emotions of others for selfish ends, demonstrating how passion, when bent to ambition, can destroy everything it touches.

But Russian literature, with its profound psychological depth, offers equally powerful examples. In *Anna Karenina* by Lev Tolstoy, the protagonist embodies the tragedy of a woman torn between duty and a love that consumes her. Her relationship with Vronsky, as intense as it is fatal, leads her to challenge conventions but also to pay a steep price—the cost of isolation and personal destruction. Tolstoy keenly probes Anna's emotional fragility, making her a universal symbol of the conflict between feeling and society.

In Dostoevsky's *White Nights*, love becomes a dream and an obsession. The protagonist falls in love with a woman he can never have, turning his feeling into a poignant experience of solitude. The author, with his unique sensitivity, explores unrequited love as a mental prison, where desire never finds peace.

Finally, Pushkin's *Eugene Onegin* offers a disillusioned view of passions. Tatiana, genuinely in love with Onegin, is rejected. Years later, when he finally realizes he loves

her, it is too late. The woman, still in love with him, refuses to betray her principles, showing that love can also be sacrifice and dignity.
Among these works, the dramas of *Jane Eyre* by Charlotte Brontë and *Manfred* by Lord Byron intertwine, where love and guilt, passion and secrets form a kaleidoscope of contrasting emotions. The literature of this era does not merely tell love stories: it unveils the fragility of the human soul, the contradictions of society, and the cost of desire, which often leads to ruin.

WHEN LOVE BECOMES A DRUG

Emotional dependencies, also known as co-dependency or "love addiction," occur when a person develops an excessive emotional attachment to their partner, to the point where they lose control over the relationship itself. But what happens in our brain when love takes on the characteristics of an addiction? When we fall in love, our brain triggers a series of chemical reactions similar to those that occur when drugs are taken. At the core of this phenomenon is what is known as the "reward circuit," a network of brain areas that controls the sensation of pleasure. Specifically, our brain releases dopamine, the chemical responsible for euphoria and gratification. This happens every time we think about our loved one or interact with them, much like when a person addicted to substances gets their "fix."
Oxytocin, often referred to as the "love hormone," plays a crucial role, especially during physical contact, strengthening emotional bonds. However, when oxytocin levels become excessive, they can foster an emotional attachment so strong that it turns into a true

dependency. Another element involved is serotonin, which regulates mood and helps maintain our emotional balance. When we fall in love, serotonin levels can drop, explaining the obsessive and anxious behaviors that often accompany emotional dependencies.

In the case of emotional addiction, the brain becomes accustomed to receiving pleasure and gratification from the relationship with the partner and begins to treat this connection as a vital necessity. As a result, when the partner is unavailable or the relationship becomes unstable, the brain experiences a sort of withdrawal crisis, similar to the one felt by those addicted to substances like alcohol or drugs. This withdrawal can manifest in symptoms such as anxiety, depression, insomnia, and even panic attacks.

Emotional dependencies are difficult to break because they follow a cycle alternating between euphoria and despair. When the partner is present, the brain gets its "dose" of emotional reward, but when the partner withdraws or fails to meet emotional needs, the dependent person experiences a sense of emptiness. This emotional rollercoaster creates a mechanism similar to what occurs in toxic relationships, keeping the person trapped in the bond.

In summary, emotional dependencies are not just about the heart; they also involve the brain. When love becomes obsessive and dysfunctional, it activates the same mechanisms found in substance addictions, making it extremely difficult to break the cycle of excessive attachment. Recognizing these patterns is the first step toward building healthier and more balanced relationships.

EATING DISORDERS: THE NEED FOR CONTROL IN A RAPIDLY CHANGING WORLD

Between the Industrial Revolution, the Enlightenment, and Romanticism, eating disorders began to emerge in more complex forms.

With industrialization and urbanization, people's relationship with food changed radically. The hectic life in the cities and growing alienation led to dysfunctional eating behaviors. As we've seen, stress has a significant impact on our relationship with food.

In the context of the Enlightenment, the body began to be seen as something to be rationally controlled. Food became part of a broader discussion on physical and mental well-being, but the inability to control excesses, inherent in eating disorders, coexisted with the search for control.

With Romanticism, the relationship with food took on a more emotional dimension, closely linked to personal identity.

Elisabeth of Austria, known as Sissi, perfectly embodies this conflict. Obsessed with slimness and her public image, Sissi followed rigid diets and engaged in intense physical activity, foreshadowing modern eating disorders.

THE ADVENT OF COCAINE AND HEROIN

As we've seen, between the 19th and 20th centuries, Europe and the Western world underwent profound economic, social, and cultural transformations. During this period, the Enlightenment and the Industrial Revolution redefined the concept of human progress, and science and medicine began to play an increasingly central role. The search for effective solutions to pain and chronic illnesses became crucial, paving the way for the introduction of new substances into medical practice.

It was during this time that the psychoactive substances that would continue to afflict the world to this day made their debut.

Cocaine, derived from coca leaves, arrived in Europe in the 19th century, just as European powers were intensifying their exploitation of colonial resources, particularly in Latin America.

Initially hailed as a revolutionary discovery for its stimulating and analgesic effects, cocaine found applications both among the working classes, worn out by industrial labor, and the elite, seeking remedies for anxiety and depression. Even influential figures like Sigmund Freud praised its benefits, helping spread it within academic and medical circles. However, Freud himself would later acknowledge the dependency issues associated with the substance.

With the Industrial Revolution, productivity became the focus of economic life, and the need for substances that could alleviate fatigue found fertile ground. International trade, driven by colonial exploitation, facilitated the importation of opiates and stimulants like cocaine, which were integrated into medicine without full awareness of their side effects.

Among the wealthier classes, the white powder soon became a popular recreational substance. Products like Vin Mariani and the first version of Coca-Cola, which contained traces of coca leaves, further fueled its popularity. At the same time, Bayer synthesized heroin at the end of the 19th century, marketing it as a miracle remedy for pain and even as a treatment for morphine addiction.

Heroin soon found its way into medical use, but it quickly proved to be highly addictive, contributing to a new wave of substance dependencies.

Urbanization and industrialization, with their harsh living conditions, created a perfect storm for the spread of these substances. The working classes, grappling with difficult physical and psychological conditions, and the elite, in search of new stimulants, fueled a growing demand. Meanwhile, the medicine of the time, lacking a modern understanding of addiction, promoted their use without fully understanding the consequences.

By the turn of the 19th and 20th centuries, both heroin and cocaine had transitioned from being regarded as "medical miracles" to becoming sources of serious social concern, laying the groundwork for the battles against drug addiction that continue to this day.

FROM COCA LEAF TO GLOBAL EPIDEMIC

Cocaine has its origins in the high valleys of the Andes in South America, where indigenous populations, such as the Incas, have been chewing coca leaves for centuries to alleviate hunger and fatigue, a practice made possible thanks to the stimulating alkaloids present in the plant.

The substance was introduced to Europe only in the 19th century, when Albert Niemann isolated it in pure form in 1860. Initially considered a medical miracle, cocaine was used as a local anesthetic and to treat disorders such as depression and addiction, but its side effects and its ability to cause addiction were not yet well understood.

Sigmund Freud had a significant relationship with the white powder, using it and recommending it in the early years of his career. In 1884, he published *Über Coca*, praising its therapeutic use for a wide range of disorders, including morphine addiction. Unfortunately, he administered it to a morphine-addicted friend, Ernst von Fleischl-Marxow, which severely worsened his condition and gave him a new, powerful addiction. This episode changed Freud's attitude toward cocaine, making him aware of its risks.

Over time, the unregulated use of "snow" revealed its devastating side effects. While initially used for medical and recreational purposes, by the end of the 19th century, its addictive potential began to be understood, and the first laws were introduced to limit its use.

THE IMPACT OF COCAINE ON THE HUMAN BODY

Cocaine is a stimulant substance that, although it initially causes euphoria

and an increase in energy, leads to severe physical and mental consequences with repeated use.
Physically, it raises the heart rate and blood pressure, exposing the user to cardiovascular risks such as arrhythmias, heart attacks, and strokes. Additionally, prolonged inhalation can damage the nasal septum.
Neurologically, cocaine acts on the dopaminergic system, causing a massive release of dopamine, the neurotransmitter of pleasure. This overload leads to excessive stimulation and permanent damage to neurons, especially in the areas of the brain responsible for memory, impulse control, and judgment. Long-term use alters the functionality of the prefrontal cortex, compromising impulse control and leading to impulsive behaviors and poor decision-making. Many chronic users develop cognitive problems, such as concentration difficulties, memory loss, and mood disorders. At advanced stages, it can induce episodes of psychosis, paranoia, and violent behaviors, severely impacting social and family relationships.

HEROIN: FROM THE PLANT OF JOY, TO A SOCIAL PLAGUE

As we have seen in previous chapters, opium, derived from *Papaver somniferum*, has played a crucial role in the medicinal and ritual practices of many ancient civilizations. As far back as 5,000 years ago, the Sumerians referred to it as the "plant of joy" for its analgesic and sedative properties. Since then, the cultivation and use of opium spread among various cultures, such as the Greeks, Romans, and Egyptians, who used it to treat pain and calm children, as reported in the famous *Ebers Papyrus*. Opium was also employed in religious contexts due to its ability to alter the mental state.

In the 18th and 19th centuries, the Western world experienced a radical shift in its perception of opium. With the expansion of European colonial powers, the substance was no longer just a medical remedy, but became a cornerstone of international trade, with disastrous consequences. The discovery of morphine in the 19th century marked a pivotal moment in the history of opiates.

In 1804, German chemist Friedrich Sertürner first isolated this substance, which was named after Morpheus, the Greek god of dreams, for its potent sedative and analgesic effects. This discovery represented a significant medical innovation, as it allowed for more precise dosing compared to crude opium.

The substance became the treatment of choice for acute and chronic pain, especially during the wars of the 19th century, such as the American Civil War. However, its widespread use soon revealed its strong potential for addiction, a problem that worsened further with the synthesis of an even more powerful derivative: diacetylmorphine, better known as heroin, by the end of the century. The name was chosen precisely because "heroin" derives from the German word *heroisch*, meaning "heroic." The powerful effects of the drug, which provided immediate relief from pain and elevated mood, were interpreted as something "heroic."

The synthesis of this new compound, which occurred in 1874 by English chemist C.R. Alder Wright, initially did not generate much interest until the German pharmaceutical company Bayer marketed it in 1898. This compound was promoted as a safer alternative to morphine, particularly effective in treating pain and chronic cough, and was even advertised as a non-addictive drug. Heroin was even recommended to calm children.

However, the reality proved to be very different. This morphine derivative quickly demonstrated its ability to create an even faster dependency.

In both the United States and Europe, its use spread rapidly, initially among patients to whom it was prescribed, and later among marginalized populations due to its easy availability. Diacetylmorphine, with its devastating physical and psychological effects, led to its rapid criminalization.

Throughout the 20th century, its global spread created vast criminal networks involved in the illegal trade of opiates, turning it into one of the major public health issues. The symbol of the syringe became the very image of the devastation caused by the abuse of this substance, and the fight against addiction became one of the top priorities for governments worldwide.

THE OPIUM WARS

The vast profits from the opium trade led to two wars: the Opium Wars. These two conflicts saw China and Great Britain clash in the mid-19th century, marking a pivotal moment in the history of international trade and Western-Asian relations.

In the 18th and 19th centuries, Great Britain imported large quantities of Chinese goods, such as tea, silk, and porcelain, which were highly prized in Europe. However, China demanded payments in silver for these goods, a precious and limited resource for the British. As a result, a significant trade imbalance was created: Britain imported large quantities of Chinese products but exported little to China, further aggravating its economy.

To solve this problem, London found an economically advantageous solution in opium. The poppy was cultivated in India, then a British colony, under the control of the East India Company. Despite the official ban on the trade of this substance imposed by the Chinese Empire, the opium black market thrived, causing a growing addiction among the Chinese population.

Addiction quickly became a problem of alarming proportions in China. Millions of people, including men and women from all social classes, began using it, with devastating effects on physical and mental health. Productivity plummeted, family structures deteriorated, and entire communities were destroyed. The Chinese treasury was drained as vast amounts of silver left the country to pay for opium.

The government in Beijing, under Emperor Daoguang, attempted to counteract the phenomenon.

In 1839, Lin Zexu, an official tasked with stopping the opium trade, seized and destroyed over 20,000 chests of opium in Canton, an act that was seen as a direct challenge to British economic interests.

Britain's response was swift: the destruction of the opium was an unsustainable economic loss, and the British decided to intervene militarily to protect their trade, sparking the First Opium War (1839-1842).

The war ended with China's defeat and the signing of the Treaty of Nanjing in 1842, which opened several Chinese ports to British trade and ceded Hong Kong to Britain. This treaty represented another humiliation for the Chinese Empire, which saw its sovereignty drastically reduced.

TOWARDS THE 20TH CENTURY

The journey through the history of addiction has shown us how humanity, from ancient times to the dawn of the 20th century, has had a complex and ambivalent relationship with psychoactive substances. From the ritualistic and medicinal practices of opium in ancient civilizations, to the global spread of cocaine and heroin in the 19th century, we have seen how the use of these substances evolved from a medical and spiritual context to a mass addiction problem, fueled by the economic and geopolitical dynamics of the time. However, the beginning of the 20th century marks a significant turning point.

The evolution of science and the growing understanding of the nature of addiction led to a new therapeutic and social approach. Substances once considered miraculous remedies began to be recognized for their devastating addictive potential, prompting societies to seek more informed solutions. In the next chapter, we will explore the evolution of drugs and addiction in the contemporary world, from the 20th to the 21st century. We will see how science, government policies, and cultural changes have transformed the way we approach addiction, with the introduction of new synthetic drugs, advances in therapeutic treatments, and the ongoing battle against the illicit drug trade.

CHAPTER 3

ADDICTION IN THE MODERN WORLD
TOWARDS A DEEPER UNDERSTANDING

In the 20th and 21st centuries, we have witnessed a dramatic rise in pathological addictions worldwide, but also significant progress in understanding this disease. However, the path toward effective addiction management has been—and still is—far from straightforward. The recognition of addiction as a pathology goes hand in hand with the emergence of new, often more lethal substances, and with socio-cultural situations that favor compulsive behaviors.

Navigating the complex world of new substances is not easy, as past and present often overlap. In this regard, it is essential to remember that addiction is not an isolated deviance from the social and cultural context in which it manifests.

As outlined in this book, the drama of addiction has accompanied humankind since its origins and reflects its historical and social evolution. Addictions are by no means a vice but a profound phenomenon that involves the physical, emotional, mental, and spiritual spheres of the individual. Over time, positive and negative aspects have often merged, making it difficult to draw a clear line between the two dimensions.

Humankind has discovered and used psychoactive substances to experience intense spiritual journeys. However, outside of ritual contexts, these substances have often consumed the human being itself, depriving it not only of its spirituality but also of its physical, emotional, and mental health.

In this context, drawing a linear historical narrative is complicated, as the different substances and practices related to addiction have overlapped throughout various eras.

I have generally tried to follow a chronological account to simplify the analysis, but there were cases where this was not possible. In historical reality, many of the substances and situations described have overlapped and intersected.

Before we resume the narrative, however, it is necessary to take a pause.

Pathological addictions are a physical, mental, emotional, and spiritual disease. Only an integrated understanding of these four dimensions of the human being can lead to an effective cure for pathological addiction. Science has sought and continues to seek to understand how the disease "works" physically; psychiatry and neuroscience have done the same regarding mental mechanisms; psychology and other disciplines, such as coaching and counseling, look at the emotional aspect. We will discuss these scientific branches in detail in the last chapter of the first part.

The spiritual realm has long been the domain and monopoly of religions. However, in the 20th and 21st centuries, these structures have shifted.

THE SPIRITUAL VOID OF THE 20TH CENTURY

Explaining what spirituality an almost impossible task can be. Mental categories alone are insufficient to grasp its full depth. However, given the essential role this dimension of the human experience plays in understanding and combating pathological addictions, an attempt must be made.

Spirituality is the deep breath of the soul, the invisible force that fills the void of existence and connects us to something greater and transcendent. It is the inner compass that guides humanity toward a more authentic and meaningful life, allowing individuals to feel part of a universal design. Without it, one experiences a profound disconnection, which cannot be filled by professional success or material pleasures.

When one neglects their spiritual dimension, an absence of meaning arises, leading to confusion and alienation. This sense of existential disconnection, rooted in the absence of a deeper purpose, drives individuals to desperately seek something to fill this feeling of incompleteness. However, no success or material possession can replace the authentic connection with one's own spirituality.

In the Western world, spirituality has often been confused with religion. While the two are closely linked, they are not synonymous. Religion, with its structured system of beliefs, rituals, and dogmas, can provide a pathway to cultivate spirituality, but spirituality itself is an intimate and personal experience that can exist outside religious institutions.

Throughout the 20th century, Western man began to distance himself from a spirituality tied to the dogmatism of the Church. The idea of *Nulla salus extra ecclesiam* (no salvation outside the Church), introduced by Saint Augustine and promoted for centuries by Catholic tradition, no longer responded to the spiritual needs of an evolving society. Dogmatic certainties were challenged by new scientific, philosophical, and ideological perspectives, making it increasingly difficult for modern man to identify with a rigid and absolutist religious vision. The Second Vatican Council addressed this challenge by reinterpreting doctrine in a more inclusive manner, as seen in the document *Lumen Gentium*. While the Catholic Church retained the fullness of the means of salvation, the Council recognized that other religions and Christian communities could also be instruments of divine grace.

At the same time, secular ideologies such as Humanism and Communism emerged as alternatives to traditional religion. Humanism, while promoting the dignity and autonomy of the individual, placed man at the center of the universe, thereby reducing space for a broader spiritual vision. Communism, on the other hand, exalted ideals of solidarity and social justice but saw religion as an obstacle to revolution, as expressed by Karl Marx's famous phrase: "Religion is the opium of the people."

In this process, humanity became distanced not only from religion but also from spirituality, creating a profound inner void. This separation had devastating consequences. Faced with historical crises and personal suffering, without a transcendent meaning, life in the 20th century appeared sterile and purposeless. This existential void contributed to the spread of addictions, both substance-related and behavioral.

Starting in the 1960s, drug use became a response to the growing spiritual crisis, a temporary escape to try to fill the inner emptiness many were experiencing. However, these escapes, rather than offering solutions, often led only to further alienation and destruction, reflecting the increasingly evident spiritual crisis of our time.

The heroin epidemic of the 1960s-1980s spread in a context of deep social distress, exacerbated by the absence of spiritual references and the weakening of traditional institutions like family and religion. Even the Counterculture of the 1960s, which had sought new meanings and alternatives to institutions, lost momentum in the following decade, leaving many young people disoriented and without clear points of reference.

In the 1980s, as consumerism and materialism took over, the promises of the Counterculture shattered. Many alternative spiritual movements—Hippies, Flower Children, Eastern philosophies, etc.—turned into commercial industries, and drug use, initially exploratory, morphed into destructive dependencies, as seen with heroin and cocaine.

Spirituality became a more individual, fragmented quest, while neoliberalism and the race for personal success dominated the cultural landscape.

In summary, the spiritual crisis of the 20th century, fueled by secularization, political disillusionment, and the search for new existential meanings, left many people disoriented and uncertain about how to reconcile a rapidly changing world with their deeper spiritual needs. And addictions found fertile ground to proliferate.

BARBITURATES AND BENZODIAZEPINES: "UNPLUGGING" FOR RELIEF

The period from the 1930s to the 1950s was marked by great turmoil: economic crises, world wars, and the arduous task of rebuilding. The 1930s, in particular, were defined by the Great Depression, which devastated the global economy, causing mass unemployment and uncertainty. As if that wasn't enough, totalitarian regimes made their way to power, sowing political instability and setting the stage for World War II.

When the war ended in 1945, the world began the slow process of rebuilding a new equilibrium. The 1940s and 1950s were a time of recovery and renewal, with Europe benefiting from the Marshall Plan, and the defeated countries—Italy among them—forced to reckon with a limited sovereignty, sometimes only on paper. This marked the beginning of an era of economic prosperity, with the rise of consumerism and the growth of the middle class.

In this climate of change, the use of psychoactive substances began to make its way into the spotlight, though still relatively quietly compared to the boom it would experience in the 1960s.

By the 1950s, with the introduction of tranquilizers and antidepressants, the potential risks of abusing these new "pharmacological solutions" started to be debated in a society desperately seeking balance.

Meanwhile, as early as the 1930s, the pharmaceutical industry had introduced barbiturates, a class of depressant drugs capable of slowing down the central nervous system. Although barbituric acid had been synthesized back in 1864 by Adolf von Baeyer, it wasn't until later that these substances entered widespread medical use. They were employed to treat conditions like insomnia, anxiety, epilepsy, and as anesthetics.

What was their effect? They slowed down brain activity, "turning off the light," so to speak, but with severe side effects. It didn't take long for the other side of the coin to emerge. Initially hailed as a revolution, barbiturates turned out to be a ticking time bomb. Tolerance developed quickly, forcing patients to increase their doses, with the ever-present risk of overdose becoming more tangible. In the 1950s and 1960s, their use expanded outside of medical settings, with people turning to them as a way to escape daily stress, leading to a full-blown epidemic of addiction. And it wasn't just ordinary people who fell victim to these drugs. The entertainment world saw some of its most famous figures succumb to barbiturate abuse. Marilyn Monroe, Judy Garland, and Jimi Hendrix are just a few of the names tragically linked to overdoses involving these substances. Marilyn Monroe's death in 1962 remains shrouded in mystery, while Judy Garland, after years of battling addiction, passed away in 1969. Even Jimi Hendrix, who died in 1970, ingested a fatal combination of alcohol and barbiturates.

With the rise in deaths and dependencies, the search for safer alternatives began.

Today, barbiturates are still used, but only in specific cases such as treating severe epilepsy or as anesthetics. Their use as sedatives or sleeping pills has almost disappeared.

By the late 1950s, benzodiazepines emerged, seen as the "safe solution." The first marketed drugs were Librium and Valium, enthusiastically welcomed for treating anxiety, insomnia, and panic attacks.

Compared to barbiturates, benzodiazepines had a better safety profile: a lower risk of fatal overdose and less sedative effect.

From a scientific standpoint, benzodiazepines work by enhancing the action of GABA, the neurotransmitter that reduces neuronal activity, creating a calming effect. They are highly useful for acute anxiety, but they are not without dangers.

Outside of limited use, addiction is just around the corner. After just four weeks of regular use, the risk of developing an addiction becomes significant, and it only takes two weeks to start developing tolerance. Prolonged use? Memory problems, difficulty concentrating, and risks of excessive sedation that can interfere with daily life.

Combining benzodiazepines with other substances, like alcohol or opioids, is a recipe for disaster: respiratory depression and overdose become very real risks.

Despite the dangers, benzodiazepines are still widely prescribed for acute anxiety and insomnia, but for chronic disorders, alternative therapies such as psychotherapy or antidepressants with a lower risk of dependency are preferred.

These drugs are also heavily regulated in other European countries and the United States. However, in some countries, like Mexico or Southeast Asian states, they can be bought with fewer restrictions, creating fertile ground for abuse.

Many people report falling victim to benzodiazepine addiction without being fully informed of the long-term risks. "My doctor told me it was a mild substance, to take as needed!" This is one of the recurring phrases that emerged during interviews conducted for this essay. The problem is that, if the underlying issues of anxiety, insomnia, or panic attacks are not addressed, the need becomes constant... and so, addiction is inevitable.

"THE HANDBRAKE" FOR EMOTIONS

Benzodiazepines are drugs known for their ability to "calm the waters" in the brain. Primarily used to treat anxiety, insomnia, and panic attacks, they act as tranquilizers for those whose minds are racing at full speed. But how exactly do they work, and what effects

do they have on our body and, more importantly, our brain?
When you take a benzodiazepine, what happens in the brain is quite surprising. These drugs enhance the action of a neurotransmitter called GABA (gamma-aminobutyric acid). GABA acts as a natural brake for our brain: its main function is to slow down neuronal activity.
The result is a feeling of relaxation, reduced anxiety, and, in some cases, drowsiness. This is why these drugs are so effective against insomnia and anxiety: they quiet the constant noise in the brain, putting it into "rest" mode. When taking these substances, worries seem to slip away.
However, there is a downside. The brain quickly becomes accustomed to this "enhanced brake" and starts depending on the drug to maintain calm. This is where tolerance comes into play: over time, the dose that once calmed you becomes insufficient, and you need larger quantities to achieve the same effect.
Withdrawal from benzodiazepines is long and difficult. The brain struggles to "brake" on its own. This can lead to insomnia, intense anxiety, irritability, and, in severe cases, seizures or panic attacks.
On the body, the effects of benzodiazepines are similar to those of a sedative. Prolonged use can lead to issues such as muscle weakness, loss of coordination, and, in some cases, breathing difficulties.
When taken in combination with alcohol or other depressants of the nervous system, the risk of overdose increases dramatically, as the respiratory system may slow down to the point of stopping altogether.

Benzodiazepines, therefore, are a double-edged sword. On one hand, they can be incredibly effective if used properly and for very short periods. On the other, their abuse or prolonged use can lead to dependence, serious health issues, and a cycle that's hard to break.

Recovery from benzodiazepine dependence often requires a long detox process under strict medical supervision. Stopping suddenly can be dangerous, so discontinuing these drugs must be done gradually. It's a challenging journey, but not impossible.

FALLEN STARS: A FATAL PILL POP

One of the most well-known cases is that of Australian actor Heath Ledger, who passed away in 2008 at the age of just 28. He is famous for his roles in films such as *The Dark Knight*, where he played the legendary Joker, and *Brokeback Mountain*. Ledger's life was tragically cut short due to an accidental overdose caused by a lethal mix of prescribed medications, including benzodiazepines, opioids, and sleeping pills. His death highlighted the dangers of combining benzodiazepines with other substances, raising public awareness of the risks involved.

Among the stars claimed by the reckless use of prescription drugs, we also remember Elvis Presley, who died in 1977. Although the official cause of death was cardiac arrest, it is well-known that Presley had been using large amounts of medications, including sedatives and benzodiazepines. These drugs contributed to his physical deterioration in the final years of his life.

Another tragic case is that of Whitney Houston, who was found dead in 2012 with traces of benzodiazepines and alcohol in her system. The artist had long struggled with drug addiction, and the combination of benzodiazepines and alcohol may have played a key role in her death.

Similarly, Michael Jackson, who died in 2009, was the victim of a lethal combination of drugs, including benzodiazepines and propofol, which led to his death from respiratory depression. His case sparked a widespread debate about medical responsibility in managing drug dependencies.

Thus, despite their therapeutic potential, the abuse of these drugs can have tragic consequences. The deaths of these famous figures have sparked a debate about the dangers of improper use of prescribed medications and the need for better information from doctors, as well as greater awareness from those who take them.

AMPHETAMINES - METHAMPHETAMINES
SOLDIERS AS WAR MACHINES

In war and love, anything goes? It certainly seems so. When the stakes are high, ethics can become a luxury. During World War II, amphetamines and methamphetamines evolved from medical drugs to war tools, maximizing soldiers' performance at a very high cost. Initially developed to treat issues like narcolepsy, these stimulants were mass-distributed in armies to boost energy, reduce sleep, and enhance vigilance.

Amphetamines, synthesized in the late 19th century, were primarily used by the United States and the United Kingdom, who provided their soldiers with Benzedrine to keep them battle-ready. However, it was Nazi Germany that took it a step further: with the infamous Pervitin, a powerful methamphetamine, they transformed their soldiers into tireless war machines. The blitzkriegs, lightning-fast attacks, were fueled by these pills promising superhuman endurance. Japan also adopted similar strategies, administering methamphetamines to soldiers and even factory workers.

However, the side effects were quick to show: addiction, paranoia, and physical damage marked the lives of many

veterans.
In Italy, the use of stimulants was more limited and mostly documented among pilots and special forces. Still, the sacrifice demanded of these generations—fighting not only the enemy but also their own bodies and minds—left indelible scars.

FATAL CRYSTALS: THE EVOLUTION OF THE THREAT

After World War II, "combat doping" left the battlefields and infiltrated civilian life. In the 1950s, methamphetamines were promoted in the medical field to treat conditions like obesity, narcolepsy, and ADHD. Pharmacies and manufacturers marketed these substances as "energy pills," encouraging students, workers, and housewives to use them to tackle daily fatigue.
This popularity quickly led to widespread abuse. In the 1980s, the underground drug industry seized control of methamphetamine production, giving birth to "crystal meth" or "ice." Its crystallized form, more potent and cheaper, devastated vulnerable communities, both urban and rural. Users sought the euphoria and endurance this substance provided, ignoring its devastating side effects: from "meth mouth" (tooth loss) to "meth face" (skin deterioration), and even permanent neurological damage. The battle against crystal meth remains a global challenge. Despite laws and operations targeting clandestine labs, the low cost and easy availability of the chemicals needed continue to fuel a thriving market, leaving millions trapped in a cycle of addiction and destruction.

THE CHEMICAL "TURBO" THAT DEVOURS MIND AND BODY

Amphetamines and methamphetamines are powerful stimulants that act on the central nervous system, increasing energy, concentration, and alertness. These substances work by releasing massive amounts of dopamine and norepinephrine, which causes a feeling of invincibility and seemingly improved performance. However,

their effect on the brain is devastating: chronic use undermines the nervous system's ability to produce dopamine naturally, leading to depression, anxiety, and an unbearable sense of emptiness.
Methamphetamines, more potent and destructive than amphetamines, amplify these effects. Prolonged abuse leads to severe and often irreversible brain damage, including psychosis, paranoia, and loss of cognitive abilities. Neuroimaging studies have shown significant reductions in brain volume, particularly affecting areas involved in emotional control and learning. The cardiovascular system also suffers enormous damage: heart attacks, strokes, and hypertension are common risks.
Physical symptoms, such as "meth mouth" and extreme weight loss, are just the tip of the iceberg. The complexity of addiction requires integrated medical and psychological interventions to facilitate recovery, which, unfortunately, is often partial. Science continues to study the mechanisms of these substances to develop effective therapies, but the battle against the "chemical turbo" remains a huge challenge for public health.

HEROIN, FROM MEDICAL MIRACLE TO GLOBAL CRISIS

One of the most significant tragedies of the 20th century, in terms of both its spread and impact, was undoubtedly the heroin epidemic. In the previous chapter, we discussed opium, morphine, and the discovery of this derivative, initially marketed as a "miracle drug."
Now, it’s time to pick up that thread and see what happened next.

In the 19th century, opioids like morphine were primarily used in medical contexts and were considered a cure-all for many conditions. But over time, the side effects—particularly addiction—became an increasingly visible problem. This situation exploded in the 20th century, and it was a grim sight.

In 1898, the pharmaceutical company Bayer introduced heroin as a treatment for morphine addiction and other medical conditions.

It sounds absurd, doesn't it? But at the time, the understanding of the risks associated with these substances was limited, and experimental protocols were nearly non-existent. Agencies like the FDA or EMA, which now monitor every drug released to the market, didn't exist yet. Pharmaceutical companies often relied on empirical observations and unbridled enthusiasm.

Heroin was welcomed as a kind of salvation, believed to be less dangerous than morphine, and was prescribed to treat ailments like cough and pain. However, it didn't take long for people to realize that this "remedy" was worse than the disease. Heroin's addictive potential proved to be devastating, and the physical damage soon became apparent.

The substance attacks nearly every system in the body. Cardiovascularly, repeated injections destroy veins, leading to venous collapses and severe infections like endocarditis, a life-threatening infection of the heart valves. Not only that, but blood pressure and heart rate decrease over time, with the constant risk of collapse or sudden death.

The respiratory system doesn't fare any better. Heroin depresses respiration, and many overdoses are caused by respiratory failure. But that's not all: chronic use compromises lung capacity, leaving users exposed to diseases like pneumonia, all compounded by a weakened immune system.

The liver and kidneys are also victims of this substance. The liver, which metabolizes heroin, can suffer enormous damage, including liver failure or cirrhosis, especially

when heroin is mixed with other toxic substances. The kidneys, on the other hand, can develop chronic inflammation and toxin accumulation, which leads to kidney failure.
Then there's the brain, the most affected organ. Heroin acts on opioid receptors, inducing both physical and psychological dependence. The body develops tolerance quickly, so users need larger doses to achieve the same effects. And with increased doses comes the heightened risk of overdose. When respiration slows down, the brain receives less oxygen, which can lead to permanent damage, coma, or, in the worst cases, brain death.
Even the digestive system isn't immune to heroin's effects. The drug slows down intestinal function, causing chronic constipation and more severe issues like intestinal blockages. Long-term users often suffer from malnutrition and general physical deterioration.
Heroin also has a powerful immunosuppressive effect, raising the risk of infections. The use of contaminated needles exposes users to diseases like HIV and hepatitis C. And there's the damage to teeth: reduced saliva production causes dry mouth, making cavities and gum disease more likely. Bruxism, common among heroin users, further damages dental enamel.
Finally, the skin. Frequent injections cause abscesses, skin infections, and permanent scarring. The skin loses elasticity and integrity, making heroin users vulnerable to severe bacterial infections.
In conclusion, heroin is far from the "miracle drug" it was once thought to be. The damage it causes to both body and mind is immense, and its legacy is one of devastation, not salvation. The global crisis sparked by heroin use continues to affect millions of people, highlighting the urgent need for comprehensive treatment, prevention, and support systems to combat addiction and its far-reaching consequences.

THE "WARM EMBRACE"

Heroin addiction, as we'll see in the final chapter, is a complex disease. Here, we'll focus on one fundamental aspect: the immediate sensations this opium derivative products, which make it so difficult to break free from. Understanding how this "enemy" works is essential in combating it.

Heroin, like all opioids, acts on our brain similarly to endorphins, substances that, as we've already seen, the body naturally produces to manage pain and stress. When heroin enters the body, it binds to opioid receptors, blocking pain and reducing the activity of GABAergic neurons, which regulate dopamine release. With this regulation disabled, the brain is flooded with dopamine, which has effects primarily in the nucleus accumbens—the pleasure center—tied, as we know, to the reward system. This rush of dopamine creates an intense feeling of euphoria.

In the short term, this euphoria can feel irresistible, but it's precisely this exaggerated dopamine release that alters the brain's natural system. With repeated use, the brain reduces its natural production of dopamine, and the dopamine receptors become less sensitive. The result? Without the drug, it's almost impossible to experience pleasure. This leads to tolerance and dependence: the brain requires increasingly larger doses to achieve the same euphoric effect.

One of the most well-known immediate effects of heroin is the so-called "rush," a strong and intense wave of euphoria. This effect is short-lived but so powerful that those who experience it often seek to relive it, over and over.

Immediately following this peak, many users describe a sensation of enveloping warmth, which provides a feeling of fulfillment and security—almost like a protective embrace. This sense of well-being, though deceptive and temporary, is what drives many to return to the drug.

In addition to the euphoria and warmth, heroin also induces a deep state of relaxation. It depresses the central nervous system, reducing anxiety, and allows users to disconnect from daily worries. For some, this temporary "escape" represents relief from an otherwise oppressive existence.

Another aspect that makes heroin so attractive is the sense of security it can offer. Some users report feeling safer and less inhibited socially, with a reduction in feelings of inadequacy.

In other words, the drug creates a false sense of confidence and well-being, momentarily masking emotional emptiness or personal struggles.

And beyond the immediate pleasure, heroin is also a powerful analgesic. Pain relief is almost instantaneous, and for those suffering from chronic or acute pain, this effect can seem like a blessing.

However, the price to pay for these brief moments of relief is extremely high: the physical and psychological dependence that develops makes it increasingly difficult to turn back.

The big difference between the natural release of endorphins and the effect of heroin lies in how these substances interact with our brain. Endorphins are released in balanced amounts, only when the body truly needs them. Once their job is done, they naturally degrade without causing an imbalance. Heroin, on the other hand, completely upends this system: the release of dopamine is disproportionate and out of control, leaving the brain unable to function properly without the substance.

At this point, perhaps we should ask another question: What pain and what need led so many people to try and force the reward system? Generations from the '60s to the present day have not suffered from hunger or other ancient physical needs. Let's leave this question open!

THE SILENT AND DEADLY WAR

The 20th century experienced two World Wars, the Cold War, and dozens of "minor" conflicts, each with its own toll of victims. The First World War caused between 15 and 20 million deaths, while the Second World War claimed over 80 million lives. Even conflicts like the Vietnam War left their mark, with a death toll between 2 and 4 million.

At the same time, a "silent war" has continued to take its toll worldwide: heroin and opioids are responsible for between 100,000 and 110,000 deaths every year. When we add in deaths caused by other psychoactive substances (including alcohol), the number rises to over 3 million deaths annually. Considering the trends of the last four decades, deaths related to psychoactive substances exceed those of many wars. And this toll does not even include the victims of other behavioral addictions, which further exacerbate the global crisis.

The heroin crisis began to emerge in the 1960s, initially spreading among Vietnam War veterans before rapidly reaching all social strata in the United States. War contexts, such as Southeast Asia, provided fertile ground for the spread of this substance, which infiltrated every corner of society.

THE "THREE J" AND THE "27 CLUB"

The "Three J" – Jimi Hendrix, Janis Joplin, and Jim Morrison – are three rock legends who defined an era of cultural and musical revolution in the 1960s. However, they also shared a tragic fate: the premature death at the age of 27, which earned them a place in the so-called "27 Club." This term refers to a group of artists who passed away at this young age, often due to substance abuse and self-destructive lifestyles, in a time marked by radical changes and experimentation.

Jimi Hendrix, with his revolutionary guitar talent, redefined psychedelic rock. His innovative techniques and creative use of feedback and pedals transformed the electric guitar into a tool for unprecedented sonic exploration. At the peak of his success, Hendrix became a rock icon, with historic performances like his set at the 1969 Woodstock festival. However, the lethal mix of alcohol and sleeping pills led to his premature death in 1970.

Janis Joplin, with her powerful and raspy voice, captivated audiences with deep interpretations of blues and rock songs. A rebellious spirit and an icon of the 1960s counterculture, Janis became one of the first great female stars of rock. But behind the success lay deep insecurities and addictions. She died from a heroin overdose just a few weeks after Hendrix, in 1970, silencing one of the most powerful voices of that generation.

Jim Morrison, the charismatic leader of The Doors, was known for his hypnotic voice as much as for his poetic and visionary lyrics. An emblematic figure of avant-garde rock, Morrison infused his songs with existential reflections and a dark aura that mirrored the chaos of those turbulent years. His life was marked by addictions and personal struggles, culminating in his tragic death in Paris in 1971. The circumstances of his passing remain shrouded in mystery to this day, fueling the myth that surrounds his figure.

The "Three J" not only defined a musical era, but their early deaths turned them into symbols of human vulnerability behind the myth of rock'n'roll. These figures embodied the aspirations, contradictions, and dangers of an era, becoming icons not only of creative freedom but also of self-destruction.

Another famous name associated with the "27 Club" is Kurt Cobain, the leader of Nirvana and an iconic voice of grunge music. Cobain struggled with physical and mental health issues, using heroin to alleviate his pain. His addiction, combined with personal difficulties, led him into a self-destructive spiral that culminated in his death by suicide in 1994, at just 27 years old.

Amy Winehouse, one of the brightest voices in contemporary music, also met a tragic end at 27. She died on July 23, 2011, from acute alcohol poisoning, with her blood alcohol level five times the legal driving limit in the UK. The singer had a long and tumultuous history of battling drug and alcohol addictions, with numerous rehabilitations attempts that, tragically, were not enough to save her.

Finally, we cannot forget Philip Seymour Hoffman, one of the most talented actors of his generation, who died in 2014 at the age of 46 from a heroin overdose. His passing further emphasized the tragic pattern of addiction that claimed yet another brilliant mind. Hoffman's death, like that of others in the "27 Club," serves as a stark reminder of the dark side of fame and the destructive power of substance abuse.

Heroin and other substances temporarily filled the existential void that many artists experienced, but at a devastating cost. Today, it's crucial to remember how important it is to address the spiritual and emotional needs of society to prevent new forms of alienation and addiction.

METHADONE: FROM GERMAN TRENCHES TO THE WAR ON HEROIN

The heroin crisis led to the development of new therapies, including methadone.
Born in a wartime context, methadone has become, over the years, one of the most widely used and simultaneously most controversial substances in addiction treatment for relieving withdrawal symptoms.
The substance was first synthesized in 1937 by German chemists Max Bockmühl and Gustav Ehrhart at the IG Farben laboratories, the same company notoriously known for producing Zyklon B, used in concentration camps.
At the time, Germany was facing a dramatic shortage of morphine due to the commercial difficulties caused by the war, and methadone was developed as a synthetic alternative to natural opioids.
After the war, the formula was discovered by the Allies, who introduced it to the United States, where the drug was initially used for pain management. However, in the 1960s, two doctors, Vincent Dole and Marie Nyswander, revolutionized its use by proposing it as a substitution therapy for heroin addicts. Their goal was simple: to replace a more potent and illegal substance—heroin—with a less harmful and legal alternative.
In fact, the relief provided by methadone lasts longer than that of heroin. Its long half-life helps manage withdrawal

symptoms for 24 hours, unlike heroin, which acts quickly and requires frequent dosing.

However, it remains an opioid, and as such, still carries the risk of addiction.

In the 1970s, methadone treatment programs spread quickly across the United States and other countries. While the drug has helped reduce crime associated with drug use, allowing patients to avoid illegal behaviors to obtain heroin, it is not without controversy.

Methadone is not a cure; it's a substitution. Many patients remain on this treatment for years, some even for life, unable to fully discontinue it. Methadone withdrawal syndrome, though less intense than heroin withdrawal, can last weeks or months, with symptoms like anxiety, muscle pain, and insomnia.

Moreover, long-term use can cause side effects such as heart problems, sexual dysfunction, and damage to the liver and bones.

Despite these risks, methadone remains one of the most widely used treatments today, still within harm-reduction strategies.

BUPRENORPHINE AND HARM REDUCTION POLICIES

At the same time, alternatives like buprenorphine are being developed, which seem to carry a lower risk of dependence and a less severe withdrawal syndrome compared to other opioids.

However, buprenorphine also belongs to the opioid class. Specifically, it is a partial agonist, meaning it binds to opioid receptors in the brain but activates them less powerfully than full opioids like heroin or morphine.

One of the main advantages of buprenorphine is that it produces a more controlled and less euphoric opioid effect. It also has what is known as a "ceiling effect": beyond a certain dose, its effects do not significantly increase, thus reducing the risk of overdose compared to other opioids.

Buprenorphine is available in various forms, such as sublingual tablets and transdermal patches. In many cases, it is combined with naloxone (as in Suboxone) to prevent

misuse. This combination is designed to further reduce the risk of improper use, as naloxone counteracts the euphoric effects of opioids if buprenorphine is taken incorrectly, such as through intravenous injection.
The transition from buprenorphine treatment is often considered easier than from other opioids, due to less intense withdrawal symptoms.
This drug is also used in Italy. It can only be prescribed by authorized doctors, and the treatment is often closely monitored.

THE OPIOID EPIDEMIC: THE "4 WAVES"

After the tragic spread of heroin in the 1980s, four waves of the opioid epidemic have followed from the 1990s to the present day.
The first wave began in the final decade of the 20th century, when the use of prescription medications such as oxycodone and hydrocodone dramatically increased. This rise was partly due to aggressive marketing campaigns by pharmaceutical companies, which promoted these painkillers as safe and effective for chronic pain treatment while downplaying the risk of addiction. Many people developed a strong dependence on these drugs, leading to widespread abuse.
When prescriptions for these opioids were reduced in the early 2000s in an effort to curb the damage caused by addiction, many dependent patients turned to heroin, which was cheaper and more readily available. This phase, known as the second wave, saw an exponential rise in overdoses.
The third wave began around 2013, with the appearance of fentanyl and other synthetic opioids on the illegal market. Even small amounts of this drug can be fatal, and its spread has had a devastating impact.
Currently, the crisis has entered a new phase, the so-called fourth wave, marked by the combined use of fentanyl with stimulant drugs such as cocaine and methamphetamines. But we will discuss this phase in more detail later, after exploring the effects of these substances.

THE FATAL CYCLE OF OPIOIDS

History doesn't always teach… or perhaps it would be better to say that, even when history does teach, some choose other masters to follow.

And the God of Money is often more inspiring than History or Conscience.

In fact, looking at the events surrounding the spread of drugs, one might get the impression of being catapulted into the famous song by Italian singer-songwriter Angelo Branduardi, which started something like this: "*At the fair of the East, for a few pennies, a little mouse was bought... then came the cat that ate the mouse... then came the dog that bit the cat... the stick that beat the dog...*" and so on... until death came with its sickle...

What a strange coincidence! Opium also comes from the East.

Well, the colorful poppy plant produced opium... which devastated entire nations, but mankind did not stop, and didn't keep away from that plant. From opium, morphine was extracted... which soothed pain and drove thousands and thousands of people mad. To limit the damage caused by morphine, heroin was introduced, the "miraculous remedy" by Bayer, even recommended for children, which, however, caused and continues to cause devastation. Then, from the magician's hat, came methadone—less loud, but capable of chaining people for life—and then, and then, and then… until today's oxycodone and fentanyl. Each solution, in this deadly chain, has created more drama than the problem it was supposed to solve. History teaches, but perhaps some pages are best left unread.

OXYCODONE: AN AVOIDABLE TRAGEDY

One thing is certain: by the 1990s, the pharmaceutical industry was fully aware of what it was doing. With all the medical and scientific resources available, there was no justification for promoting drugs like oxycodone, fully aware of their devastating potential for addiction. At the end of the 19th century, Bayer could still be "justified" for advertising heroin as a therapeutic miracle, but by 1996, with oxycodone, the situation was completely different. The tools to avoid another global epidemic of addiction were all available, yet the warning signs were ignored in the name of profit. Judicial rulings have revealed how Purdue Pharma, with its OxyContin brand, raked in over $35 billion in the United States by manipulating clinical data and downplaying the addictive risks of oxycodone. Promoted as a safe drug for managing chronic pain, OxyContin generated astronomical profits thanks to aggressive marketing, leading to its widespread distribution, with sales representatives incentivized to promote increasingly higher dosages. In 2010 alone, annual sales reached $3.1 billion, with additional profits generated globally from generic versions of the drug. To put these profits into perspective, the launch of this drug generated an economic value equivalent to the GDP of Latvia. These earnings are comparable to those of giants like Visa. With such a sum, one could finance the military expenditures of a small country like Estonia for over 50 years.

However, these enormous profits came at an incalculable human cost.

For the judges, this behavior was not only irresponsible but criminal.

Today, oxycodone continues to be prescribed in many countries, including Italy, but hopefully with greater caution. Still, this crisis raises questions about how to prevent similar disasters in the future. It seems hard to imagine that a pharmaceutical company, no matter how "evil and ruthless," could have caused such a massacre on its own. One question remains: where were the drug control agencies while all this was happening? And the doctors, when they signed those prescriptions, what were they thinking? It can be said that clinical trial data was manipulated, but the fact that opioids cause addiction is a well-known truth:

any opioid, even those distributed by the healthcare system like methadone, has a destructive potential, even when sold in the name of "harm reduction."
Prescribing these drugs to a terminally ill patient can be justified as an act of mercy, but for those suffering from addiction, there are other hopes. Treatment options exist, even if they require effort, suffering, and commitment. One thing is certain: for the massacre caused by oxycodone, beyond the condemnation of Purdue Pharma, no criminal verdicts were issued against FDA officials (the agency responsible for drug regulation in the US), politicians, or doctors, even though there have been numerous trials against individual healthcare professionals accused of prescribing the drug irresponsibly.

FENTANYL: THE LATEST LETHAL FRONTIER

Fentanyl, developed in the 1960s by Belgian chemist Paul Janssen, is a synthetic opioid of devastating potency. Originally designed to relieve acute pain in cancer patients, it has found a dangerous path onto the illegal market. Its chemical structure allows it to cross the blood-brain barrier rapidly, providing immediate relief but also an equally swift risk of death.
This drug is 100 times more potent than morphine and 50 times more than heroin. This means that even a tiny dose can be fatal.
On the black market, it is often mixed with other drugs like heroin or cocaine, multiplying the risk of overdose for unsuspecting users unaware of its presence.
In the United States, fentanyl has been one of the main drivers of the opioid epidemic, contributing to a shocking number of deaths.
Despite its legitimate medical use for alleviating pain in the most severe patients, out of control it has become a deadly weapon. Abused as a powder or liquid, it has triggered an unprecedented health crisis, leading to the deaths of thousands.

And it's not alone: derivatives like sufentanil, alfentanil, and carfentanil are even more lethal. Carfentanil, used to sedate elephants, can kill a human with an infinitesimal dose.

To combat this emergency, life-saving drugs like naloxone (Narcan) have been used, capable of temporarily reversing the effects of an overdose. But fentanyl's potency is such that often, multiple doses of naloxone are required to save a life.

Since this substance is often mixed with other drugs without the user's knowledge, reactive strips are also distributed in the U.S. to detect its presence.

This opioid is not just a threat: it's a ticking time bomb. Health authorities are trying to contain the wave, but the battle is far from over.

We will see what the future holds. For now, to continue our overview, it's necessary to take a step back in time.

CULTURAL REVOLUTION AND PSYCHEDELICS

The 1960s and 1970s were a period of profound transformation, especially in the West, where the economic boom and industrialization had led to greater availability of consumer goods. However, this prosperity came to a sudden halt with the 1973 oil crisis, marking the beginning of a period of stagflation and uncertainty.

As the economy slowed, society went into turmoil. Youth movements emerged everywhere, demanding civil rights and protesting the Vietnam War, in an atmosphere of rebellion and rejection of old norms.

The youth of that era were children of a generation marked by the Second World War, a collective trauma that didn't dissolve with the economic boom. The scars of war, often suppressed or ignored, clashed with material compensation that failed to meet the deeper needs for authenticity and meaning. For many, the consumerist model seemed empty—a conformist cage suffocating higher ideals like peace, love, and freedom.

This climate of dissatisfaction gave rise to the Counterculture, a movement that challenged traditional norms and sought radical alternatives in politics, art, and lifestyles. It was not just about rebellion, but a true cultural experiment aimed at rewriting the rules of society.

The use of psychoactive drugs, such as LSD, mescaline, and marijuana, became a symbol of this change. These substances were not just seen as an escape, but as tools for expanding consciousness, breaking conventions, and accessing a deeper reality.

Yet, the Counterculture was not just a journey through hallucinogens. It was a much broader phenomenon, intertwined with music, art, philosophy, and a worldview centered on personal freedom. It was an attempt to imagine a life less bound by imposed rules and more faithful to individual desires and aspirations.

While the dominant society sought to maintain a pre-established order—especially as another war, though "Cold," was underway—the new generations sought to build a world made of rock music, brightly painted canvases, and ideals of universal peace.

Despite its contradictions and limitations, the Counterculture of the 1960s and 1970s marked a unique moment of rupture and experimentation, leaving a legacy that still inspires movements and ideals today.

LSD: FROM MEDICINE TO TOOL OF REBELLION

In this climate of protest and the search for new values, LSD became a symbol of youth rebellion. Ironically, this substance, which promised to open the doors of perception, was discovered almost by accident, and its journey began with a bicycle ride that led to hallucinations. It was 1938, in the laboratory of Albert Hofmann, a Swiss

chemist with a passion for mushrooms… and, above all, for *Claviceps purpurea*, the famous ergot.
The scientist was trying to create drugs to improve circulation and respiration, but his LSD-25 didn't seem very useful, so it was put aside. Then, in 1943, Hofmann decided to give it a second chance. The result? A groundbreaking discovery: just a tiny amount was enough to send him on an unforgettable psychedelic trip, right as he was riding his bike home. The famous "Bicycle Day" is not just an anecdote, but the official birth of the substance that would color the years of the counterculture.
In the following years, LSD also made its way into the medical world. Psychiatrists used it to treat depression, anxiety, and trauma, especially in war veterans. It seemed promising, but there was a small problem: acid is not an easy substance to manage. If it works, it can open the doors to a universe of perceptions; if it goes wrong, it can open the doors to nightmares that feel all too real—the infamous "bad trips."
And what about addiction? LSD doesn't create physical dependency with withdrawal symptoms, but it's not entirely harmless. Tolerance builds up quickly: the more it's used, the less effective it becomes.
Fortunately, the body just needs a break from usage to recover, but the mind? If used to "escape" reality, it can become an obsession, even without the physical signs of addiction.
Yet, its dual nature continues to intrigue on one hand, therapeutic promise, on the other, a ticking time bomb. Acid doesn't just break conventions; it shatters them with kaleidoscopic visions and endless introspections. A gift for some, a danger for others.
Definitely a substance best not toyed with, because you never know what's waiting on the other side of the mirror.

PSYCHEDELIC COUNTERCULTURE'S INFLUENCE ON ART, MUSIC, AND LITERATURE

LSD didn't just unlock the doors of individual perception; it also flung open the doors to music, art, and culture. During the years of the Counterculture, the ability of this molecule to transform sounds, colors, and emotions into kaleidoscopic experiences made it an irresistible muse for artists of all kinds.

Music became fertile ground for expressing this new consciousness. The Beatles, undisputed icons of the era, drew inspiration from LSD to create the legendary *Sgt. Pepper's Lonely Hearts Club Band* in 1967. Not all of the tracks on that album were born under the influence of acid, of course, but songs like *Lucy in the Sky with Diamonds* and *A Day in Life* ooze surreal imagery and bold sonic experimentation. And they weren't alone: The Grateful Dead, Jefferson Airplane, and Pink Floyd turned their concerts into multi-sensory experiences, with light shows, hypnotic projections, and sounds that seemed to come straight from a cosmic trip.

Visual art was also deeply impacted by this revolution. Psychedelic posters, with vibrant colors and flowing lines, became the graphic symbol of an entire generation. Artists like Wes Wilson and Victor Moscoso captured in their works the hallucinogenic visions of an era, while cinema and literature weren't left behind. Films like *Easy Rider* (1969) embodied the rebellious spirit of American youth, and masterpieces like Stanley Kubrick's *2001: A Space Odyssey* brought the expansion of consciousness to the big screen, turning it into a visual odyssey. Ultimately, LSD was a lens through which the world seemed bigger, more colorful, and definitely stranger. And even though its legacy is controversial, its impact on art and culture is impossible to ignore.

Politics and Heroin: Quelling Cultural Unrest

LSD wasn't just a drug—it became a symbol of political rebellion. Seen as a tool to break free from the constraints of a conformist, authoritarian society, the psychedelic culture was all about transcending societal norms, opening doors to new forms of consciousness and spirituality. But the authorities didn't see it that way. They saw it as a threat.

By 1968, the United States had launched its full-scale "War on Drugs," and LSD was banned. European governments followed suit, with countries like the UK and Italy enforcing strict anti-drug measures.
Despite these restrictions, heroin began to devastate communities, particularly those on the margins of society.
Some theories suggest that, in the U.S., the heroin epidemic wasn't just a consequence of addiction—it was part of a deliberate strategy "from above" to stamp out the cultural unrest and youth rebellion movements of the 1960s and 1970s. While there's no solid proof of a government conspiracy to push heroin use as a means of silencing dissent, suspicious ties to the drug trade in the Golden Triangle and the CIA's covert activities during the Vietnam War raise serious questions about the role of the authorities in fueling the crisis.

Repression of Social Movements. Another theory claims that the spread of heroin among African American communities and politically active youth wasn't by chance. Activists like Huey P. Newton, co-founder of the Black Panther Party, believed the drug epidemic was deliberately targeted at Black communities to break up their social unity and dismantle the revolutionary potential of these movements.
But we'll delve deeper into this in the next chapter...

DECLINE OF THE COUNTERCULTURE

By the early 1970s, the Counterculture began to lose momentum. Government repression, the radicalization of some factions within the movement, and the commercialization of its ideas all contributed to its weakening.
However, the values it promoted continued to influence society, leaving an important legacy still visible today in struggles for the environment, social justice, and civil rights.

THE BIRTH OF THERAPEUTIC COMMUNITIES

Until the 1950s and 1960s, people suffering from pathological addictions, who became a problem for themselves or society, were often confined to prisons or asylums. These institutions represented the primary solutions for containing those suffering from this crisis. The methods used reflected an extremely limited understanding of addiction as a disease.

In the United States and Europe, drug addicts were placed in psychiatric hospitals, prisons, or correctional institutions. Addiction, particularly to opioids and alcohol, was considered a problem of moral deviance, often linked to criminality or character weakness. Consequently, addicted individuals were segregated from society, with no access to appropriate treatments.

For wealthier patients, there were private clinics and specialized healthcare institutions where they received treatments like detoxification, hypnotherapy, and psychiatric sessions. However, these treatments were often short-term, and there were no real rehabilitation or social reintegration programs.

In some countries, like the UK, doctors began experimenting with more specific treatments, such as the use of heroin substitutes, including morphine and later methadone. This approach, known as the "British System," involved the controlled administration of these substances under medical supervision. While helpful in managing addiction, this method did not represent a rehabilitative cure but a form of "harm reduction."

Let's not forget that morphine and methadone are also highly addictive substances.

An important innovation came from the 12-Step groups, with the Alcoholics Anonymous (AA) model, founded in the United States in the 1930s by Bill Wilson, Bob Smith, and their "brothers." This approach, based on mutual aid

and peer support, proved revolutionary. Although the initial focus was on alcoholism, the model later influenced the treatment of other addictions.
In the 1960s and 1970s, the approach to drug addiction changed significantly. With the crisis caused by the heroin epidemic, many nations sought alternatives to incarceration and psychiatric treatment. Therapeutic communities and outpatient treatment programs emerged, promoting a more humane and medical view of addiction. While these facilities represented a more compassionate alternative, they were not without their challenges.

THE FIRST EXPERIENCES

The first therapeutic communities for drug addicts, which emerged in the 1950s and 1960s, represent a pivotal moment in the history of addiction treatment. However, their approach was often rigid, punitive, and far from empathetic. Structures such as Synanon, Daytop Village, and Phoenix House were based on a philosophy that viewed addiction as a behavioral or moral failure, to be corrected through strict discipline and aggressive confrontations among patients.
Synanon, founded in California in 1958 by Charles Dederich, developed around communal living and intense group therapies, such as "game therapy." This technique involved group members verbally attacking each other to "break" their psychological defenses. The goal was not to explore personal traumas or promote empathy, but to confront issues head-on through public accusations and humiliations.
Although Synanon initially had success, over time it transformed into a cult, with increasing control over its members. It was eventually closed in the 1990s due to scandals involving violence and abuse of power.
Daytop Village, founded in 1963 in Staten Island, had a philosophy similar to Synanon's but was less extreme. Paticnts lived in residential communities, participating in

group work and collective therapy sessions, where confrontations were still harsh. However, Daytop sought to be more inclusive, involving families in the recovery process and trying to reintegrate patients into society through professional training.

Phoenix House, founded in 1967 in New York, adopted a similar approach. Patients lived in a highly regulated environment, with an emphasis on peer support and self-discipline. While offering professional training and social reintegration pathways, Phoenix House maintained a strict approach, leaving little room for understanding the emotional and psychological needs of the patients.

These therapeutic communities were primarily funded through government grants, both federal and state, especially as drug addiction among youth and Vietnam veterans increased. Public funds allowed structures like Daytop and Phoenix House to expand and offer free or low-cost treatment. Synanon, in addition to public funds, was self-financed through internal economic activities managed by its members.

The duration of treatment in these communities was often long, with programs that could last from one to two years. Synanon, in particular, allowed many members to stay indefinitely, contributing to the management of the community. In contrast, Daytop and Phoenix House often set limits to the length of treatment, emphasizing the importance of reintegration into society.

While these early therapeutic communities played a crucial role in offering some form of structured support for addicts, they were far from perfect.

Their strict, sometimes dehumanizing methods raised important questions about the ethical treatment of individuals struggling with addiction. Nevertheless, they laid the groundwork for the development of more humane and innovative treatment models in the decades that followed.

AFTER VIETNAM: THE BARRACKS-COMMUNITY MODEL

As we've seen, during World War II, soldiers from various countries were often given amphetamines to boost physical and mental performance, a common practice designed to improve their effectiveness rather than a form of intentional abuse.

The situation worsened during the Vietnam War, where heroin addiction among military personnel became a significant concern for U.S. authorities. Drug use was widespread among soldiers, partly due to the ease of obtaining these substances, given the proximity to the Golden Triangle, and also as a way to escape the harrowing realities of war.

It's estimated that around 15-20% of U.S. soldiers in Vietnam developed a heroin addiction, while 40% tried it at least once. With 2.7 million soldiers deployed to Vietnam, over 500,000 veterans returned home with addiction problems—an alarming number that underscored the scale of the crisis therapeutic communities were now tasked with addressing.

Along with addiction, many veterans also suffered from post-traumatic stress disorder (PTSD), further complicating their reintegration into civilian life.

To tackle the crisis, the U.S. government launched rehabilitation programs such as the 1971 Operation Golden Flow, which involved mandatory drug tests for soldiers returning from Vietnam. Those who tested positive were required to undergo detoxification before they could re-enter the U.S.

By the 1970s, therapeutic communities inspired by existing models for civilian addicts, like Phoenix House and Daytop Village, were created to help veterans.

Treatment often began with a harsh detox process, with no medication to ease withdrawal symptoms, which led to additional suffering.

The approach to emotional and psychological recovery was no less traumatic. These communities typically used a rigid, punitive model, often borrowing from military discipline—something the veterans were trying to escape.

"Confrontation therapy," a group therapy technique, was particularly aggressive. Participants were verbally attacked to break down their emotional defenses. Veterans who didn't adhere to the rules could be publicly criticized, accused of "weakness" or "irresponsibility," with the belief that such emotional reactions would lead to personal change. However, this approach often exacerbated their trauma rather than healing it. The rigid, militaristic structure of these therapeutic communities, designed to break down emotional defenses, was far from the empathy-based models that were beginning to emerge in civilian treatment centers.

Many veterans, already struggling with the aftereffects of war and addiction, found that the harsh confrontations and punitive methods led to a sense of powerlessness, rather than empowerment. The goal of reintegrating them into society often seemed secondary to the emphasis on "correcting" their behavior through emotional and psychological breakdowns.

As a result, these communities became places of intense conflict, not only between the patients and staff but also within the individuals themselves, as they struggled to reconcile the trauma of war with the demands of recovery. Although some veterans did find recovery within these systems, the long-term effectiveness of this approach was questionable, and many critics pointed out the lack of genuine therapeutic support.

In the years that followed, the approach to addiction treatment for veterans evolved, with more focus on understanding the root causes of addiction and trauma. The punitive models gave way to more compassionate, holistic methods that addressed both the physical and emotional aspects of addiction recovery.

IN EUROPE

Unfortunately, the methods used in the early therapeutic communities across the Atlantic, as well as those in veteran rehabilitation centers, were also adopted in Europe.

In fact, their use may still be present in certain environments today.
One of the first European experiments with therapeutic communities, although not exclusively for drug addicts, was the model proposed by British psychiatrist Maxwell Jones. In the 1950s, Jones developed the concept of a therapeutic community for the treatment of psychiatric patients in a collaborative environment. His approach actively involved patients in the management of the community, promoting a strong sense of individual and collective responsibility.
Although initially not aimed at drug addicts, Jones' idea deeply influenced the development of therapeutic communities in Europe, which would later become a key reference model for addiction recovery.
During the 1960s and 1970s, the first therapeutic communities for drug addicts began to emerge in Europe, inspired by American models. However, the early approaches did not fully recognize addiction as a complex condition that affects not only the body but also the mind, emotions, and social environment—let alone spiritual needs. It wasn't until later that a more integrated understanding developed, leading to the creation of facilities that offered psychological and social support alongside medical treatment.
One of the most influential communities in Europe was Daytop Lodge, founded in 1966 in the United Kingdom through the collaboration between the American organization Daytop Village and British authorities. Shortly after, in 1967, Phoenix House UK was established as part of a global network of therapeutic communities focused on residential treatment and individual responsibility.

THE 12-STEP-BASED TREATMENT CENTERS

The 12-Step method, which will be explored in more detail in the second part of this book, has over time influenced the creation of professional treatment centers for addiction. These therapeutic facilities adopt a hybrid approach, integrating the 12-Step Program with psychological and medical interventions, distinguishing them from traditional recovery communities.

The philosophy behind the 12 Steps, and the centers that follow this model, is based on the goal of providing patients with the tools necessary to live without the use of substances within society. Consequently, residential treatment periods are relatively short, while external support is permanent, thanks to the possibility of attending self-help groups for free.

12-Step-based treatment centers offer a safe and controlled environment where the principles of the 12 Steps are combined with psychological, medical, and pharmacological interventions. Although the 12 Steps are a cornerstone of the program, therapeutic pathways are personalized and may include cognitive-behavioral therapies, family therapy, and other psychological techniques.

The programs can vary in length, with short-term treatments ranging from 28 to 90 days, or longer periods, depending on the severity of the addiction and the specific needs of the patient. During treatment, patients participate in 12-Step-based groups within the center, while also receiving additional support to sustain their recovery process. One limitation of traditional recovery communities is maintaining "sobriety" in the outside world. Here, treatment centers offer more structured and lasting support.

The first treatment center inspired by the 12 Steps was established in the United States in the 1940s, shortly after the founding of Alcoholics Anonymous. The model spread particularly in the 1950s and 1960s, with the creation of formal structures that integrated the 12 Steps with medical and psychological assistance. One of the most well-known programs was the Minnesota Model. This model became a benchmark for many treatment centers in the United States and Europe. Over time, Bill's method and that of his fellows was extended to other addictions, such as drug and medication abuse.

FROM LABORATORIES TO NIGHTCLUBS THE DOUBLE FACE OF ECSTASY

Staying within the realm of psychedelics, it was in the 1970s that MDMA (3,4-methylenedioxymethamphetamine) began to spread. Commonly known as "Ecstasy" when sold in pill form, it is both a psychedelic and a stimulant substance that has attracted significant interest in both medical and cultural fields from the 1970s to the present day.

Originally synthesized in the early 20th century, MDMA went through several phases, evolving from an almost unknown compound to a recreational drug of mass use and, more recently, into a promising therapeutic tool.

It was first synthesized in 1912 by chemists at Merck, a German pharmaceutical company. The initial purpose was not to develop a psychedelic drug, but rather to create a compound useful for the pharmaceutical industry, likely as a precursor to other medications. Although patented in 1914, the substance did not undergo further study until the 1950s and 1960s, when it was rediscovered by some chemists and psychotherapists who saw its potential for psychological therapies.

PSYCHOTHERAPEUTIC USE IN THE 1970S AND 1980S

In the 1970s, MDMA was experimentally used by some psychotherapists in the United States as an adjunct in the treatment of various psychological conditions. In therapeutic settings, the drug helped break down emotional barriers, allowing patients to openly discuss trauma and improve interpersonal connections.

MDMA proved particularly effective in treating disorders such as post-traumatic stress disorder (PTSD) and depression, thanks to its ability to induce feelings of empathy and well-being.

One of the main advocates for the therapeutic use of MDMA was Dr. Alexander Shulgin, who extensively explored the potential of psychedelic substances. Shulgin, along with his colleague Ann Shulgin, experimented with MDMA in therapeutic settings, helping to spread its use among other therapists.

SOCIAL IMPACT AND CRIMINALIZATION

In the 1980s, MDMA began to spread as a recreational drug, particularly in party settings and nightclubs. The substance was valued for its ability to increase energy, empathy, and the sense of well-being, becoming popular in clubbing circles and the rave movement, which was strongly associated with electronic music.

The phenomenon helped define the identity of a generation of young people in the 1980s and 1990s, with collective partying experiences that strengthened a sense of community and belonging, but also of profound alienation.

The rise in recreational use inevitably attracted the attention of authorities. In 1985, MDMA was added to the list of controlled substances in the United States, and the same occurred in Italy in 1988, making its production, possession, and distribution illegal. Authorities justified this decision by citing the risks associated with recreational use of MDMA, especially when the substance was sold on the black market and cut with other drugs, which increased the likelihood of dangerous side effects such as hyperthermia, dehydration, and, in some cases, death.

REBIRTH AS A THERAPEUTIC TOOL

In the last twenty years, there has been a renewed scientific interest in MDMA as a potential therapeutic tool. Organizations such as MAPS (Multidisciplinary Association for Psychedelic Studies) have conducted and funded numerous clinical studies on the use of this substance in combination with psychotherapy.

The results have shown that MDMA can be particularly effective in the treatment of PTSD, a condition affecting millions of people worldwide. Administered in a controlled environment, the substance helps patients confront deep-rooted issues, reducing anxiety and fear associated with traumatic memories. These studies are so promising that MDMA is now in advanced clinical trials and could be approved in the U.S. as a legal treatment for PTSD in the coming years. However, the FDA recently rejected the final approval of the therapy.

This decision was made after an advisory committee of the U.S. Food and Drug Administration raised concerns about the validity of the clinical trial data and the safety of the treatment. In particular, concerns were expressed regarding the lack of sufficient evidence on long-term effectiveness and potential risks, such as cardiovascular issues and the possibility of abuse.

Despite this rejection, the FDA has requested an additional study phase, and Lykos Therapeutics, the sponsoring company, has stated that it hopes to resolve the raised concerns through further discussions with the agency. However, the realization of new studies will take several years.

In summary, despite its potential therapeutic benefits, MDMA is not without risks. Recreational use, especially without medical supervision, can cause serious side effects, including heart problems, neurotoxicity, and, in some cases, psychological dependence. Furthermore, the spread of adulterated MDMA, mixed with other substances, has increased these risks.

In addition to MDMA, other psychedelic substances are currently at the centre of scientific studies for their potential therapeutic benefits. Psilocybin, found in hallucinogenic mushrooms, has shown effectiveness in treating treatment-resistant depression and addictions.

COCAINE - IN THE TUNNEL **OF THE "WINNERS'" DRUG**

In the previous chapters, we traced the evolution of cocaine's spread up to the early 20th century. We left off with yet another discovery of the "pharmacological miracle" that had ensnared even Sigmund Freud. However, the father of psychoanalysis was soon forced to

rethink his enthusiasm for the "magical tonic" that promised to erase depression and fatigue, transforming humans into superheroes.
The severe dependence issues, along with the physical and mental damage caused by the drug, became apparent very quickly. The negative effects of cocaine have already been discussed, but it's worth reiterating them here. **Repetita Juvat!**

THE EFFECTS OF THE "GLAMOUR" DRUG

This work is dedicated not only to those who have experienced substance use firsthand but also to those who fight against the addiction of a loved one. To truly understand the problem, it is crucial to also describe the sensations perceived as "positive" by users, as they form the heart of cocaine's destructive trap.
The white powder is known for its rapid and powerful effect on the brain. At first, it triggers an intense euphoria, caused by the massive release of dopamine, the neurotransmitter associated with pleasure. This exhilaration brings an immediate sense of happiness, energy, and an amplified perception of one's abilities. It is no surprise that in competitive work environments or during social events, cocaine seems like a formidable ally. The "snow" can make users feel confident, talkative, and irresistible. Additionally, because it suppresses appetite, it has been exploited as a shortcut for weight loss, especially in the fashion world. However, these effects are short-lived and illusory. The toll on the body and

mind is devastating. Prolonged use has dramatic consequences, especially on the cardiovascular system: it causes extreme vasoconstriction, increasing the risk of heart attacks and strokes. Those who abuse it can develop hypertension, fatal arrhythmias, and heart failure.

Even visible physical damage is severe: prolonged inhalation destroys nasal tissues, causing ulcerations and perforations in the septum.

The impact on the brain is even more devastating. Cocaine blocks the reabsorption of dopamine, serotonin, and norepinephrine, leaving the user in a state of heightened euphoria followed by a profound emptiness. With continued use, the brain adapts by reducing sensitivity to these neurotransmitters, leading to tolerance: higher doses are needed to achieve the same pleasure. This cycle of addiction impairs memory, attention, and decision-making ability. The prefrontal cortex, responsible for impulse control, becomes damaged, leading to irrational choices and reckless behavior. The user's judgment becomes clouded, and their ability to assess risks is severely impaired. Over time, emotional and mental health deteriorate as the addiction takes hold. Anxiety, paranoia, and depression often replace the initial euphoria, leaving the individual trapped in a cycle of cravings and despair. The initial allure of increased energy, confidence, and pleasure gradually turns into an insatiable need for more, with increasingly severe

consequences for both physical and mental health.
Cocaine's destructive nature is not only evident in the lives of users but also in the broader social impact it has. What begins as a seemingly glamorous escape turns into a relentless pursuit of a high that can never be fully satisfied, leading to long-term damage that can last a lifetime.

CRIMINALIZATION AND BOOM – 1970S-1980S

Having explored the action and effects of cocaine on the human body, we can continue with our historical overview.
Starting with the Harrison Narcotics Tax Act of 1914, the United States began regulating and restricting the distribution of cocaine and other drugs, leading to its gradual criminalization. With the ban, production and sales shifted to the black market.
After a period of relative marginalization, in the 1970s, cocaine began to resurface widely as a recreational drug, particularly among urban elites in the United States and Europe. Known as "snow," it became synonymous with glamour, associated with wealth, success, and power. It was primarily used in social and artistic circles, promoted as a substance that enhanced concentration and creativity without the debilitating effects of alcohol or heroin. This "positive" perception undoubtedly fueled its spread.
As supply and demand are closely tied, the 1970s saw the rise of powerful drug cartels—criminal organizations that controlled and monopolized the production, distribution, and sale of illegal drugs. The most famous of these were the Medellín cartel, led by Pablo Escobar, and the Cali cartel, which became the primary suppliers of cocaine to North American and European markets.
Cocaine trafficking expanded rapidly due to the globalization of illicit trade and the complicity of criminal organizations, which took advantage of networks of political and

economic corruption to facilitate the international transport of drugs.

Interestingly, during these same years, while the harms of other substances, particularly opiates, were rightfully highlighted by the media, very little was said about cocaine. The white powder circulated almost like a ghost, present everywhere. The damage caused by it, however, remained largely under the radar.

THE CRACK EPIDEMIC: THE COCAINE OF THE POOR

In the 1980s, the drug market found a more affordable—and criminally democratic—way to make cocaine accessible to the lower social classes. Thus, crack was born: a solid, crystalline form of cocaine, with effects that were faster and more intense than regular powdered cocaine.

Crack is produced by mixing cocaine with sodium bicarbonate or ammonia, then heating it to form crystals that, when smoked, emit a characteristic crackling sound—hence the name.

The method of consumption, usually through inhalation, allows for rapid absorption through the lungs, resulting in an almost instantaneous effect.

Users experience an intense euphoria, but it lasts only 5-10 minutes. This cycle of brief exhilaration followed by a sudden crash drives users to continuously repeat the process, fueling a highly addictive dependency.

The spread of crack was driven by its low cost compared to powdered cocaine, which made it accessible to the poorer segments of the population, particularly in marginalized urban areas. In the United States, the crack epidemic hit African American and Latino communities hard, bringing devastating social and health consequences. Entire communities were torn apart by this addiction, which in many cases led to an escalation of crime and overcrowded prisons.

The physical effects of crack are like those of powdered cocaine, but they are more intense and short-lived. Psychologically, the impact is even more devastating: paranoia, hallucinations, and in severe cases, crack psychosis, a condition in which one's perception of reality is profoundly altered. Withdrawal symptoms include severe depression, anxiety, extreme fatigue, and a compulsive desire for the drug.

Critical note

The crack epidemic and the U.S. government's response raise questions about possible political motivations behind the handling of the crisis. The disproportionate sentencing for crack versus powdered cocaine, which was not justified by significant differences in the danger posed by the two forms, disproportionately affected African American and Latino communities. These fuelled theories suggesting that the spread of crack may have been exploited to decimate certain already marginalized segments of the population, thereby consolidating a structure of social and racial inequality.

While direct evidence remains a topic of debate, it is undeniable that the "war on drugs" exacerbated the crisis rather than resolving it, contributing to the destruction of entire communities and perpetuating cycles of poverty and crime.

THE PLAGUE OF BASUCO IN PRODUCING COUNTRIES

As if things couldn’t get any worse, the 1990s saw two major developments in relation to coca plant-related substances.

Suddenly, the gravity of the drug trade became undeniable, and the United States decided to take action directly in the countries of Latin America where the substance was being produced. Colombia, the leading producer of cocaine, was militarized in an operation we'll discuss further in the "thinking badly" chapter.

At the same time, a new epidemic broke out in South America, tied to the consumption of basuco, a derivative of cocaine that is even more harmful than crack.

Basuco is an impure and toxic substance, a byproduct of the cocaine refining process, containing highly dangerous chemical residues such as industrial solvents and kerosene. It is smoked, and its effects are similar to crack, but even more devastating for both body and mind.

Unlike powdered cocaine, basuco is incredibly cheap and quickly spread among the most marginalized groups, worsening the social crisis in Latin America.

Let's briefly consider its effects. Those who use it quickly develop an addiction, accompanied by severe health issues, including malnutrition, lung damage, and mental deterioration, with episodes of paranoia and hallucinations.

The war on coca wasn't very successful, despite the involvement of the world's greatest military power at the time.

As the basuco crisis grew in Latin America, North America and Europe became increasingly profitable markets for drug traffickers, with cities like London, Madrid, and Amsterdam becoming key destinations for the influx of cocaine products. This expansion exacerbated the global problem, transforming the drug trade into a sprawling, multinational crisis.

Basuco's devastating impact on public health and social stability in Latin America serves as a grim reminder that the fight against drugs is a complex and ongoing struggle, with no simple solutions in sight.

THE RISE OF COCAINE TRAFFICKING IN THE 21ST CENTURY

Since the dawn of the new millennium, cocaine trafficking has skyrocketed, with a significant impact on emerging economies like Brazil and Mexico.

Brazil, with its borders shared by coca-producing countries such as Colombia, Peru, and Bolivia, has become a key strategic point for transatlantic trafficking to Europe and Africa, leveraging ports like Santos.

In Mexico, the cartels, particularly the Sinaloa cartel, have strengthened direct ties with Andean producers, positioning themselves as key players in the global drug trade.

In West Africa, countries like Guinea-Bissau have become crucial hubs for the smuggling of the white powder. Political instability and weak institutional structures in the region have made it easier for drug merchants to operate freely. However, local consumption remains low, with the continent primarily serving as a transit point to Europe.
As for Europe, Italy has unfortunately established itself as a critical node, both for trafficking routes originating from the Americas and for imports coming from the East.
But the new routes and shifting power dynamics in the drug trade will be explored in the next chapter, which aims to analyze the changes in narcotrafficking in relation to the geopolitical shifts that have occurred since the end of World War II.

SPEEDBALLING: THE COMBINATION OF COCAINE AND OPIOIDS

When it comes to the focus of this chapter, dedicated to the evolution of drug use in the contemporary age, a section must certainly be devoted to the rise of speedballing. This term refers to the combined use of cocaine and opioids.
It is an extremely dangerous practice, as it mixes two drugs with opposite physiological mechanisms. Cocaine, as we've seen, is a powerful stimulant that increases heart rate, blood pressure, and energy, while opioids, such as heroin or fentanyl, are central nervous system depressants; they slow down respiration and induce a sense of relaxation and euphoria.
The simultaneous use of both substances creates a conflict within the body: cocaine speeds up vital functions, while opioids slow them down. This contrast can lead to serious physical problems, with a high risk of respiratory failure.
One of the most dangerous aspects of this combination is that the stimulating effect of cocaine can temporarily mask the sedative effects of opioids, making the user feel less "intoxicated" than they actually are. This can lead to opioid overdose, with potentially fatal consequences.
When the effects of cocaine wear off, the remaining opioids in the body could cause severe respiratory depression, especially if the opioid used is fentanyl, which, as we know, is a

synthetic substance up to 100 times more potent than morphine.

In the United States, the increase in fatal overdoses from cocaine is closely linked to the growing prevalence of speedballing. The combination of cocaine and opioids, particularly fentanyl, has significantly contributed to the sharp rise in overdose deaths. Fentanyl, a synthetic opioid much stronger than heroin, is often mixed with cocaine to enhance the effects, but this also amplifies the risks of overdose. The stimulant effect of cocaine can hide the sedative effects of fentanyl, causing users to unknowingly consume a lethal dose of the opioid.

This deadly combination has become a major public health issue, with emergency responders and healthcare providers facing an unprecedented number of overdose cases. The challenge lies in the fact that the use of speedballs often leads to delayed recognition of overdose symptoms. While the user may feel the initial stimulant rush from the cocaine, the depressant effect of the opioid only becomes apparent after the cocaine wears off, leaving little time to react before respiratory failure occurs.

The widespread availability of fentanyl has made speedballing more accessible and more dangerous, as it is often mixed into illicit cocaine without the user's knowledge. This has made the opioid crisis even more complex, as people who typically use cocaine are now at an increased risk of fatal overdose, something that was less common before the rise of fentanyl.

This phenomenon highlights the increasingly dangerous nature of contemporary drug use, where the lines between different types of substances have blurred, creating new, unpredictable risks. The growing prevalence of speedballing is a stark reminder of the need for effective harm reduction strategies, education, and better public health responses to address the changing dynamics of the global drug trade.

WHEN "SNOW" ALSO DIRTIES THE STARS

Many famous figures have admitted to being overwhelmed by cocaine use, sharing the devastating consequences this drug had on their lives.

Among them, Elton John confessed to being a slave to cocaine for years. He openly discussed how this addiction negatively affected many aspects of his personal and professional life. Only through the 12-step program, used by Alcoholics Anonymous and Narcotics Anonymous, was he able to break the cycle of self-destruction.

The British pop legend has repeatedly emphasized how crucial this recovery program was for his rebirth, allowing him to dedicate himself to philanthropic projects like the Elton John AIDS Foundation and rediscover balance in all areas of his life.

The "master of horror," Stephen King, has also never hidden his battle with cocaine in the 1980s, a period in which he wrote many of his most iconic works. Although he initially used the drug to maintain a high work pace, King has shared how the white powder contributed to his descent into a dark spiral of addiction and personal crisis. In his writings, such as *On Writing*, the author describes his recovery journey and how the drug nearly jeopardized both his career and his life.

Robin Williams, on the other hand, faced alcohol and cocaine head-on in the 1970s and 1980s. The celebrated protagonist of *Dead Poets Society* often spoke candidly about his addiction, even using his characteristic humour to reduce the stigma surrounding sensitive topics like mental health. Williams openly acknowledged how the pressures of fame and the constant need to perform had fuelled his struggles with substance abuse, yet he also emphasized how his recovery, which included rehabilitation and therapy, allowed him to regain control of his life and career.

These stories of addiction among high-profile figures shed light on the darker side of fame, where the pressures of success can lead to devastating consequences. They also highlight the importance of recovery programs and personal strength in overcoming addiction. For many of these celebrities, the path to recovery was long and difficult, but it ultimately allowed them to rebuild their lives, regain their health, and continue to inspire others in new ways.

NPS, GHOST DRUGS AND THE DARK WEB

New Psychoactive Substances (NPS) are an emerging phenomenon in the world of drugs, attracting the attention of authorities and public health experts due to the speed at which these substances spread and the risks they pose to health.

Also known as designer drugs, NPS are synthetic chemicals created to mimic the effects of illegal drugs such as cannabis, cocaine, ecstasy, and LSD. They are called "designer" because their molecules are intentionally modified to bypass laws regulating narcotics.

These chemical alterations allow them to sidestep the legal classification of banned substances, creating a "new" version of the drug that is not immediately recognized as illegal under current regulations.

NPS were developed with the goal of staying "one step ahead" of legislation. Since most drugs are banned through specific lists of substances, NPS producers slightly alter the chemical structure of an illegal substance to create a new molecule that has not yet been outlawed. This makes NPS not only difficult to detect and monitor, but also particularly dangerous, as the chemical modifications can amplify negative effects or introduce unforeseen risks.

One of the most concerning aspects is their unpredictability. Unlike traditional drugs, which have been studied for decades, NPS have never undergone clinical testing. Often, the long-term effects of these substances are unknown, and consumers expose themselves to serious risks, including psychosis, permanent brain damage, and even death.

The spread of NPS has been further fueled by the rise of the dark web, an online marketplace where users can purchase illegal substances anonymously. The dark web has provided a new and largely unregulated platform for the distribution of NPS, making it easier for users to access these dangerous drugs. Since the chemical composition of NPS can be altered quickly and easily, dealers can often

offer a wide range of substances that are difficult for authorities to track.
The availability of NPS on the dark web has also led to concerns about the lack of quality control. Unlike traditional drugs, which often come from established networks with some degree of quality assurance, NPS are often produced in unregulated environments, making it difficult to know what is being consumed. This increases the likelihood of contamination and accidental overdoses.
As the number of NPS continues to grow, so does the challenge for law enforcement and public health authorities. Monitoring and controlling these substances have become a complex task, with new variants appearing faster than regulations can be updated. In the face of this rapidly evolving threat, prevention efforts, public awareness campaigns, and international cooperation will be crucial in addressing the dangers posed by these so-called "ghost drugs."

IN SUMMARY

We have reached the end of our historical journey. We have traveled through space and time, following humanity's relationship with substances capable of altering mood and mind since the dawn of history. We have seen psychotropic plants and the nectar of the gods as allies in humanity's quest for contact with what lies beyond the visible and the material. We have observed ancient societies and their respective religions acting as guardians and protective umbrellas against the risks inherent in these practices. At a certain point, we could not help but notice how the "demon" had slipped out of control.
From that moment on, drug use spiralled out of control, and every attempt by humankind to remedy the damage proved more harmful than the problem it sought to solve.
From the 1990s to the present day, pathological addictions have become a global emergency, extending not only to

the abuse of traditional psychoactive substances like alcohol, heroin, and cocaine, but also to new forms of addiction linked to emerging behaviors and technologies.
The phenomenon is complex and multifaceted, as always intertwined with the profound social, economic, and cultural changes in the societies involved.
The last decade of the 20th century represented a transitional phase in the landscape of addiction. While traditional drugs such as heroin and cocaine continued to present significant problems, there was also an increase in the use of synthetic drugs. This led to changes in the geography of consumption.
In these years, drug trafficking and production became a global phenomenon, facilitated by new technologies, the expansion of the internet and the growth of online markets. The rise of these digital spaces made it easier for users to access illegal substances from virtually anywhere, complicating efforts to combat drug abuse.
Synthetic drugs, in particular, have posed new challenges. These substances are often more potent and harder to monitor than traditional narcotics. The creation of new psychoactive substances (NPS) in labs has allowed producers to evade existing drug laws, adding layers of complexity to the problem.
Along with the spread of these substances, there has been a significant rise in prescription opioid abuse. Drugs like OxyContin and Fentanyl have led to an alarming increase in fatal overdoses. This opioid epidemic has affected people from all walks of life, but particularly young people and vulnerable populations.
The opioid crisis has shown us that pathological addiction is not confined to illegal substances; it can be aggravated by improper medical practices, aggressive pharmaceutical marketing, and failures within the systems and organizations that are supposed to protect the public.
The opioid crisis has shown that pathological addiction is not just about illegal drugs, but can also be aggravated by improper medical practices, aggressive pharmaceutical

marketing, and failures within the systems and organizations that should protect the public.

At the same time, in recent years, behavioral addictions have emerged with increasing intensity. Pathological gambling has become one of the most widespread forms of non-substance-related addiction, especially with the liberalization of online gambling and the indiscriminate opening of casinos everywhere. Despite not involving substance use, gambling addiction has devastating psychological, economic, and social consequences, particularly affecting young people and vulnerable individuals.

Another phenomenon linked to behavioral addictions is the addiction to the internet and digital technologies. The compulsive use of social media, video games, and online platforms has led to complex psychological problems such as social isolation and depression, often associated with other forms of addiction.

Meanwhile, technological addiction has continued to grow with the advent of smartphones, streaming platforms, and social media. Issues like nomophobia (the fear of being without your phone) and doomscrolling (the compulsive scrolling through negative news) have become central problems for mental health, especially among young people.

The COVID-19 pandemic has further exacerbated these addictions, due to the social isolation it caused.

Responses to pathological addictions have evolved over the years.

In the past, most treatment options focused on abstinence and punishment, but today there is a more nuanced understanding of addiction as a chronic condition that requires comprehensive treatment. Modern approaches emphasize harm reduction, therapy, and social reintegration, along with prevention strategies aimed at addressing the root causes of addiction.

As we continue to face the global challenges posed by addiction, it is clear that the problem is no longer just about individual behavior, but also about the broader social, economic, and cultural factors that fuel it. In this context, understanding addiction as a multi-dimensional issue is key to finding effective solutions.

Programs such as needle exchange, the controlled distribution of methadone, and the establishment of safe consumption spaces for drug users have proven insufficient. This does not mean that nothing is being done. Behavioral addictions have seen the development of prevention and treatment initiatives, with the adoption of psychological support programs, self-help groups, and targeted therapeutic interventions (such as cognitive-behavioral therapy) to address gambling, technology addiction, and other compulsive behaviours.

The use of medication-assisted therapy to combat opioid abuse and the improvement of access to care are important steps to tackle the crisis. However, they are clearly not enough.

In a world where news, thanks to the internet and social media, travels faster than light, information is scarce and incomplete. Indeed, in the first quarter of the 21st century, it is still necessary to write an essay to settle a question that should be self-evident and obvious: is pathological addiction a vice or a disease?

In the last chapter of this first part of the book, we will explore what science really thinks.

Before moving on, however, I would like to involve readers in a small mental exercise. As we have seen, training the mind never hurts. So, let's try to soar a little higher and look at the drug phenomenon from a different perspective.

CHAPTER 4

THINKING BADLY IS A SIN...

In writing this essay, I started with one certainty. Actually, two.
First certainty: pathological addictions are diseases, and as such, they must be treated.
Second: there is still a lot of ignorance on this topic (in the positive sense of the word, meaning "lack of knowledge"). Prejudices, in fact, are hard to die, and the information we receive from those who should be tackling the issue is scarce or inadequate.
Two certainties that, by the end of writing this essay, remained intact.
In the meantime, however, the research conducted for this work has raised quite a few questions.
Here are some: Is it really possible that so little can be done about drugs? Is it possible that, in a hyper-controlled world, the death dealers manage to move around the planet with their loads of poison, undisturbed? Is it plausible that there are vast plantations of psychotropic plants that no one notices? Is it possible that the astronomical sums of money generated by these traffics just disappear into thin air? Is it possible that the information system fails to provide clear and accurate data?
As the old Italian statesman Giulio Andreotti used to say, “thinking badly is a sin...”
But sometimes, the temptation is strong.
So, perhaps, we can sidestep the issue, avoiding the inevitable sentence of eternal damnation... for those who think badly!
And, since we live in a part of the world where freedom of thought is guaranteed, let’s take advantage of it and let our

minds wander, exploring the questions that remain unanswered. After all, as Andreotti said, thinking badly may be a sin—but it's often the only way to get closer to the truth.

FROM DUST TO GOLD AND LEAD

The many films about mafias and drug trafficking have taught us one fundamental lesson: to find the culprits, just follow the money. For ordinary citizens like us, actually tracing its path is impossible, but we can at least imagine the sums at stake.

The global drug market is estimated to be between 400 and 600 billion dollars annually, including cocaine, heroin, methamphetamines, cannabis, and new psychoactive substances (NPS), figures that rival national budgets. Cocaine and methamphetamines dominate the market, each generating over 100 billion dollars, followed by heroin and cannabis. However, these figures provided by organizations such as the UNODC and Europol are just estimates; the real market is much more complex and ever-changing, influenced by trafficking routes, cartels, and the increasing involvement of criminal groups operating from South America to Asia, passing through Africa, and flooding the rest of the world.

From the Golden Crescent to the Balkans

In the context of the Middle East, it is impossible not to mention Afghanistan, which produces about 90% of the world's heroin, with an estimated value between 40 and 50 billion dollars annually. The profits generated in the Golden Crescent (Afghanistan, Pakistan, and Iran) fuel the entire global heroin trade. And how does this "merchandise" reach Europe? Through the Balkan Route, a corridor that passes through Kosovo, Albania, and Serbia, involving both local and international criminal networks. This route generates between 15 and 20 billion dollars annually, making the Balkans a key transit point for heroin destined for Western Europe.

Asia and the Golden Triangle: Empires of Methamphetamine and Heroin. In Asia, the trade in methamphetamines and heroin generates an estimated turnover between 125 and 150 billion dollars. The Golden Triangle (Myanmar, Laos, and Thailand) is a historic production hub that meets the demand in China, Japan, and the Philippines, making the synthetic drug trade in Asia one of the most profitable in the world. In fact, the "powder" produced in the Golden Triangle could financially support millions of Italian retirees, at least from an economic perspective.

South America and the Kingdom of Cocaine. From South America comes another 80-120 billion dollars annually, thanks to cocaine produced in Colombia, Peru, and Bolivia. South American cartels collaborate with Mexican cartels to manage the traffic to the United States and Europe, keeping cocaine at the center of an ever-expanding empire. To put it into perspective: if the annual budget of Colombian cocaine were allocated to education and research, it would cover the entire needs of Italy's educational and scientific systems.

Middle East: Captagon and War Funding. In the Middle East, especially in Syria, Captagon has become the cornerstone of a thriving trade, generating around 5-6 billion dollars annually. It is a powerful amphetamine, often enriched with other stimulants, known for increasing physical endurance and reducing fatigue and hunger, which is why it is particularly popular in conflict zones. The profits from Captagon finance wars and armed groups in the region and provide a livelihood for many local groups, especially in the Gulf countries, where demand is growing. In practice, Captagon not only enriches traffickers but also fuels conflicts and finances armed groups.

USA and Europe: Fentanyl and Methamphetamine DIY Laboratories. In the United States and Europe, clandestine laboratories specializing in methamphetamines and fentanyl generate between 50 and 100 billion dollars annually, an amount rivaling Italy's budget for infrastructure and transportation. Imagine what could be achieved by investing these funds in highways and railways, instead of in a business that sows death.

THE DARK SIDE OF THE GLOBAL ECONOMY

Beyond the economic impact, the drug market fuels crime, corruption, and political instability. Many experts believe that the estimates of 400-600 billion dollars are still conservative, and that the true volume of business exceeds 1,000 billion dollars, a figure that also includes money laundering through cryptocurrencies and transactions on the dark web. It is important to remember that no one has central control over cryptocurrencies because they are decentralized. There are no banks, governments, or companies managing the system.

In addition to illicit profits, there are also the costs of the corruption necessary to keep this trade active. In short, the global drug market is a colossal entity that flows powerfully and silently, influencing aspects of our society that we often ignore.

HOW DIRTY MONEY ENTERS THE SYSTEM

We cannot ignore the role of money laundering, which allows drug traffickers to reintegrate their profits into the legitimate financial system. Regulations in Europe and the United States heavily restrict the use of cash to prevent untraceable transactions. For example, many EU countries set a ceiling of between 1,000 and 3,000 euros per individual cash transaction, while in the United States, transactions over 10,000 dollars must be reported. Yet, those involved in money laundering manage to circumvent these controls by breaking up deposits, multiplying bank accounts, or investing in businesses with high cash flow such as bars, restaurants, and casinos.

The "Stratification" and Integration of Proceeds. Money laundering operates through what is known as "stratification": the money travels around the world, moving from account to account, between offshore companies and tax havens, often via investment funds that complicate traceability. In countries like the United States and the United Kingdom, anti-money laundering regulations are strict, but in tax havens—such as the Cayman Islands, Switzerland, Luxembourg, the Vatican, and others—controls are more lenient, making it easier to hide the origin of funds.

The Role of Cryptocurrencies and the Dark Web. Cryptocurrencies, stocks, and bonds are also used to conceal illicit proceeds. Each transaction is a "cleaning" step that makes the money appear more legitimate. The process culminates in the "integration" phase, where the money enters the legitimate economy as legitimate income. The drug trafficker can then appear as a real estate entrepreneur, ready to invest in villas and restaurants with capital that is now "clean."

The Elegance of Dirty Money. Tax havens and complacent banks are central to this system, with offshore accounts and laws that guarantee anonymity. Cryptocurrencies and the dark web add another layer of security, allowing illicit funds to blend seamlessly with legitimate capital. Every year, billions of dollars from drug trafficking, corruption, and other shady dealings infiltrate the global economy, bypassing anti-money laundering controls. It's hard to believe that banks and governments are completely unaware of this: political power over banks does exist, though not absolutely. Banks, operating across multiple countries, often manage to sidestep the strictest regulations.

Thus, drug money, with a silent elegance, continues to flow undisturbed.

CUI PRODEST? WHO BENEFITS?

The teachers of our childhood, who entered our homes

every evening through the television, taught us a fundamental lesson. With different methods, uniforms, and hairdos, all of them—from Sherlock Holmes to Lieutenant Columbo, and even Jessica Fletcher—showed us that to solve a case, one must always start with a question: *Cui prodest?* — Who benefits?

Our question now is: who benefits from the drug trade?

Let's try to answer, starting with the facts.

Even those who tend to think well would have a hard time arguing that logistics and economic giants, such as the holdings behind deadly drugs, have operated almost undisturbed and resisted the various "wars on drugs" from the 1960s to today as parallel and autonomous entities. The cynics suggest that the drug world is something more than just a criminal issue; it's a phenomenon intertwined with the dynamics of international politics and the underground economies.

If we accept this hypothesis, a question naturally arises: why would democratic, just, and transparent governments play along? What do they gain from it?

To try to answer, even as a mental exercise, it might be useful to reopen history books, especially those recent chapters that are quickly glossed over in school, near the end of the year.

An observation immediately catches the eye: the territories and main routes of the drug trade have often been the scene of bloody conflicts.

Let's broaden our perspective to understand how geopolitical alignments have evolved from the 1960s to the present day.

During those years, marked by the global spread of the scourge of drug addiction, the planet was divided into three main areas: two in open antagonism with each other, and a third, unofficially unaligned, but fluctuating between the two blocks.

The great powers—the Atlantic Alliance, led by the United States, and the Soviet bloc, dominated by Moscow—competed to maintain their power while avoiding the outbreak of a third world war.

It was the era of the Cold War, the time of 007 agents with licenses to kill, if you will.
The world was divided by an invisible but palpable boundary: the line between the communist bloc and NATO countries.
In Europe, the Berlin Wall split Germany in two, separating East Berlin from West Berlin like a scalpel cutting through raw flesh. In the heart of the continent, Italy, an integral part of NATO, bordered socialist Yugoslavia and ultra-communist Albania, two countries formally neutral but close to the Soviet bloc. To the north, the border between Norway and the USSR represented a strategic key: here, the two blocs spied on each other relentlessly, while nuclear submarines silently crossed the icy waters like shadows.
Moving further south, Turkey kept watch over its border with the USSR and controlled the Bosporus Strait, crucial for maritime routes between the Black Sea and the Mediterranean. In the Middle East, Iran shifted from being a Western ally to an Islamic revolutionary state, further inflaming the region with ideological and tactical tensions. In Asia, North and South Korea faced off, divided by a precarious armistice, while Vietnam became a symbolic theatre of the Cold War, turning a local conflict into a global struggle where powers poured in weapons, soldiers, and ideologies.
Across the Atlantic, in Latin America, Cuba, aligned with Moscow, represented a thorn in the side for the United States, while Africa became the battleground for civil wars sponsored by the superpowers.
At this point, you might ask, "Interesting reconstruction, but what does all this have to do with drugs?"
It has everything to do with it.
War requires money, and drug trafficking has always been an effective method for generating cash reserves that no democratic state would officially allocate. How could a parliament pass a vote to provide weapons and hard cash to groups that embody everything except the ideals of democracy?

Beyond thinking well or thinking badly, it is a fact that wars are fought on multiple levels. The troops in the field are only the tip of the iceberg; the success of open conflicts is also determined in the underbrush of intelligence operations, where rules are bent or broken in the name of the ultimate goal.
The former are funded by official budgets, while the latter—well, it's unclear.
To try to answer the initial question, "Why are drug trafficking operations so difficult to eradicate?" we will examine three emblematic situations: Latin America, the homeland of cocaine; Afghanistan and the Balkan Route, the realm of heroin; and Italy, the land of the author, but also the heart of the Old Continent.

LATIN AMERICA, KINGDOM OF COCA

In the 1970s, South America began to emerge as the global center of cocaine production. Colombia, Peru, and Bolivia quickly became the capitals of the cultivation of the miraculous plant that, transformed into white powder, would be exported everywhere.
The main markets? Europe and the United States, where demand skyrocketed, along with profits.
It's important to remember the world division at that time: NATO, led by the United States on one side, and the USSR and the communist bloc on the other, with neutral countries in between.
For the United States, the red line was right on their doorstep. Cuba, just a few miles away, and Latin America were highly unstable regions, marked by political turbulence that seemed ready to overturn any equilibrium. In addition to Che's and Fidel's island, Nicaragua was the only country with a left-wing government; in the rest of the region, however, right-wing regimes dominated, often authoritarian, but strategically supported by the United States under the well-known principle of "the enemy of my enemy is my friend."

One of the most well-known cases was Chile: Salvador Allende, elected democratically, was overthrown in the 1973 coup that brought Augusto Pinochet to power. Argentina followed shortly after, falling under a military dictatorship from 1976 to 1983, while Brazil was under a military junta from 1964 to 1985. In Paraguay, Alfredo Stroessner, a right-wing dictator and loyal ally of the United States, ruled unchallenged from 1954 to 1989. Uruguay, also under a dictatorship, received American support, while in Guatemala and El Salvador, the United States actively fueled the fight against Marxist factions. Keeping all these regimes in check required aid and concessions. During the Salvadoran civil war of the 1980s, for instance, the right-wing government received funding and training to counter the Farabundo Martí National Liberation Front (FMLN), a Marxist guerrilla movement. Moreover, Honduras became a key pawn, hosting American bases and supporting the Nicaraguan Contras against the Sandinista government.
If the Soviet Union had succeeded in establishing strong alliances or, even worse, direct control over these countries, it would have opened up a threatening scenario for Uncle Sam: Soviet missiles could have hit them directly from the American continent itself.

In simple terms, South America was a mosaic of unstable areas, where the stakes were as simple as they were dramatic: control or defeat.
It is in this context that the alleged “tolerance” policies adopted by the CIA to maintain control over Latin America come into play.
There are many theories, few confirmations – but after all, the CIA, the United States' foreign intelligence agency, isn't called "secret service" by accident.

OPERATION CONDOR

Operation Condor was the dark side of the Cold War in South America, a political repression laboratory disguised as a fight against communism. Coordinated between the dictatorships of Argentina, Chile, Brazil, Uruguay, Paraguay, and occasionally Bolivia, this network of terror had a clear objective: to eliminate political dissidents who dared to challenge the authoritarian regimes. But behind the scenes, the real puppeteer was often another: the United States.

With the CIA as the unofficial director, Washington provided tacit approval, logistical and technical support, and even the shadow of its know-how for methods of torture and assassination, all in the name of fighting the "Red Menace."

One of the darkest chapters in this story is the so-called "Cocaine Coup" in Bolivia in 1980. It wasn't just a coup: it was a business. Led by General Luis García Meza and Colonel Luis Arce Gómez, the coup had close ties to the cartel of Roberto Suárez Gómez, one of the most powerful drug traffickers of the time.

In a grim symbiosis, the profits from the drug trade were used to fund political repression, creating a vicious circle of drugs, blood, and power. Arce Gómez, in particular, transformed Bolivia into a cocaine crossroads while eliminating anyone who represented a threat to the regime.

The consequences of this toxic connection between dictatorships and the drug trade didn't take long to surface.

García Meza and Arce Gómez were prosecuted for crimes against humanity and drug trafficking. Colonel Arce Gómez was even extradited to the United States, where he served a lengthy sentence for his role in the cocaine trade.

Though less known than the rest of Operation Condor, these events reveal an even more disturbing reality: some dictatorships not only trampled on human rights but did so by exploiting drug trafficking as a tool of repression and power. All of this, of course, with the blessing of a powerful and interested partner: the United States, committed to using the continent as a geopolitical shield against communist expansion. History judges, but as always, it was the people who paid the price.

The United States played a significant, though complex and controversial, role in the events surrounding Operation Condor and the South American dictatorships of the 1970s and 1980s. Declassified documents from the National Security Archive reveal that the CIA and the State Department were fully aware of the coordinated activities between the authoritarian regimes aimed at eliminating political dissidents. While there is no evidence that the United States directly orchestrated Operation Condor, there was clear indirect support: they provided intelligence, technical assistance, and, in many cases, tacit approval of human rights violations.

An emblematic example is the so-called "Operation Condor Cable" from 1976, a diplomatic cable that shows how the United States was aware of the repressive plans of the South American dictatorships. In addition, documents related to CIA manuals reveal that military personnel from the region were trained in interrogation techniques and counterrevolutionary tactics, some of which included practices akin to torture.

In the case of the 1980 coup in Bolivia, and the already mentioned "cocaine coup," the direct involvement of the United States is not proven. However, during the Cold War, U.S. support for authoritarian regimes claiming to be engaged in the fight against communism was a well-established practice. This approach often involved turning a blind eye to these governments' ties to criminal activities, such as drug trafficking.

While the documentation is not always explicit, there is little doubt that the United States supported, directly or indirectly, authoritarian regimes in Latin America. Their goal was clear: to block the communist advance in the region, even at the cost of sacrificing human rights and democracy.

THE IRAN-CONTRA SCANDAL

Among the numerous secrets that emerged from the fog of the Cold War, the Iran-Contra scandal represents one of the murkiest chapters, an explosive cocktail of arms trafficking, ideology, and state interests.

The United States, champions of the fight against communism, found themselves at the center of a scandal that seemed straight out of a spy novel. The plot? Arms were sold to Iran—not the Iran of today, dominated by the ayatollahs, but an Iran led by a Shah who embodied the decadent allure of the East. The proceeds from these sales, rather than ending up in American coffers, were used to finance the Contras, Nicaraguan rebels trying to overthrow the Marxist Sandinista government. A geopolitical chess game, played at the expense of civilians.

But this is only the tip of the iceberg. Some researchers argue that the Contras were supported not only by the proceeds from arms sales but also by the profits from cocaine trafficking.

The suspicion? The CIA may have turned a blind eye—if not both eyes—toward the flow of drugs from Central America fueling the U.S. market. In this tangled mess, the Medellín cartel stands out as a presumed ally in the distribution of the white powder—a "necessary compromise" to finance the war against communism.

The journalist Gary Webb stoked the flames in 1996 when he published a series of articles titled *Dark Alliance* in the *San Jose Mercury News*. Webb exposed that the CIA was not only aware of the cocaine trafficking orchestrated by the Contras but that these rebels had used the profits to fund their activities, indirectly contributing to the crack epidemic that devastated African American communities in the 1980s, particularly in Los Angeles.

The reaction? A media and political uproar, with the CIA vigorously denying any responsibility. However, an internal investigation by the Office of the Inspector General confirmed that the Agency was aware of the links between the Contras and drug trafficking, though it claimed not to have been actively involved.

Behind all of this, geopolitical power plays were at work. Nicaragua, after overthrowing the dictatorship of Anastasio Somoza in 1979, had come under the control of the

Sandinista National Liberation Front, a Marxist-Leninist government supported by the Soviet Union and Cuba. For Washington, the Sandinistas represented an intolerable threat—a pro-Soviet stronghold in America's "backyard." Support for the Contras, however morally questionable, was seen as a strategic necessity to contain the spread of communism in Central America.

Journalists such as Alexander Cockburn and Jeffrey St. Clair, in their book *Whiteout: The CIA, Drugs, and the Press*, and scholars like Peter Dale Scott, author of *Cocaine Politics*, further explored the links between American intelligence and drug trafficking. Their research suggested that drug trafficking was not only tolerated but sometimes even encouraged as a "lesser evil" to counter the communist threat.

Although the theories remain controversial, the investigations by Webb and others have lifted the veil on a dark chapter of American foreign policy. In the name of fighting communism, alliances with drug traffickers and actions that left deep scars were justified, not only in Central America but also within the United States itself. Ideology, in this case, seems to have been used as a pretext to legitimize unacceptable compromises.

History offers few certainties but one bitter lesson: when empires are built, the costs—evidently—are always paid by the weakest.

THEN THE WALL FELL AND THE AIR CHANGED

1985 is a crucial year for understanding recent history. In that year, Mikhail Gorbachev, the last president of the Soviet Union, was forced to initiate a series of reforms encapsulated in two words: *perestroika* (economic restructuring) and *glasnost* (openness). These changes marked the beginning of the end for the USSR, the fall of the Berlin Wall, and the Cold War. The Soviet collapse was the result of a deadly combination of economic inefficiencies, political rigidity, social pressures, and failures in managing reforms.

Centralized planning could no longer support a competitive economy, while the arms race with the United States drained vital resources away from consumer goods. Added to this were a corrupt bureaucracy and an elite disconnected from the needs of the people, fueling mistrust and disillusionment.

Gorbachev's reforms aimed to modernize the system, but without a real market to support them, they further destabilized the country. *Glasnost* encouraged a wave of independence movements in the Soviet republics, inevitably leading to the collapse of the USSR in 1991. Gorbachev had to step aside, and in his place, Boris Yeltsin, decidedly more pro-American, took power.

Explaining the reasons behind this dramatic change would require an entire encyclopedia, but what matters for our story is that by the mid-1980s, tensions began to ease. With the fall of the Berlin Wall in 1989 and the dissolution of the USSR in 1991, for the West – led by the United States – it was no longer necessary to keep Latin American countries "onside."

Suddenly, consciences were awakened: the brutality of human rights violations perpetrated by the "friendly" Latin American governments was revealed, and cocaine began to be seen as a serious problem.

It was under the presidency of Ronald Reagan that the United States launched yet another "war on drugs." As the right-wing dictatorships in Latin America fell one after another, public opinion in the West also began to realize the devastating effects of cocaine.

Before 1989, public information about the white powder in the West was sparse and often distorted: as we've seen, it was considered a "drug of the elite," associated with famous figures, and its destructive potential was not deeply discussed. In short, cocaine was the "chic" drug, perceived as less dangerous than heroin, which had dominated public narratives about narcotics in the preceding decades. Public opinion was fascinated by – yet simultaneously ignorant of – the "snow" of cultural elites.

Then, with the fall of the Wall, the veil that had concealed the price paid in lives and brains due to the white powder also fell. From that moment on, the drug began to be associated not only with glamorous circles but also with the social disasters in the poorest communities, particularly among African Americans and Latinos. The media coverage, however, remained ambiguous, focusing on drug trafficking and crime without delving into the economic and geopolitical dynamics of drug trafficking.
In 1986, Reagan signed the Anti-Drug Abuse Act, which harshened the penalties for drug-related crimes. And because, for Americans, "war" really means war, he sent military forces to Colombia, the birthplace of coca.
The more suspicious, and the usual cynics, speculate that, with the fall of the USSR, the old agreements with Latin American governments to contain communism were no longer necessary. It was no longer necessary to "turn a blind eye" to their sources of funding derived from the coca exported to the West.

THE COLOMBIA PLAN

The Colombia Plan, launched in 2000 as a collaboration between Colombia and the United States, officially aimed at fighting drug trafficking and illegal armed groups in the country. However, behind the label of the fight against drugs, this plan became one of the most controversial interventions in Latin America.
With an investment of over 7.5 billion dollars, primarily from the U.S., the program involved strengthening the Colombian army and using aerial herbicides to destroy coca crops. However, the glyphosate used caused serious environmental damage and severely impacted local communities, including indigenous populations dependent on those lands.
The results were mixed: on one hand, it was possible to strike at the cartels (but only the Colombian ones, while Mexican cartels began to thrive) and weaken guerrilla groups like the FARC (Revolutionary Armed Forces of Colombia); on the other hand, the increased militarization

led to human rights violations and favored the expansion of paramilitary groups. Although coca cultivation decreased in some areas, many crops shifted to other regions or to neighboring Peru and Bolivia.
Critics, always suspicious, argue that the Colombia Plan was not only an anti-drug crusade but also a tool for the United States to exercise geopolitical control in South America and curb anti-American movements.

THE END OF LATIN AMERICAN DICTATORSHIPS

With the end of the Cold War, Latin American dictators who had enjoyed decades of tacit support from the United States began to fall, one after another. The military regimes, long justified as anti-communist strongholds, no longer had a reason to exist in the eyes of Washington, which was now focused on promoting democracy and human rights as its new geopolitical priorities. The rhetoric of the "communist enemy" could no longer justify repression. The very populations of these countries were urged to rise up forcefully, demanding change and freedom.
However, the authenticity of these democracies has often been called into question. Between black and white, there can, in fact, be infinite shades of grey. In reality, only history will tell us how and where real democratic progress has occurred—or is occurring.
In Argentina, the military dictatorship—responsible for tens of thousands of desaparecidos during the "Dirty War"—began to falter in the early '80s. The defeat in the Falklands War against the United Kingdom in 1982 accelerated the process, and in 1983, the country returned to democracy, electing Raúl Alfonsín as president. Argentina was one of the first countries to put its former military leaders on trial, revealing to the world the horror of state repression.
Chile followed soon after. Augusto Pinochet, the dictator who came to power after the 1973 coup, found himself under growing pressure. In 1988, a public referendum officially voted against him, and by 1990, he was forced to relinquish power, though he remained in control of the

armed forces for several more years. Chile began a slow process of democratization, which brought to light the human rights violations committed under his regime, with a ripple of justice that still echoes today.

In Paraguay, Alfredo Stroessner, the long-time dictator who ruled from 1954, was overthrown in 1989 by a military coup. After 35 years of authoritarian rule, his regime fell amid international isolation and growing popular discontent. The end of his dictatorship marked Paraguay's transition to democracy, though the legacy of his authoritarian system continued to leave scars on the country.

A chapter apart is represented by Panama under Manuel Noriega. This former CIA agent had maintained close ties with the United States while engaging in illicit activities, including drug trafficking and internal repression. However, by the late 1980s, with the changing international context, the United States could no longer tolerate his actions. In 1989, Operation Just Cause led to an American invasion of Panama, culminating in the capture of Noriega, who was tried and convicted for drug trafficking in the United States. This event marked the symbolic end of an era of complicity between Washington and the region's authoritarian regimes. One note: Panama is one of the famous "tax havens" deemed "necessary" for the process of laundering "dirty" money from narcotrafficking.

In the 1980s and 1990s, Brazil and Uruguay also freed themselves from military dictatorships. In Brazil, power gradually shifted to civilian governments, with the official end of the dictatorship in 1985 and the subsequent adoption of a new democratic Constitution. Uruguay, notorious for brutal repression and the systematic use of torture, returned to democracy in 1985, bringing the voice of the people back to the center of politics after years of imposed silence.

The wave of democratization, however, did not erase the dark legacy left by the dictatorial regimes. Countries like Argentina, Chile, Paraguay, and Uruguay found themselves grappling with deep social divisions and scars left by years of repression, torture, and state violence. The road to healing and reconciliation was long and painful, with many still seeking justice for the victims of the brutal regimes that once held power in the region.

THE EASTERN FRONT: HOME OF HEROIN

Let's change latitude and time zone: we're heading east. Still in the Cold War era, the beating heart of the other superpower, the Soviet Union, was surrounded by alliances and rivalries.

To fully grasp the boundaries of the Red Bloc and the power dynamics of the time, it's important to remember the division of the world into three blocks: the Atlantic Alliance (NATO), the USSR, and the floating nations.

In the pro-Western orbit, there were NATO member states, an alliance that included the United States, Canada, and much of Western Europe, with West Germany surrounded by the Berlin Wall. In the Middle East, Israel was a staunch ally of the United States, as were Saudi Arabia, Jordan, and Iran (until 1979), tied to Washington for economic and security reasons. In Asia, Japan was a pillar of the Western camp, alongside South Korea, the Philippines, Taiwan, Thailand, Australia, and New Zealand.

On the opposite side, the Soviet bloc revolved around the Warsaw Pact, which included the Soviet Union (15 republics led by Russia) and countries such as Poland, East Germany, Czechoslovakia, Hungary, Bulgaria, and Romania. In the Middle East and North Africa, countries like Egypt (until the late 1970s), Syria, and Iraq received economic and military support from the USSR.

In Asia, China, initially an ally, distanced itself in the 1960s, while Vietnam and North Korea remained solid Soviet partners.

Finally, the non-aligned countries, such as India, Indonesia, Yugoslavia, and many African nations (like Ghana and Algeria), sought to maintain strategic neutrality while often showing socialist sympathies. In this group, Iran and Iraq maintained special relationships with both blocs, trying to balance autonomy and alliances.

Anyone over 40 will likely remember how these countries have been at the center of wars over the years. The longest of these, which directly involved NATO countries, including Italy, was the war in Afghanistan.
Let's try to understand why this barren, steppe-like country has attracted so much attention.

AFGHANISTAN, THE BRIDGE STATE

Today, Afghanistan seems almost like a land forgotten by both God and man, a place lost in time. Dusty roads, crumbling houses, men with beards wearing turbans, women cloaked from head to toe in burqas, and malnourished children sketch a picture of daily survival.
Yet, in this setting, where even a decent meal is a challenge, the drug industry has thrived undisturbed—before, during, and after the Cold War.
Afghanistan is not only the world's largest producer of heroin; it is also a geopolitical and strategic crossroads.
Bordering Iran, Pakistan, China, and the former Soviet republics (Turkmenistan, Uzbekistan, and Tajikistan), the country acts as a "natural bridge" between South Asia, Central Asia, and the Middle East. Each neighbor plays its part: Iran resists Western influence, Pakistan recalibrates its alliances after a long partnership with the U.S., moving closer to China, while the latter emerges as a rising superpower.
Thus, the unique combination of mineral resources, instability, and strategic location makes Afghanistan a pivotal node.
As early as the 19th century, Afghanistan was the focal point of the "Great Game" between the British Empire and Tsarist Russia, both vying for control of Central Asia. Today, this game involves the United States and China, with one new factor: Afghanistan's underground wealth, rich in copper, lithium, and rare earth minerals. These resources, vital for modern technologies like electric car batteries and electronic devices, turn the country into a key player in global energy and industrial politics.

In summary, dominating Afghanistan is not just about controlling its resources—it's about gaining a geopolitical advantage with the potential to influence critical balances in the Middle East and South Asia.

CLASH USA-USSR: THE CYCLONE OPERATION

Let's revisit the history of Afghanistan through this lens. During the Cold War, the country was the stage for a devastating conflict between the two superpowers. In the 1960s and 1970s, Afghanistan sought to maintain a facade of neutrality while the Soviet Union and the United States exerted their influence over Kabul through economic and diplomatic aid.

Governed by monarchs and moderate leaders, the land of the poppy became a contested pawn in the great geopolitical game. In 1978, the Marxist-Leninist People's Democratic Party of Afghanistan, backed by Moscow, seized power in the Saur Revolution. This pro-Soviet shift triggered a reaction from the West, which, however, could not intervene directly, as the legitimate Afghan government supported it.

As is often the case, the West's intervention took place on a different level. Western intelligence agencies stepped in, attempting to fight the enemy by fomenting discontent and insurgencies.

These underground currents also played on the sentiments tied to the beliefs of these people. It's important to remember that the Soviet Union and communism in general were not fond of religions, viewing them as the opium of the people.

In the next section, we will see how the foundations for the radicalization of Islamism were laid during the war. But for now, let's return to the historical account. Faced with this situation, in 1979, the Soviet Union intervened militarily to support the Afghan government against these insurgencies. Although Moscow's intervention was legitimized by Kabul, the United States considered it an invasion aimed at expanding Soviet influence toward the Middle East and the Indian Ocean.

The American response was relentless: alongside Saudi Arabia, Pakistan, and other allies, they began to fund and arm the mujahideen, Islamic resistance groups fighting the Soviet occupation. This support materialized in the famous Operation Cyclone, one of the most expensive operations in CIA history. Thousands of fighters were trained with Saudi funding and Pakistani logistical assistance.
During the Soviet occupation and the war against the mujahideen backed by the West, opium production in Afghanistan grew exponentially.
Those who are considered the "bad guys" today were, at the time, the "good guys," and much of their resistance was funded through the trafficking of poppy, which was transformed into heroin for global markets. This brings us to a controversial point. There is no documented evidence directly linking drug trafficking to the CIA or other Western intelligence agencies.
However, as a mental exercise, let’s apply a basic principle of formal logical reasoning: the Aristotelian syllogism.

- Major premise: The mujahideen were funded through opium trafficking.
- Minor premise: The United States supported the mujahideen.
- Conclusion: The United States supported the opium trade.

This line of reasoning will surely be dismissed by the well-meaning as flawed, due to the potential for a fallacy of improper association. Simply put, in a syllogism, even if both premises are true, the conclusion may not necessarily be valid.
The cynics, on the other hand, will revel in this! But the point is not to determine who is right: the value of this exercise lies in training critical thinking. History may, one day, tell us more.
What we do know for certain is that funds from opium were crucial in financing the mujahideen’s resistance. The cultivation of poppies and the production of heroin be-

came pillars of the Afghan economy, sustained by the difficult geography, local tribal structures, and the absence of central control over large areas of the country. This parallel economy, fueled by war and international alliances, left a deep mark on Afghanistan's history and its role in the global drug trade.

HOW TO BUILD A TERRORIST

At this point, younger readers might feel a bit disoriented. They were born and raised in a world where Islamic extremists are the enemy to fight. The ones who brought down the Twin Towers and, for decades, turned European cities into places of terror, with continuous bombings and massacres.

How is it possible that the West supported these fanatics? What seems like a paradox is, in fact, not one. Because in history, it doesn't take much to go from being the "good guys" to being the "bad guys."

Now, let's try to understand how this could have happened.

During the Cold War, the United States, wisely, used every possible weapon against their communist enemies. As we've mentioned, one area where the USSR was vulnerable was its negative view of any kind of belief system. Let's not forget that for Karl Marx, religion was the opium of the people.

In this context, the U.S. leveraged this point to win over Arab countries. After all, while religious freedom is considered an inalienable right for all, it's even more so for those cultures that do not embrace the secular concept of the state.

To put it simply, while for a Westerner, of Christian culture, the rule of separation between government and spirituality prevails, based on the saying "Render unto Caesar the things that are Caesar's, and unto God the things that are God's," in the Islamic world, this division is not conceived. The Quran is the law, and the law cannot violate the dictates of the Quran.

Coincidentally, it was precisely during these years that the U.S. was making official statements about the sacred right to respect all religious faiths, Islam included. Words certainly noble, spoken by presidents like Dwight D. Eisenhower, who in 1957 declared: “We recognize the importance of Islam in the lives of the Arab people and support the right of every individual to practice his or her faith freely.”

As always, for the cynics, these words might have had a specific goal: to use religion as an ideological weapon to counter the Soviet bloc, which made atheism its banner. Sincerity aside, Eisenhower’s, the Arab world, which was predominantly Muslim, was highly sensitive to these issues. Therefore, the use of propaganda can only be seen as a smart move. It was essential to paint the Soviet Union as the enemy of spirituality, contrasting it with the image of the Western bloc as the bastion of faith.

It’s no surprise that in the 1980s, Ronald Reagan praised the Afghan mujahideen as "freedom fighters." Of course, at the time, he probably couldn’t have imagined that those jihad warriors, supported by the U.S. against the Soviets, would later be seen as the seed of global terrorism. Cynics often point to another aspect of the politics of those years to demonstrate its alleged hypocrisy. While proclaiming respect for Islam, the United States supported authoritarian regimes in the Middle East and North Africa that brutally suppressed any dissent. Saudi Arabia, for example, received millions of dollars in aid while maintaining a repressive and conservative system of government. In Egypt, the regime of Hosni Mubarak crushed Islamist movements with Washington’s blessing, while in Algeria, a military coup annulled elections won by an Islamist party, supported by popular consent.

This dichotomy did not go unnoticed by a figure we will analyze later. While the U.S. proclaimed itself the liberator, it was, in fact, sowing the resentment that would later manifest in devastating ways.

The statements about religious freedom were, to some, seen as tools of a cynical calculation. They were not meant to guarantee universal rights, but to fuel an ideological war—sometimes literally armed—against communist atheism.

If there's one thing history teaches, it's that the fire of anger sometimes burns even those who start it.

THEN THE WALL FELL...

With the fall of the Berlin Wall and the implosion of the Soviet Union, the spotlight on Afghanistan seemed to fade.

No longer a strategic borderland, the country was left in the hands of the mujahideen, who, despite imposing the burqa on women and marrying off daughters at ages 10-12, had fought for the Western cause. Armed and supported by NATO, they had challenged Soviet forces, earning the right to do with the country as they saw fit. As we've seen, this war-torn yet far from impoverished land was already a powerhouse in the opium industry. During the Cold War, poppy plantations had thrived, and continued to do so even after the Soviet withdrawal in 1989.

Divided among factions of mujahideen, the country became a mosaic of warlords, armed with American rifles and funded through Pakistan's intelligence service, the ISI (close to the U.S.). Among the most significant groups were Hezb-e Islami, led by the radical Gulbuddin Hekmatyar, and the Northern Alliance, commanded by Ahmad Shah Massoud, a respected but less extreme leader. Alongside them were other smaller factions.

The United States, now distant, left the task of managing the new balance of power to Pakistan and Saudi Arabia, delegating the oversight of the "loyal" factions to regional allies.

However, it was not easy to bring the mujahideen together: internal fragmentation, ideological differences, and personal ambitions prevented any form of unification. The American dream of a moderate and controllable Afghanistan collided with the reality of groups where the religious component was deeply rooted. In this regard, it's worth remembering that in Islam, the affairs of God and the affairs of men cannot be disconnected. In other words, our "Render unto Caesar the things that are Caesar's (the state) and unto God the things that are God's (religion)" is not recognized.

The same mujahideen leaders, despite the support they received, saw American influence as a threat to Islamic sovereignty.

It was in this chaotic context that Osama bin Laden emerged, a Saudi billionaire who found ideological affinity with the Taliban (from "talib," meaning students), a movement born in the madrassas (koranic schools) of Pakistan and Afghanistan. But we will discuss him in the next section.

The Taliban, logistically supported by the Pakistani ISI and funded by Saudi Arabia, adopted a strict interpretation of Sunni Islam and aimed to consolidate internal power. When they took Kabul in 1996, they established control over much of the opium production, which became crucial to their economy.

Initially, the United States considered them as potential partners for stabilizing the region, even evaluating economic projects such as an oil pipeline crossing Afghanistan. However, the deal fell through, and in the next section, we will explore why.

THE RISE OF OSAMA BIN LADEN

Sometimes, in an apparently perfect system, a wild card slips in. What mathematicians call a random variable, represented in equations by the famous letters X, Y, Z. In our story, X has a magnetic face, deep, dark eyes, an ethereal figure with refined features.

His name was Osama bin Laden.

Just when Afghanistan seemed destined to fade into the forgotten pages of history, with everyone having had their share and all seemingly happy and content, this X variable entered the scene.

Remember that the most powerful mujahideen factions controlled the opium trade, Saudi Arabia and Pakistan had free rein in the region, and the U.S. watched from above. In this almost perfect picture, our "prince" could have followed in the footsteps of his family and lived a life of luxury, in the true sense of the word.

Born in Saudi Arabia, the son of a powerful construction magnate close to the royal family, he was raised in luxury, with a future ahead of him that was mapped out and free of uncertainties.
He could have had four wives at once (as the Quran allows, though they can be rotated), dream cars, and villas scattered everywhere.
Instead, despite a background in economics, he decided to delve deeper into his religion.
In 1979, at just 22 years old, he left his family's castles and supersonic yachts to join the mujahideen, engaged in resistance against the Soviet invasion of Afghanistan. Follies that only a young man, born under the dreamy sign of Pisces, could conceive.
At first, everything followed the script.
During the Cold War, Bin Laden used his wealth to fund the Islamic fighters, operating in a context where even the United States was supporting the mujahideen to counter the USSR. But then, something changed.
The young man with eyes like embers began to look with growing disdain at Western politics in the region. Although active in the same theater, he refused to accept direct funding from the United States, preferring to build an autonomous support network, fueled by donations from supporters in the Gulf countries and funds from his own family.
In 1988, as the Soviet war was coming to an end, Bin Laden founded Al-Qaeda, an organization designed to unite veterans of the Afghan conflict in a project for global "jihad." It's worth noting that the term "jihad" has multiple meanings: it can refer to a spiritual effort to follow the teachings of the Quran, but also to an armed struggle against influences seen as contrary to Islam. Bin Laden embraced both interpretations.

After the Soviet withdrawal, the relationship between our variable X and the United States rapidly deteriorated. The 1990-1991 Desert Storm operation, with the arrival of American military bases in the Gulf, particularly in Saudi Arabia, was something he could not tolerate.

For Osama, this meant the desecration of Islam's holy lands by foreign military presence. Moreover, he strongly opposed the U.S.'s unconditional support for Israel and its backing of repressive regimes in the Middle East and North Africa.

Here, perhaps, a brief historical digression is in order. In the 1980s and 1990s, the Middle East and North Africa were the stage for an American strategy that prioritized authoritarian stability over democratic progress. Nothing new: the same script had already been seen in Latin America. Repressive regimes, supported by substantial U.S. economic and military aid, became bulwarks against communism at first, and later against Islamic radicalism, while simultaneously suffocating any popular aspirations. Bin Laden saw these pro-American governments not only as enemies of Islam but as tools of Western hegemony that perpetuated oppression under the guise of stability.

Saudi Arabia, his homeland, became for him the symbol of betrayal: a monarchy willing to host American bases in the name of security. In Egypt, Mubarak's regime brutally repressed any Islamist movement, growing fat on U.S. dollars. In Algeria, a democratically elected Islamic government was overturned in a coup supported by Western powers. In Tunisia and Jordan, repression went hand in hand with diplomatic smiles toward Washington. Bin Laden saw these regimes not just as oppressors, but as the reflection of a short-sighted American strategy, one destined to sow resentment. That resentment found its fiercest interpreter in him: a man determined to turn anger into a global war against the "Great Satan" and its local allies. The rogue element had found its target.

THE SHIFT OF THE TALIBAN FROM GOOD TO BAD

Let's take a step back. Remember the failed oil pipeline deal? Now we know who had a hand in it. Despite being involved, like all other mujahideen groups, in the opium trade, the United States initially considered the Taliban as potential partners for stabilization, even proposing joint economic projects. However, with the growing influence of Bin Laden and his organization, everything fell apart.

The alliance between Al-Qaeda and the Taliban was complex but complementary: the Taliban focused on consolidating internal power, while Al-Qaeda used Afghan territory as a base to train troops needed for its vision of Islamic unification and independence from the West. What happened next, once again, leads one to think the worst.

By the end of the 1990s, the international community, including states, organizations like the United Nations, and NGOs, launched a media campaign against Afghanistan for its role in the global trade of opium and heroin. Horror!

Suddenly – as had happened in Latin America – the country, governed by the Taliban, was seen as one of the world's main sources of opium, fueling a large heroin trade.

Murderers!

The international community united in a coordinated effort to raise awareness, focusing attention on the links between the proceeds of opium and the funding of Taliban activities.

This coalition, justly and finally, emphasized the devastating effects of heroin and connected the Taliban regime to drug trafficking, highlighting the precarious conditions of Afghan farmers for whom opium represented a stable source of income, given the lack of economic alternatives.

The campaign was not limited to raising awareness; it included diplomatic pressure, sanctions, and proposals for development programs aimed at reducing opium cultivation.

Reports and official statements described the impact of the drug trade on regional stability and the emerging threats to international security, considering Afghanistan a potential hotspot for radicalism and terrorism.
Today, many analysts believe the campaign was also a geopolitical tool, useful for raising global public awareness. In fact, this was happening at the same time as the United States and other international actors were starting to reassess the security risks linked to the growing presence of radical groups in Afghanistan, anticipating a more direct and strategic engagement in the region.

THE BOLD MOVE OF THE TURBANED MEN

In response to international pressure, on July 7, 2000, amidst many questionable actions, the Taliban made a bold move: they proclaimed a ban on opium poppy cultivation, complete with the destruction of remaining crops and stockpiles. This measure, imposed by Mullah Omar, the Taliban leader, led to a dramatic reduction in the production of the "magic capsule" in the following season. For once, a group of "madmen" driven by mystical delusions managed to achieve something the West had never been able to do.
There has been much debate about the reasons behind this decision. In fact, the ban came at a time when the Taliban were heavily isolated on the global stage. As we have seen, the international community, with the United States leading the charge, was not exactly giving them good press. Some argue that it was an economic strategy, as international funding was scarce. Destroying the opium and thus "purifying" the regime's image could have had a longer-term strategic goal: to position Afghanistan as a "worthy" partner to receive humanitarian and economic aid from the United Nations or foreign countries.
As some analysts have noted, this move could have turned the drug problem into an opportunity to attract resources from abroad and, potentially, ease the economic sanctions weighing on the local population. This interpretation holds water, too, though there is also a more straightforward

view: the decision was part of the Taliban's religious ideology, which saw the opium trade as contrary to Islamic principles.
This strategy proved to be quite effective.
The following year, various organizations and countries began exploring options to provide economic aid and alternative development programs to support the Afghan population. However, the Taliban had overlooked one crucial fact: history had already shown that burning opium doesn't bode well. It's somewhat akin to pouring oil onto the fire.
The same action, carried out by China in the mid-1800s, had attracted Britain's intervention and cost them two wars—the Opium Wars we've already discussed—resulting in tens of thousands of deaths and the loss of strategically important ports.
One could only hope for a different outcome, but that wasn't the case.
The United States, which had already exerted strong indirect influence in the region during the Cold War, chose to intervene directly just over a year later. At that point, they dragged NATO into the conflict, making Afghanistan the theater of a new phase of wars and military interventions. The official reason, however, was not the opium trade.

THE ATTACK ON THE TWIN TOWERS

One year and two months after the burning of the poppy crops, on September 9, 2001, Ahmed Shah Massoud, the leader of the Northern Alliance, the main ally of the U.S. and the primary opponent of the Taliban, was assassinated. Just two days later, on September 11, 2001, between 8:46 and 10:03 in the morning, four commercial airplanes were hijacked in U.S. airspace. Two crashed into the Twin Towers in New York, one hit the Pentagon in Washington, and the fourth plunged into Pennsylvania after passengers attempted to regain control.
The attacks resulted in around 3,000 deaths and thousands of injuries, shocking the world and radically altering international politics.

Osama bin Laden, who was immediately identified as the mastermind behind the attacks, strangely did not claim responsibility right away—a departure from the usual practice of an organization that would have seen an assault on the heart of the United States not only as a major victory but as an act of justice for the suffering of Muslim peoples and the desecration of Islam's holy lands.

Instead, he initially denied Al-Qaeda's involvement. A month later, on October 7, the man with the burning eyes publicly praised the hijackers, calling them "Muslim heroes" in a video broadcast by Al Jazeera, but still refrained from claiming credit for the attack. What followed was a global shift in U.S. foreign policy and security measures, leading to the War on Terror and the invasion of Afghanistan in October 2001. The events of 9/11 marked the beginning of a new era of conflict and geopolitical realignment.

The writer, unfortunately, does not know Arabic, but it would be interesting to hear, word for word, what the Prince of Terror had to say.

In the video from October 29, 2004, our variable X appears with a look that blends authority and simplicity. He wears a traditional white Arab robe, over which he dons a camouflage military jacket, symbolizing his commitment to armed struggle. His beard is well-groomed and dyed black. He does not wear a turban, which is quite unusual, given that this headgear holds significant symbolic value in Islam: it represents faith, tradition, and political authority. It's not exactly as if the Pope were to say Mass on Christmas Eve in beach shorts, but it's close.

The background of the video is neutral, likely a beige cloth or a uniform wall. Osama's posture is upright and composed, his steady gaze into the camera amplifying the gravity of his words. He speaks calmly, with a measured, almost didactic tone, in sharp contrast to the aggressive image typically associated with his public persona.

The leader addresses the American people directly, trying to explain and justify the September 11 attacks as a response to what he considers the injustices suffered by the

Islamic world. His gestures are measured, reinforcing the impression of a solemn figure rather than a fanatic consumed by fervor. With articulate language and a firm tone, he constructs a message that is not only a claim of responsibility but also an attempt to convey to the public the reasons behind the Jihad.

He attributed the attacks to the need to respond to American "aggressions" against the Islamic world, particularly citing U.S. support for Israel and the difficult conditions of the Palestinians and those in Lebanon. Some of his words strike at the heart.

In any case, this claim of responsibility did not change the course of history. The condemnation of the wealthy Saudi was already in place, and his sentence had long been in execution.

In response to the attacks, by November 2001, the United States, with NATO's support, invaded Afghanistan under "Operation Enduring Freedom." The goal of the operation was to dismantle Al-Qaeda and remove the Taliban, who were harboring bin Laden and his organization.

The military campaign achieved quick initial success, with coalition forces, supported by the Northern Alliance, managing to drive the Taliban out of major cities, including Kabul, by the end of 2001.

Curiously, opium production—the only activity the Taliban had restricted—immediately resumed at full capacity. Ten years later, in 2011, it was revealed that bin Laden was no longer in Afghanistan but had been living in Pakistan, a U.S. ally. There, he was killed by U.S. special forces.

Despite his elimination, international forces remained in Afghanistan for another ten years, focused on stabilizing the country and attempting to prevent it from becoming a base for international terrorism once again.

The war officially ended in August 2021, when the United States and NATO quietly withdrew their troops. Shortly after, the Taliban regained control of the country, retaking Kabul on August 15 with little resistance.

On August 30, 2021, the last American military flight left Kabul airport, marking the definitive end of a twenty-year conflict, with the return of the Taliban to power. The war in Afghanistan was one of the longest and most costly military operations in modern history. It involved over 50 nations under the leadership of NATO and the United States. The U.S. alone bore a cost of over 2.3 trillion dollars, while allied countries like Italy contributed significant economic and military resources.
In any case, the war was lost, and by the first year of the conflict, the opium trade not only resumed but reached even higher levels.
One tries not to think the worst... but sometimes it's hard.

LESS HEROIN, MORE OXYCODONE AND FENTANYL

Returning history to the historians, let's return to the focus of our book: addiction and what fuels it.
The media campaign against Afghanistan and its role in the global opium trade in the 1990s partially coincided with the opioid crisis in the West.
The direct connections are complex, but with a bit of "thinking the worst," it's hard not to see some possible link.
When the Taliban imposed the poppy cultivation ban in 2000, opium production in Afghanistan plummeted, dropping by up to 75%. This led to a sharp rise in the cost of heroin, following the simplest of market laws: less supply, higher price. The drop in production caused a spike in global drug prices and a temporary shortage on the market. However, the ban didn't last long. By 2001, coinciding with the launch of the U.S.-NATO Operation Enduring Freedom, poppy cultivation resumed at full speed. The Afghan people, despite being under attack by a coalition of more than 50 countries—at times with peaks of 130,000 Western soldiers in the field—managed with only tens of thousands of their own to hold their positions and even cultivate opium.

Meanwhile, in the West, a parallel phenomenon was observed: the rise in prescriptions for opioid-based painkillers like oxycodone, which in the following years would become a key driver of the opioid epidemic. At the same time, fentanyl, a synthetic opioid far stronger than heroin, began to appear in the drug markets. This shift was partly the result of the West's growing reliance on prescription opioids, and it would go on to fuel the deadly opioid crisis we now face.

LITTLE ITALY AND THE BALKAN ROUTE

We've explored the western front, with cocaine-producing countries to the south and major consumers to the north, and then ventured into the eastern front, home of heroin. Now, let's focus on the center: Europe, and particularly Italy.

The policies that shaped Europe and Italy after World War II were crucial in constructing our recent history. Understanding how the "best youth" of those years were transformed into an army of zombies, obsessed with the search for a fix, is essential to making sense of this essay. The plague of drugs decimated generations, tearing away their dignity, their souls, and their very lives. It was a war after the war, with a death toll still impossible to calculate. The "kids from the Berlin Zoo" could be found everywhere: Rome, Paris, London, Canicattì, and in every corner of what was once glorious Europe.

It won't be easy to understand the causes of all this, but we will try. Let's start with the facts, with what is written in the history books.

During the years of widespread drug use, the Old Continent bore a deep wound: the Iron Curtain, which divided the West, led by the United States, from the Soviet bloc under the USSR. This line cut through Germany, crossed neutral Switzerland, and descended, splitting the Adriatic in two, with Italy straddling both sides.

Italy, just out of the war, found itself for several years floating between the two blocs.

As often happens to countries on the border, it became a battleground.
It's important to remember that both the Atlantic Alliance and the Soviet Union were victors of the conflict, while Germany and Italy emerged as the defeated nations. For Germany, the solution was drastic: a wall divided Berlin and everything around it. For Italy, the path seemed softer. After all, the country had turned its back on fascism and opened its doors to the Allies. But mercy and politics never walk hand in hand.
In short, defeat erased Italy's ambitions for international power, but not its strategic importance for the great powers. Positioned at the heart of the Mediterranean, on the fault line between East and West, the Peninsula became crucial in the Cold War chessboard, long before the Italians themselves were aware of it.
The 1947 Paris Peace Treaty stripped Italy of strategic territories and imposed heavy military restrictions. But the United States wasted no time: with the Marshall Plan, the country received an economic boost that enabled its reconstruction, but also firmly tied it to the West.
This tool, which revived the Italian economy, transformed the Bel Paese into a crucial piece of the Atlantic alliance, solidified by its entry into NATO in 1949.
However, the process was not straightforward. The Italian Communist Party, at the time one of the strongest in Europe, represented a real ideological threat. It was led by political figures whose presence in today's halls of power would be a dream.
In simple terms, after the World War ended, the country risked civil war. The resistance against the fascist dictatorships, which had seen partisans of all political colors fight side by side, dissolved. The Communists began looking East, while the moderates, led by the Catholic Church, chose the West.
The Christian Democratic Party, created to meet this need, became the stronghold against the Communist Party and governed the country for nearly half a century. The 1948 elections were an ideological referendum, a turning point

that marked the dominance of DC, but also the need to make concessions to the PCI to avoid irreparable fractures. An important protagonist is missing from this narrative, one whom we intentionally leave in the shadows for now. We will bring him out when the shift within his power structures becomes more relevant to the focus of our book: the spread of death in powder form and the institutions' failure to combat its slow drip.

For now, it is enough to know that not only the formal economy, but also the criminal one, regained strength after the end of the conflict.

During the fascist regime, a truly dark era without a shadow of doubt, too many things were done that should be ashamed of, but organized crime also suffered, losing much of its power.

Once Benito Mussolini was hung upside down, along with his Claretta, in Piazzale Loreto, many let out a sigh of relief, and among them was organized crime.

A dictatorship is the worst thing a person can wish for. Worst still are dictatorships that are masked.

THE DIVISION OF THE "PIE"

Post-war Italy was a time of material reconstruction but also a crucial moment for redefining the country's power dynamics. The "pie," made up of cultural, political, and economic influences, was on the table, and there was no shortage of diners eager to claim their share. Many had contributed to the fall of Nazifascism and now wanted their portion. However, the feast was far from harmonious. In simple terms, the **Christian Democracy (Democrazia Cristiana)** party secured the largest slice. As the guarantor of the interests of the United States and the Catholic Church, the DC took control of the government, the state apparatus, and social policies. Primary education also fell under its domain—a sector as crucial then as it is today for shaping society.

The **Vatican**, an unshakable ally of the DC, was not content with a marginal role. A long-standing pillar of Italian identity, the Catholic Church wielded influence far beyond parish walls. Through a network of oratories, Catholic schools, and organizations like **Azione Cattolica**, the Vatican maintained an active presence in Italians' daily lives, becoming a nearly unassailable moral and political force. Its hands firmly gripped social policies and basic education, reinforcing the bond between faith and political power.

The **Italian Communist Party (PCI)**, confined to opposition, was assigned an apparently lesser portion: culture and universities. A sector that, at first glance, served to appease without threatening. Yet, as history would show, that "minor slice" proved pivotal in shaping new generations of intellectuals, artists, and professionals. This "could have" made all the difference.

Culture, in the hands of the PCI, became fertile ground for ideas and movements alternative to Christian Democratic dominance.

The control of the working class, then a significant force, was divided among the unions.

Finally, there was one slice of the pie that no one openly claimed but was essential to completing the feast: the management of the **shadow economy**. Cynics argue that every democratic state requires unofficial funds to support operations that could never be discussed or approved by an elected Parliament in broad daylight.

But who managed that power and how? That will be explored later.

Returning to the focus of this essay, the Cold War era translated into a time of heightened tensions at all levels in Italy. Coincidentally—or not—it was precisely in the areas where the struggle was most intense that the scourge of **heroin** eventually took root.

YEARS OF LEAD AND THE STRATEGY OF TENSION

Before the Daughter of Opium took control, Italy lived through a period of constant turmoil. It was a laboratory of ideas, clashes, and contradictions. These were years when the streets filled with students, workers, and intellectuals, each with their own banner and their own fight, driven by ideologies that were as strong as they were often incapable of compromise.

The economic boom of the early 1960s had transformed a post-war, rural country into an industrial, urban nation, ready to consume and eager for change. But beneath this apparent vitality, tensions simmered, poised to erupt.

Ideologies dominated the public discourse—sometimes in a toxic way, other times as a vehicle of hope.

On the left, the Italian Communist Party gained support among workers and students, advancing a revolutionary agenda aimed at overturning the old capitalist order. On the right, the Italian Social Movement nurtured a nostalgic opposition to fascism, while the center, with the Christian Democrats, struggled to maintain an impossible balance between these two centrifugal forces.

Then more radical movements emerged: the Red Brigades, Prima Linea, and on the other side, New Order and National Vanguard. Politics became violence, and violence became a strategy.

The streets became the stage for a social conflict that at times spilled over into bloodshed. Students and workers, united in 1968, marched for a more just world, against capitalism and imperialism. Demonstrations turned into clashes with the police, and every stone thrown became a symbol of resistance. But the long wave of those ideals shattered against a wall of disillusionment in the 1970s, a period in which the "historical compromise"—an attempt to bring together the Christian Democrats and the Communist Party to form a government of national solidarity in a time of great political and social instability—ended with the kidnapping and execution of the man who had tried to realize it, the number one of the Christian Democrats, Aldo Moro.

In this case, one could easily indulge in suspicion, but this isn't the place for in-depth analysis. The focus of the book is elsewhere.

So, back to the matter at hand. It was in this climate of uncertainty and emptiness that a phenomenon began to spread, one that would mark an entire generation: the widespread use of drugs. Heroin, in particular, made its way into the urban peripheries and among the youth who had lost faith in the very ideologies that once set their hearts on fire.

People still wonder whether this was a historical coincidence, or if there were specific interests in promoting a social numbness that would defuse political unrest.

The 1970s and 1980s saw the spread of drugs like an invisible web, suffocating the dreams of revolution. Heroin didn't just affect the marginalized: it entered universities, social centers, and cultural clubs. The young man with the keffiyeh, who once chanted slogans in support of oppressed peoples, was now bent over a spoon, a victim of a spiral from which few escaped.

The spread of heroin was so rapid it seemed orchestrated. Some documents and testimonies leave room for disturbing hypotheses: was there perhaps a plan to extinguish that rebellious generation? The "strategy of tension" didn't just stop at bombings but might have also passed through a silent dependency that emptied the streets and filled the alleys with syringes, and too often, with broken lives.

As the streets grew increasingly deserted, the centers of power looked elsewhere. The economic prosperity of the 1980s, with its neon lights and discos, offered a hollow, glittering alternative to those seeking answers: hedonism instead of commitment, pleasure instead of struggle. Ideologies crumbled under the weight of an increasingly individualistic society, and the ferment of the 1960s and 1970s gave way to a void that was hard to fill.

In the end, Italy woke up from that restless dream with broken bones. The ideologies were not entirely dead, but they had been marginalized. Drugs had claimed their victims, and consumerism had taken the place of protests. However, those years remain in memory as a time when one could believe in something, an era of great mistakes and great passions. Perhaps the bitterest lesson is that a people without ideals is a people easily manipulated, and that the void left by disillusionment can be more dangerous than any external threat.

THEN THE WALL FELL...

Anyone over fifty in Italy will certainly remember the wave of TV series and mafia-themed fiction that took over the mid-1980s in the Bel Paese. Actor Michele Placido, in the role of detective Cattani, became the national hero in the fight against the Octopus, embodying the collective desire to rid the country of the mafia's stranglehold. It was an era when a disturbing yet deeply rooted reality was uncovered – or rather, made public: men wearing flat caps and carrying shotguns were holding not only Sicily, but the entire nation in their grip.

With the fall of the Berlin Wall, an event that reshaped global geopolitical and cultural dynamics, Italy had its own epiphany. While in South America the focus shifted to the now-disgraced dictators, and in the East to the fanatical mujahideen, in Italy the spotlight turned to the Mafia. It was as if the collapse of the Wall had lifted the veil on a reality that many knew about, but few dared to speak of: the mafia was not just a regional issue, but a system that permeated every facet of power, from institutions to the economy.

At this point, one question arises: if the Latin American dictators and the mujahideen had played a crucial role in maintaining the Atlantic Order during the Cold War, could the Italian mafia have been equally functional? Did the collusion between powerful elites and organized crime perhaps serve a strategic purpose on the grand geopolitical chessboard?

To find an answer, going back to the history books might help, but only up to a point. Because in Italy, some pages were never written, or rather, they remain between the lines. However, some clues do emerge from documents preserved across the ocean, in American archives.

For some time, historians and researchers have argued that, during World War II, U.S. authorities formed a tactical alliance with the mafia to facilitate the Allied invasion of Sicily. If this relationship is confirmed, it would have laid the groundwork for a mutually beneficial connection that lasted long beyond the conflict.

FROM THE N Y'S PORT TO THE BEACHES OF SICILY: THE PACT BETWEEN USA AND LUCKY LUCIANO

During World War II, the stakes were so high that even the most unspeakable agreements became acceptable.

It is in this context that the curious – and troubling – alliance between the United States government and the Italian-American mafia, led by Charles "Lucky" Luciano, took shape. A collaboration that began in the ports of New York and culminated on the beaches of Sicily, marking one of the most controversial chapters in history.

In 1942, with the war in full swing, the United States was obsessed with the possibility of sabotage in its ports. The Port of New York, the largest and most strategic in the country, was particularly vulnerable. The fear was not unfounded: in February of that year, the transatlantic liner *Normandie*, docked in Manhattan, was devastated by a mysterious fire. Although authorities officially declared it an accident, the suspicion that German or Italian spies were behind it never left the minds of American officials.

The Naval Intelligence Office, desperate over the risk of new sabotage attempts, realized that true control of the ports was not in the hands of the government, but of organized crime. The dock workers, often tied to local bosses, answered more to the codes of the mafia than to the laws of the state.

It was then that intelligence decided to turn to a highly questionable yet effective ally: Lucky Luciano, the "king of organized crime" in New York, who was at the time incarcerated for crimes related to the prostitution racket.

Despite being behind bars, Luciano maintained a widespread influence over the city's criminal activities. American agents made him an offer: collaboration in exchange for favorable treatment.

Luciano accepted.

Through his contacts, he ensured security at the New York ports and the monitoring of suspicious activities. Sabotages ceased, and the port returned to being a controlled zone.

But the agreement didn't end there.

When the Allies began planning the invasion of Sicily, the island presented itself as a minefield of political and social complexities. In addition to enemy troops, the Allies faced a network of power deeply rooted in mafia clans that had controlled the territory for centuries. The Americans soon realized that conquering Sicily without the mafia's cooperation would have been impossible.

Thanks to Luciano, contacts with Sicilian mafia bosses were established. The local mafia ensured that the invasion went smoothly: American soldiers found clear roads and received crucial intelligence on the movements of Italian and German troops. In return, the mafia bosses were promised a return to power they had lost under the fascist regime, which had persecuted them.

The invasion of Sicily in July 1943, known as Operation Husky, was a strategic success and marked the beginning of Italy's liberation.

Up to this point, everything is backed by documents. To connect the rest, however, we must eavesdrop behind the doors of the cynics.

According to these accounts, behind the military victory lay a hidden cost: the resurgence of the Sicilian mafia, which became even more deeply embedded in the island's political and economic fabric. Eager for stability, the Allies appointed mayors and local administrators directly from the mafia ranks, creating a power structure that would have lasting consequences for decades.

The agreement between the United States and Luciano remained a well-kept secret for a long time. It was only after the war, with Luciano's sentence commuted and his extradition to Italy in 1946, that details of this collaboration began to surface.

Although U.S. authorities have always downplayed the incident, documents and testimonies gathered over the years confirm that the pact with the mafia was a strategic decision driven by wartime necessity.

Thus, the story of the Sicily landing is not just one of military triumph, but also one of moral compromise. The

United States, champions of democracy, allied with one of the symbols of organized crime to secure their success.
An operation that, on one hand, led to the liberation of Italy, but on the other, left a heavy legacy: a strengthened mafia, ready to claim its share of power in the postwar period.
This is where the famous "missing slice of cake" would land—the one that granted the right to control the management of the underground economy generated by criminal activities.
Thus, while Italy reinvented itself as a western pillar, internal contradictions grew. The apparent stability masked a system in which shadow powers and external influences moved behind the scenes. Perhaps the greatest postwar illusion was believing that Italy had fully achieved its autonomy. Rather, it had become a key pawn in a much larger game, a political and social laboratory where strategies of containment, manipulation, and control were being tested.
In the postwar years, the mafia returned to fill the void left by fascism, becoming both an economic and political player in the South. While the Christian Democracy (DC) ensured stability, mafia bosses guaranteed votes and control of the territory, often in exchange for protection and impunity.
The mafia wasn't just a local issue: its interests were intertwined with those of businessmen, politicians, and even intelligence agencies. Some conspiracy theorists, trying to piece together a picture—especially since other avenues to the truth are still sealed—have even suggested that the mafia acted as a "cleaner," removing inconvenient figures from the scene.

FALL OF THE WALL AND THE METAMORPHOSIS OF THE MAFIAS: NEW ROUTES, OLD SCHEMES

At this point, one question arises naturally: why, in the mid-1980s, was Commissioner Cattani turned into a TV hero tasked with destroying a mafia that, up until then, had been functional to the system? The answer may seem simple, but it's not: like any mechanism, the mafia has its own cycle of usefulness.

With the fall of the Berlin Wall, the old mafia was no longer needed. To be clear, the mafia is always useful, but perhaps a new version was required—one better suited to the new geopolitical balance and less compromised by the high-profile murders that had shaken public opinion, with victims being state officials who were guilty only of doing their job.

Thus, the fall of the Wall in 1989 did not just reshape the global geopolitical order, it also influenced the geography of mafia organizations in Italy. The ideological barrier separating East from West had regulated economic, political, and criminal flows. With its collapse, Cosa Nostra and the Camorra began to lose influence, while the 'Ndrangheta demonstrated an extraordinary ability to adapt to the new context, turning change into opportunity, especially in the drug trade.

The 'Ndrangheta, already a leader in cocaine trafficking due to its ties with South American cartels, further strengthened its influence by collaborating with Eastern European criminal groups. Its ability to maintain a low profile and infiltrate financial circuits allowed it to manage huge flows of money, which were laundered through both legal activities in Italy and abroad.

Cosa Nostra, weakened by investigations following the massacres of the 1990s, retained a strategic role in Sicily, acting as an intermediary between large international suppliers and local markets.

The Camorra, meanwhile, consolidated its control over heroin trafficking via Turkey and synthetic drugs produced in the Netherlands and Belgium.

Finally, the Sacra Corona Unita, thanks to its geographical position, established itself as the ideal bridge for trafficking between the Balkans and Italy.

In the 1990s, the drug market in Italy underwent a significant transformation. While heroin had dominated the 1980s, the following decade saw the rise of cocaine. This shift was driven by growing demand in urban areas and a changed social perception: cocaine, associated with success and power, replaced heroin as the drug of choice for the middle and upper classes. The 'Ndrangheta, bolstered by its ties to Colombian and Mexican cartels, became Europe's leading player in drug trafficking. Thanks to its familial structure and direct control of maritime routes, it solidified its position. Ports like Gioia Tauro, the largest container hub in the Mediterranean, became critical centers for drug trafficking, with illicit substances hidden among legitimate goods.

At the same time, the heroin market adapted to the new dynamics. Italian mafias continued to exploit Balkan routes, historically linked to opiate trafficking from Afghanistan, to meet a declining but still significant demand. With the opening of Eastern markets, criminal organizations found ideal territories in former Soviet bloc countries to manage illicit trade. Albania, in particular, became a key crossroads for smuggling, facilitating the landing of drugs on Italy's shores.

An emblematic case of this transformation is that of the Sacra Corona Unita. Its rise is largely due to the fall of the Berlin Wall and the opening of Eastern borders. The author had the privilege of being born and raised in that extraordinary land known as Salento, a region that, until the 1980s, was a paradise compared to the hells of other southern Italian regions. Drugs simply didn't circulate. The Church still held strong social control, and "drug addicts" were considered urban phenomena to be avoided. Then, with the fall of the Wall, something changed. In just a few years, the heroin invasion reached even this small corner of a lost paradise.

The less-patrolled borders and the fragile institutions of Eastern countries became decisive factors. While Italy was attempting to reinvent itself, Italian mafias and their new Eastern allies created a network of trafficking that spanned the Mediterranean and Europe, transforming the Peninsula into a crossroads for global drug trafficking.

THE BALKAN ROUTE AND THE WARS IN YUGOSLAVIA AND KOSOVO

Anyone over the age of 50 will certainly remember the devastating images of the wars in Yugoslavia: long lines of refugees, villages in flames, and cities reduced to rubble. Those who are at least 40 will recall similar scenes from the Kosovo War, a small piece of the former Yugoslavia with an Albanian majority.

During those years, many children—even those in our own homes—learned the word "genocide" before they could say "mama" or "papa," bombarded by news reports of unstoppable horrors.

But there's another, less told, and equally intricate story that intertwines with these armed conflicts: the story of drug trafficking and the notorious Balkan Route. While Croatia, Bosnia, Serbia, and Kosovo were transforming into a mosaic of ethnic and political conflicts, illegal economies found fertile ground in the chaos. In the shadows, while the West sent troops to stop ethnic cleansing, others were digging tunnels and opening "highways" to transport heroin from Afghanistan to Western markets.

The Balkan Route is not a literary invention. It is a real pathway, the main route through which Afghan heroin travels across Iran, Turkey, and the Balkans to reach Europe. With the war in Yugoslavia, this route adapted to new geopolitical realities, exploiting the lack of state control and the spreading chaos.

During the Balkan conflicts, warlords, paramilitary groups, and even government forces found drug trafficking to be an indispensable source of funding. Heroin flowed through Bosnia, Serbia, and Kosovo, enriching traffickers and militias, fueling a machine of death and destruction with the proceeds of drug trade.

In this context, Kosovo assumed a central role. After the NATO intervention in 1999, which marked the end of the war, the country fell into a state of chronic instability. In effect, the region became an operational hub for drug, arms, and human trafficking.

Meanwhile, Western Europe became the final market for this criminal network. Germany, France, Italy, and the United Kingdom, with their high heroin consumption rates, fueled a system where the proceeds from trafficking were laundered through increasingly sophisticated financial networks. Balkan criminal groups worked closely with Italian mafias—from the 'Ndrangheta to the Camorra, to the newly formed Sacra Corona Unita—transforming the profits from drug trafficking into real estate, businesses, and even political influence.

More than twenty years after the end of the Balkan wars, the region remains a crucial node for international drug trafficking. The routes have adapted, increasingly passing through Albania and Montenegro, but the Balkans continue to be one of the main arteries of global drug trafficking. Drugs, once financing wars, have left an indelible mark on the social and economic fabric of the region.

Today, while Europe views the Balkans as a frontier to stabilize, the scars from the conflicts and the criminal networks of those years still influence the geopolitics and economy of the continent.

The greatest tragedy is that the victims are not only counted among the dead, but also among the living: those who fight every day to survive in a region that has never found peace, and those who, from dawn to dusk, are possessed by a single thought: the daily dose of anesthesia, to not see, not speak, and above all, not to "feel."

CONCLUDING

It would be fascinating to review all the hotspots of the drug trade, but the goal here is different: to debunk the myth that addictions are merely “vices” and to recognize them for what they truly are—real diseases. Let’s refocus on our subject and summarize this chapter.

While wars were being fought in the East and the West, sacrificing everything at the altar of National Security, Europe was witnessing a daily drip-drip of destruction.

Until the fall of the Berlin Wall, cocaine, though officially illegal, was perceived as an “acceptable” drug, less dangerous than heroin, whose devastating effects left no doubt.
Some critical observers argue that the flood of cocaine and heroin in the 1970s and 1980s, even in Italy, may have been part of a destabilization strategy aimed at weakening social and political movements during a time marked by deep ideological tensions.
According to these theories, the spread of hard drugs among young people could have contributed to neutralizing a generation of activists and protestors.
Even Italian criminal organizations, such as the 'Ndrangheta, took advantage of the cocaine trade boom, strengthening their role in the global drug market.
From a historical perspective, there are indeed corroborating facts: studies have highlighted connections between Italian organized crime and South American cartels, with Italy quickly becoming a crucial hub for the redistribution of drugs across Europe.
Whether the conspiracy theorists are right or not is still uncertain. What is certain is that both cocaine and heroin played a major role in social and political destabilization, with production and trafficking networks tightly linked to geopolitical dynamics. These drugs still represent a threat not only to public health but also to the political stability of entire countries.

"Thinking badly is a sin... but usually, you're right," said Giulio Andreotti, a leading figure of the Christian Democracy party, who survived even the fall of the Berlin Wall. That being said, it's time to close the history book and open the science one: let’s get back on track and finally reach our destination: understanding why addiction is a real illness!

CHAPTER 5

ADDICTIONS TODAY: **WHAT SCIENCE HAS TO SAY**

By now, it's time to take stock. In the previous chapters, we explored the deep connection between humans and psychoactive substances, as well as obsessive-compulsive behaviors, dating back to ancient times. We saw how this relationship has left a significant mark on every aspect of individual and collective existence. We went further, trying to understand why it is so difficult to recognize addictions as true diseases and implement effective strategies to combat them.

EVOLUTION **OF THE CONCEPT OF ADDICTION**

The concept of addiction has undergone a profound transformation over time.
In the past, as we've seen in previous chapters, addiction was often interpreted as a sign of "moral weakness" or "lack of willpower," a perspective that contributed to deep-rooted prejudice and stigma against those who struggled with it.
However, thanks to scientific advancements, we now understand addiction as a complex, chronic disorder that involves biological, psychological, and social factors. It therefore deserves a broader, more empathetic view.
With the development of modern psychiatry between the 19th and 20th centuries, the concept of addiction began to shift. Pioneers like Dr. Benjamin Rush started to describe alcoholism as a "chronic disease," fostering a new understanding that was later embraced by movements such as

Alcoholics Anonymous and other 12-Step fellowships. These organizations adopted an empathetic approach, moving away from moral judgment. During this period, formal treatments for alcoholism were developed: specialized clinics were established, and psychological and neurological mechanisms behind addiction began to be studied, opening the door to new treatment possibilities.
In the 1960s and 1970s, neurosciences led to a further shift in perspective, demonstrating that addiction is, in fact, a brain disorder.
The discovery of the reward circuit—a network of brain areas associated with pleasure sensations—revealed that substance use not only alters these circuits but also changes the structure of the brain itself.
In particular, it was found that dopamine, a neurotransmitter central to feelings of reward, plays a key role in addiction.
The National Institute on Drug Abuse (NIDA) thus defined addiction as a "chronic, relapsing brain disease," promoting pharmacological therapies capable of restoring neurochemical balance.
Over time, the concept of addiction expanded further, embracing the biopsychosocial model, supported by organizations such as the World Health Organization and the American Medical Association.
According to this view, addiction is a chronic and complex disease in which biological (such as genetic predispositions), psychological (e.g., trauma), and social (unfavorable environments) factors are intertwined.
This model has encouraged the adoption of multidisciplinary treatments that consider the person in their entirety, combining pharmacological therapies, psychotherapy, support groups, and social interventions.
It is an approach that has definitively moved beyond moralistic views, fostering a deeper understanding and treatments based on empathy and inclusion.
Today, speaking of addiction means putting aside old judgments and adopting a scientific and complex perspective.

The WHO defines addiction as a "condition characterized by a compulsive need to continue using a substance despite harm to health, social, and work life." Dr. Nora Volkow, director of the NIDA, describes it as a "chronic brain disease," in which the need for the substance becomes uncontrollable, even in the face of severe consequences.

Addiction, in fact, works by rewriting the brain's priorities: the need for the substance is perceived as essential for survival, and the release of dopamine becomes so intense that it makes it extremely difficult to stop.

Abuse and addiction, although often confused, present important differences. While abuse refers to the risky or harmful use of a substance, addiction manifests itself with a physical and psychological need for the substance, making withdrawal extremely complex.

The American Psychiatric Association clarifies that addiction involves profound neurological changes, in which the substance is perceived as indispensable.

Ultimately, the concept of addiction has undergone a gradual but fundamental evolution: from a simple lack of willpower, it has become the subject of scientific study that has led to more humane and comprehensive treatment. This journey has allowed for a better understanding of the many facets of addiction, highlighting the importance of targeted treatments that help individuals restore balance to their lives with dignity.

THE DSM-5 DIAGNOSTIC CRITERIA FOR SUBSTANCE USE DISORDER (SUD)

"Substance Use Disorder" (SUD) is an official diagnosis based on eleven criteria from the DSM-5, used to determine the severity of the disorder (mild, moderate, or severe) based on symptoms, including:

1. Using the substance in larger amounts or for longer periods than intended.
2. Failed attempts to reduce or stop use.

3. Excessive time spent obtaining, using, or recovering from the substance.
4. Intense craving for the substance.
5. Inability to fulfill daily responsibilities.
6. Social or interpersonal problems caused by use.
7. Continued use despite health-related consequences.
8. Reduction in social or recreational activities.
9. Use in dangerous situations (e.g., driving under the influence).
10. Use despite awareness of harm.
11. Development of tolerance or withdrawal symptoms.

This classification allows for targeted, evidence-based treatment.

BEHAVIORAL ADDICTIONS: A NEW FIELD OF STUDY

The concept of addiction has expanded beyond the realm of chemical substances: today, science recognizes that certain behaviors can also lead to true addiction, with symptoms and consequences similar to those of substance use disorders.

These "behavioral addictions" include activities such as gambling, compulsive use of technology, eating disorders, and other behaviors that, when prolonged and out of control, disrupt daily life. This emerging field of study has gained increasing attention in recent years. Consequently, there has been recognition of the importance of addressing the neurobiological and psychological mechanisms shared between substance addictions and behavioral addictions.

GAMBLING ADDICTION: THE BRAIN'S FIRST RECOGNIZED BEHAVIORAL DEPENDENCY

Pathological gambling was the first behavioral addiction officially recognized by the *American Psychiatric Association's Diagnostic and Statistical Manual of Mental Disorders (DSM-5)*.

This condition shares characteristics with substance addiction: a gambler's compulsive behavior leads to tolerance (the need to wager increasingly larger amounts to achieve the same level of excitement), withdrawal symptoms (nervousness, restlessness, or irritability when abstaining from gambling), and an inability to control their actions.

Gambling exploits the brain's reward circuit: each win triggers dopamine's release, creating a "high" that gamblers strive to replicate. This cycle of exhilaration and disappointment can lead to destructive behaviors, financial ruin, and damaged relationships.

Recognizing pathological gambling as an addiction was a crucial step in understanding how seemingly harmless activities can trigger similar addictive patterns.

TECHNOLOGY ADDICTION: THE "ALWAYS CONNECTED" IMPULSE

The compulsive use of technology, particularly social media, video games, and smartphones, represents one of the most widespread and modern behavioral addictions. Social media addiction, for instance, exploits the brain's reward circuit by offering instant gratification through "likes," comments, and notifications. Each new digital interaction triggers dopamine release, compelling individuals to check their devices with increasing frequency.

Video games, in particular, pose a high risk of addiction: game mechanics, such as leveling systems, rewards, and objectives, are designed to sustain engagement and stimulate dopamine release. In some cases, this addiction leads to social isolation, concentration problems, and difficulties managing time and daily responsibilities.

Asian countries were among the first to formally recognize video game addiction, developing specialized treatment programs to address this phenomenon.

FOOD-RELATED DISORDERS AND COMPULSIVE EATING

The relationship with food can become a behavioral addiction, especially when a compulsion develops for sugary and fatty foods. This addiction is often fueled by activation of the brain's reward circuit, driving some individuals to seek immediate gratification in food to relieve stress, anxiety, or negative emotions.

Food becomes a "comfort drug," providing temporary relief while creating a cycle of dependency and suffering.

Disorders like bulimia, binge eating, and anorexia nervosa fit into this framework, sharing characteristics with substance addictions, such as loss of control, tolerance (the need to consume more to achieve the same comforting effect), and feelings of guilt. Those suffering from these conditions are often trapped in a cycle of shame and food abuse that undermines both physical and mental health.

Anorexia nervosa stands out for its extreme food restriction, leading to very low body weight, intense fear of gaining weight, and a distorted body image.

Bulimia nervosa, on the other hand, alternates binge eating with compensatory behaviors such as self-induced vomiting, laxative abuse, or excessive exercise.

In binge eating disorder, episodes of uncontrolled eating are frequent but lack compensatory behaviors, increasing the risk of overweight and obesity.

These disorders have complex roots, influenced by biological, psychological, and social factors. Research suggests that imbalances in neurotransmitters like serotonin and dopamine can affect eating behavior. At the same time, psychological factors such as low self-esteem, perfectionism, and social anxiety contribute to their onset. Social pressures, particularly cultural ideals favoring thinness, can further exacerbate the need for control over food.

The health consequences are severe, including electrolyte imbalances, gastrointestinal damage, osteoporosis, and heart problems.

Recognizing the symptoms and intervening with a targeted, multidisciplinary therapeutic approach—often involving psychological support and, in some cases, medication—is essential to breaking the cycle and restoring well-being.

OTHER COMPULSIVE BEHAVIORS: SHOPPING, DEBT, AND HOARDING

Other behaviors that can evolve into addictions include compulsive shopping and compulsive hoarding, also known as hoarding disorder. While hoarding disorder does not fall under the category of "classic" addictions, it shares several characteristics typical of addictive behaviors, such as compulsion and an inability to exercise rational control. In hoarding disorder, individuals feel an overwhelming need to save and accumulate objects, often without practical or sentimental value, fearing anxiety or distress if they discard them. For many, hoarding provides temporary relief from anxiety or a fleeting sense of gratification. Over time, this need to hold onto items becomes a routine that is difficult to break, creating a cycle of accumulation and increasing distress.

As with other addictions, hoarding disorder is influenced by psychological factors, including anxiety, perfectionism, and difficulty regulating emotions. Environmental factors also play a role: feelings of isolation or chronic stress can trigger or exacerbate hoarding behavior.

Compulsive shopping, on the other hand, is characterized by a relentless need to purchase items in pursuit of relief or momentary pleasure. Those struggling with this addiction often buy things they don't need, accumulating debt and experiencing guilt and dissatisfaction.

RELATIONAL ADDICTIONS

Relational addictions occur when an individual forms an emotional bond so intense and visceral with another person that they sacrifice their own well-being and autonomy, either consciously or unconsciously.

Two of the most recognized forms are co-dependency and emotional dependency, both characterized by an overwhelming desire for approval and affection that often leads to a symbiotic, and frequently dysfunctional, relationship.

In co-dependency, individuals build their identity and sense of self-worth around the need to "save" or "help" the other person, even at their own expense. This dynamic is common in relationships where one person struggles with an issue, such as substance addiction. The codependent individual feels responsible for the other's well-being, dedicating themselves to caregiving while suffering deeply from their emotional reliance.

Emotional dependency, on the other hand, is marked by an intense fear of loneliness and an inability to feel content without the constant presence of a significant other. Those with emotional dependency fear abandonment and often accept unfulfilling or even harmful situations to avoid losing their partner. This form of addiction also engages the brain's reward circuit: receiving attention or affection triggers dopamine production, fueling a compulsive need to stay with the other person despite conflicts or disappointments.

Both forms of relational addiction can lead to symptoms of anxiety, depression, and low self-esteem. Often, individuals struggling with these dependencies find it difficult to build a solid identity outside the relationship or to regulate their emotions.

Recognizing the signs of these dynamics and addressing them through therapeutic support is crucial to restoring balance, enhancing self-esteem, and fostering healthy, autonomous relationships.

BEHAVIORAL AND SUBSTANCE ADDICTIONS: SIMILARITIES AND DIFFERENCES

Behavioral addictions, such as gambling, social media use, or compulsive eating, share many neurobiological mechanisms with substance addictions. In both cases, the brain's reward circuit and dopamine release play a central role.

Each time an individual engages in an addictive activity—whether involving a substance or a behavior—the brain releases dopamine, creating a pleasurable sensation that encourages repetition of the experience. Over time, however, the brain adapts to these elevated dopamine levels, developing tolerance: the individual becomes less sensitive to the peaks of pleasure and feels driven to repeat the behavior more frequently.

This phenomenon leads to a compulsive cycle that is difficult to break, and in the absence of access to the addictive experience, withdrawal-like symptoms such as irritability, anxiety, and depression may arise.

The primary difference between behavioral and substance addictions lies in the absence of an external chemical in the former. However, the brain reacts similarly, and the psychological and social consequences can be just as devastating. Behavioral addiction still stimulates dopamine production and other neurotransmitters through repetitive activities that link to pleasure. As in substance addictions, behavioral addictions feature symptoms like craving (a strong desire to relive the experience), tolerance, and withdrawal. Tolerance drives individuals to seek increasingly intense stimuli to achieve the initial pleasure, while withdrawal, though more psychological than physical, can cause significant distress. For example, those addicted to gambling or social media may experience intense emotional symptoms such as irritability, anxiety, and depression, similar to those seen in substance withdrawal, albeit without severe physical effects.

The "substance-free" nature of behavioral addictions makes them harder to identify and may lead individuals to underestimate their severity. This delay in awareness can worsen the situation, making it more difficult to recognize the problem and seek help.

From a therapeutic perspective, while both behavioral and substance addictions benefit from approaches like cognitive-behavioral therapy and support programs, their interventions differ. Substance addictions often require pharmacological support to manage physical withdrawal symptoms, whereas behavioral addictions focus on psychological and behavioral interventions aimed at regulating, rather than entirely eliminating, compulsive activities—such as technology use or eating.

The physical and psychosocial consequences of behavioral addictions, though not directly involving the body as with substance use, can still be severe. For instance, compulsive gambling can lead to chronic stress and insomnia, while compulsive eating may result in obesity and metabolic health issues. Both forms of addiction can disrupt personal and professional lives, causing isolation, financial hardship, and relational difficulties.

Despite their impact, behavioral addictions tend to receive less attention, and those affected often find less understanding or support.

On a psychological level, both types of addiction share similar emotional and psychological responses, often tied to a need for "self-medication" to cope with stress, anxiety, or painful emotions. Addictive behavior becomes a way to temporarily escape reality, creating a form of emotional anesthesia that eventually adds further stress and anxiety.

Ultimately, behavioral and substance addictions share a neurobiological core and symptoms such as craving, tolerance, and withdrawal.

THE BRAIN'S CHEMISTRY **AND THE REWARD CIRCUIT**

In previous sections, we explored how the human brain is equipped with a complex system known as the reward circuit, which motivates behaviors essential for survival.

This mechanism, involving multiple brain regions and various neurotransmitters, generates sensations of pleasure and gratification, encouraging repetition of activities like eating or socializing. However, the reward circuit can be disrupted by the use of psychoactive substances, which overstimulate it and trigger a compulsive desire often leading to addiction.

The reward system operates through structures such as the nucleus accumbens, the ventral tegmental area (VTA), and the prefrontal cortex. When we experience pleasure, the VTA releases dopamine, a neurotransmitter that generates feelings of gratification. This signal spreads to the nucleus accumbens and prefrontal cortex, creating a reinforcement loop that drives us to seek pleasurable experiences. Dopamine, often referred to as the "pleasure neurotransmitter," is crucial for motivation and learning, as it signals the significance of an event.

Substances like cocaine and amphetamines directly affect dopamine, inducing temporary euphoria. However, prolonged exposure to such elevated levels results in reduced receptor sensitivity, requiring increasing amounts of the substance to achieve the same effect, thereby fueling the addiction process.

Beyond dopamine, other neurotransmitters play pivotal roles in the reward system.

- **Serotonin** regulates mood, sleep, and appetite; extended use of substances like alcohol and MDMA, which temporarily boost its production, can lead to mood imbalances.

- **Glutamate**, vital for learning and memory, works alongside dopamine to reinforce associations between behavior and gratification, solidifying the urge to repeat certain experiences.
- **GABA**, the primary inhibitory neurotransmitter, calms excitatory signals. Chronic use of benzodiazepines, which enhance GABA, can diminish its natural effectiveness, resulting in anxiety.
- **Norepinephrine**, associated with stress response, and **anandamide**, an endocannabinoid promoting relaxation, complete the picture. Prolonged cannabis use, which interacts with anandamide receptors, can impair their natural function.

Under normal conditions, the reward system maintains equilibrium within the body. However, psychoactive substances disrupt this delicate mechanism, creating an imbalance that makes it difficult to cease use and overcome addiction.

At the root of addiction are chemical processes that alter the reward circuit's normal functioning. Pleasurable substances and behaviors modify neurotransmitter levels, effectively creating a "short circuit" that fuels compulsive need. Excessive dopamine release, triggered by drugs like cocaine and alcohol, produces intense euphoria but, over time, desensitizes the brain to these peaks, diminishing the ability to derive pleasure from everyday experiences.

In this state of addiction-induced anhedonia, previously fulfilling activities lose their appeal, leaving life without the substance or behavior feeling empty. This compels individuals to seek artificial gratification. Prolonged exposure to elevated dopamine levels leads to receptor desensitization, necessitating higher doses to achieve the same effect. Simultaneously, other neurotransmitters are disrupted, negatively affecting mood, memory, stress management, and reactivity.

These changes strengthen the addiction cycle, making it increasingly challenging to break free.

THE ROLE OF NEURAL PLASTICITY

Neural plasticity, the brain's ability to adapt and reorganize itself based on experiences, plays a pivotal role in addiction.
Through repeated substance use or compulsive behaviors, the brain progressively alters its connections, reinforcing the neural circuits linked to addiction. What might initially have been a voluntary choice transforms into an automatic response. These connections become so entrenched that even when the desire to quit arises, breaking free from addictive behavior becomes an incredibly challenging task.

Ultimately, addiction profoundly disrupts the brain’s natural mechanisms. Each compulsive repetition of behaviors or substance use triggers a cascade of neurochemical adaptations that strengthen the cycle of addiction. Breaking this cycle is both difficult and painful, as the brain requires time and support to restore its balance.
Only through targeted treatment and a gradual process can the brain relearn how to find pleasure in everyday experiences, allowing individuals to reclaim a balanced and fulfilling life.

RISK FACTORS:
GENETICS AND VULNERABILITY

Addiction is a complex, chronic disease influenced not only by exposure to substances or behaviors but also by a genetic predisposition that can significantly increase individual vulnerability.
Scientific studies reveal that genetics play a substantial role in the risk of developing an addiction, accounting for as much as 50-60% of overall susceptibility.
This risk is not tied to a single gene but arises from a complex interplay of genetic variants interacting with one another and with environmental factors, uniquely shaping each individual’s vulnerability.

THE DRD2 GENE AND GRATIFICATION

Among the key genetic factors linked to addiction are genes that influence the functioning of the reward circuit. A pivotal role is played by the **DRD2 gene**, one of the most studied in this context, which encodes the dopamine D2 receptor. The D2 receptor acts as a "receiver" for dopamine, the neurotransmitter responsible for sensations of pleasure and reward. Dopamine sends gratification signals to the brain, encouraging individuals to repeat experiences deemed pleasurable or beneficial.

Certain genetic variants of the **DRD2 gene** are associated with reduced expression of the D2 receptor, meaning the brain responds less effectively to dopamine.

In other words, individuals with these variants experience pleasure and satisfaction less intensely compared to those with a "normal" dopaminergic response. This reduced sensitivity may cause the brain to demand more intense stimuli to achieve a comparable level of gratification.

As a result, individuals with these DRD2 gene variants may feel more driven to seek external sources of stimulation, such as alcohol, nicotine, or cocaine—substances that temporarily boost dopamine levels. These intense stimuli amplify the reward circuit's response, momentarily compensating for the D2 receptor's low sensitivity and providing a sense of pleasure that may feel particularly rewarding.

In this way, alcohol, nicotine, and cocaine act as "chemical compensators," helping the brain achieve a balance that would otherwise be difficult to obtain.

However, continuous use of these substances creates a vicious cycle: in the effort to constantly stimulate the reward circuit, the risk of developing addiction increases, making it progressively harder to break free from the behavior.

THE CYP2A6 GENE AND NICOTINE

Other genes influence the metabolism of substances, determining how quickly the body processes them.

For example, the **CYP2A6 gene** regulates nicotine metabolism. Individuals with a variant of CYP2A6 that slows this metabolism tend to develop less dependence, as nicotine remains active in the body for longer, reducing the urge to consume more. Conversely, those who metabolize nicotine more quickly are likely to consume it in larger amounts to maintain stable levels in the bloodstream, increasing the likelihood of addiction.

THE ADH1B AND ALDH2 GENES AND ALCOHOL

Genes such as **ADH1B** and **ALDH2**, which influence alcohol metabolism, also play a significant role. A variant of the **ALDH2 gene**, found in certain Asian populations, causes an intense and unpleasant reaction to alcohol, thereby reducing the risk of alcohol abuse.

Addiction vulnerability is also linked to genes that regulate behavioral traits like anxiety and impulsivity. Some genes modulate the neurotransmitter GABA, essential for anxiety control; lower GABA activity has been associated with higher anxiety levels and an increased propensity to use substances as a form of "self-medication" for relief. Alcohol, for instance, stimulates GABA and temporarily reduces anxiety, making individuals with a genetic predisposition to low GABA levels more likely to develop addiction.

THE MAOA GENE

Another relevant gene is **MAOA**, which regulates serotonin and norepinephrine, affecting impulsivity and risky decision-making. Specific variants of MAOA can make individuals more prone to impulsive reactions, increasing the risk of initiating substance use and developing addiction.

POLYGENIC INHERITANCE

Addiction is not determined by a single gene but is the result of complex polygenic inheritance: a combination of genetic variants that interact to increase overall risk.

Each gene contributes a small weight to the scale of vulnerability, and when an individual carries multiple predisposing variants, the likelihood of developing addiction rises, especially in the presence of unfavorable environmental factors such as chronic stress or early exposure to substances.

The genetics of addiction is, therefore, highly intricate, intertwining with life experiences, social environment, and psychological traits, making addiction a uniquely variable condition from one individual to another.

THE ROLE OF ENVIRONMENT, SOCIETY, AND CULTURE

Addiction is a complex, multidimensional condition that cannot be solely attributed to genetic or chemical predispositions. Understanding how environment, society, and culture influence its development is crucial. Factors such as family and social environment, childhood experiences, trauma, and societal pressures play a key role in shaping an individual's vulnerability to addiction. These elements create a context that can either mitigate or exacerbate susceptibility to addictive behaviors, influencing how individuals respond to challenges and stimuli.

The family environment has a profound impact. Growing up in a stable, supportive family with open communication and emotional backing often serves as a protective factor against addiction. Conversely, a dysfunctional family environment lacking emotional support and clear rules can increase vulnerability. The presence of positive role models is also critical: children who witness adults regularly using substances may develop a tolerant attitude toward consumption, making future use more likely. Additionally, easy access to drugs or alcohol heightens the risk of addiction, especially during youth—a time of heightened experimentation.

Childhood experiences, particularly early trauma, are pivotal in brain development and can significantly increase the risk of addiction later in life. Studies on Adverse Childhood Experiences (ACEs) have shown a correlation between traumatic events such as abuse, neglect, or the loss of a parent and the likelihood of developing addictions. Such traumas can disrupt the brain's neurotransmitter balance, making it more prone to stress responses and seeking relief through substances or compulsive behaviors.

Difficulty in managing emotions, often stemming from a trauma-filled childhood, drives individuals toward experiences that temporarily ease their pain but may become dangerous. The link between trauma and addiction is both direct and profound. Trauma doesn't only include extreme experiences like violence or abuse but also emotional neglect and toxic relationships, which can trigger chronic stress responses in the brain. This constant tension alters the functioning of brain regions like the amygdala and hippocampus, which are involved in emotional regulation and memory.

For many, substances or compulsive behaviors become a form of "self-medication," a temporary solution to manage otherwise unbearable emotional pain. Addiction thus evolves into a coping strategy for inner suffering, quickly becoming a cycle that is hard to break.

Social pressure and cultural norms also play a decisive role in influencing addiction-related behaviors. Modern society often glamorizes the use of certain substances, portraying them as part of leisure or as symbols of status. In many social settings, such as parties or high-stress workplaces, the use of alcohol or other substances is normalized or even encouraged, making it hard to refuse—particularly for those seeking acceptance or conformity within a group. In some cultures, alcohol consumption is tied to conviviality, while in others, substances like tobacco or cannabis are ingrained in popular culture and presented as tools for relaxation or socialization. Media, films, and music reinforce these messages, especially among young people, who may be drawn to emulate the cultural models they observe.

The relentless productivity culture in many modern societies promotes the use of stimulants to keep up with increasingly demanding lifestyles. Substances like caffeine, nicotine, and even stronger medications are used to enhance focus or reduce fatigue, particularly in competitive academic or professional environments. This reliance on stimulants can lead to addiction, fostering a psychological and physical dependency to meet societal expectations of success and performance.

Peer pressure, especially among young people, is another significant factor driving substance use. In certain social contexts, such as parties or nightlife venues, substance use becomes so prevalent that it feels like an integral part of the experience.

The fear of being excluded or judged for not participating often compels individuals to conform, leading them to adopt behaviors that may eventually evolve into addiction.

Media, especially social media, play a significant role in portraying substance use or compulsive behaviors as normal or glamorous aspects of life. Movies, TV series, and social networks contribute to crafting an image that can make addiction seem less dangerous, or even a symbol of rebellion or charisma.

Cultural norms also influence differences in risk across social groups. In some cultures, alcohol and substance use are tied to gender stereotypes, such as associating consumption with notions of masculinity. This pushes men to consume more to maintain a "virile" image. Conversely, in settings where certain substances are heavily stigmatized, users may experience shame—a feeling that often exacerbates addiction.

Poverty and social isolation are additional factors that heighten the risk of addiction, as individuals facing challenging circumstances may turn to substances as a temporary escape from the difficulties of daily life.

Fortunately, cultural contexts can also serve as protective factors against addiction. Societies that promote healthy lifestyles, social support, and positive recreational activities can reduce the likelihood of developing addictive behaviors.

In some settings, there is a growing embrace of empathetic approaches to mental health, decreasing the reliance on substances to cope with stress. Where psychological well-being is prioritized, individuals have access to alternative resources to address challenges, making them less likely to seek relief in harmful behaviors.

In summary, addiction is shaped by a complex interplay of genetic, environmental, and cultural factors. The normalization of certain behaviors, social pressures, and media representations can increase vulnerability, but environments that foster mental health and social support can make a crucial difference. Recognizing the influence of culture and social context is essential for preventing addiction and fostering a more empathetic and informed understanding of the phenomenon.

THE NEW FRONTIER:
EPIGENETICS AND GENETIC PLASTICITY

The genetic code, embedded within the DNA of cells, contains all the instructions necessary for an organism's physical and functional traits. However, the expression of these genes is not static; it can be influenced by life experiences and environmental factors.

This process, known as gene expression, determines how DNA translates into observable or functional traits, such as eye color, susceptibility to certain diseases, or even aspects of personality.

Some characteristics, like eye color, are strictly defined by DNA and remain unchanged regardless of the environment. However, other traits are more "flexible" and can be shaped by two processes: epigenetics and genetic plasticity.

Epigenetics acts as a switch that regulates gene activation without altering the DNA itself, using mechanisms such as DNA methylation or histone modifications. These changes, which can be temporary or long-lasting, are often responses to external stimuli like stress or diet and, in some cases, can even be passed on to descendants.

Genetic plasticity, on the other hand, refers to the organism's ability to adapt to varying environmental conditions without altering the DNA sequence. It allows the body to express different traits depending on the context while utilizing the same genetic blueprint—for instance, as seen when lung capacity develops more extensively in individuals living at high altitudes.
To better understand, think of DNA as a book of instructions: epigenetics and genetic plasticity represent the different ways this book is read. Epigenetics functions like a bookmarking system that "switches on" or "switches off" sections of the book, while genetic plasticity interprets the text differently depending on the context, adapting the body's functions to environmental needs.

EPIGENETICS AND GENETIC PLASTICITY IN ADDICTION

Genetic plasticity offers promising prospects for treating addiction, enabling the "reprogramming" of the body's genetic responses to reduce vulnerability to relapse.
As we've seen, certain genes may predispose individuals to addiction, but the environment and life experiences play a crucial role. The brain operates like a device that adjusts its settings based on its surroundings: prolonged substance use, for example, can activate or deactivate genes linked to addiction, making even those without a genetic predisposition vulnerable.
In the context of addiction, substance use activates specific genes associated with pleasure and reward, heightening the brain's sensitivity to such experiences. Over time, these persistent activations generate craving—a growing desire for consumption. It is as if the brain becomes accustomed to functioning with the substance, perceiving it as essential for normal operation.
Epigenetic mechanisms, through processes such as methylation and acetylation, regulate the activation and deactivation of genes. Methylation "switches off" genes, while

acetylation "switches them on." For instance, cocaine stimulates acetylation, intensifying dopamine production and the desire for consumption, whereas methylation reduces the activity of certain receptors, contributing to tolerance and driving the need for higher doses to achieve the same effect.

Another critical factor is **synaptic plasticity**, which strengthens or weakens the connections between neurons in response to stimuli. In the presence of a substance, these connections become more robust, making memories associated with consumption more persistent. This persistence hinders abstinence and increases the likelihood of relapse.

THE THEORETICAL EXAMPLE OF IDENTICAL TWINS

To understand how epigenetics and genetic plasticity interact with the environment, imagine a pair of identical twins—genetically identical—with a predisposition to addiction.

One twin grows up with their biological family, where the parents struggle with addiction, in an environment characterized by stress, emotional instability, and dysfunctional behavior. The other twin is adopted by an emotionally stable family with no addiction issues, providing a healthy and supportive context.

For the twin who remains with the biological family, the presence of emotional stress and negative influences might activate the genes predisposed to addiction. In such an environment, the brain responds to epigenetic signals by "switching on" those genetic markers associated with addiction risk. It's as if, by living in that context, the DNA's "bookmarks" that make those genes more accessible are activated, increasing the likelihood of developing addictive behaviors.

In contrast, the twin raised in a balanced family would experience the opposite. In a positive, stable environment, the epigenetic activation of addiction-predisposing genes would remain "switched off." This context acts as a biological brake, preventing the activation of traits linked to addiction. In this way, epigenetics works as a filter, modulating the activation of predisposed genes based on context, even though the DNA itself remains unchanged.

Genetic plasticity, in turn, allows each twin to adapt to their specific environment. The twin raised in a dysfunctional environment develops coping strategies and behaviors that reflect their surroundings, making them more vulnerable to addiction. On the other hand, the twin in a healthy environment develops emotional regulation skills and resilient behaviors, gaining stability and balance that reduce their risk of addiction.

Genetic plasticity, therefore, helps each twin respond to their living conditions, widening the gap between the paths they are likely to take.

A second example illustrates how epigenetics operates even in the absence of a genetic predisposition to addiction. Imagine two identical twins without an addiction predisposition. One is adopted by a family with addiction issues, while the other grows up in a stable, balanced family. In this case, the twin raised in the dysfunctional environment might develop a vulnerability to addiction through new epigenetic "bookmarks" activated in response to stress and the lack of positive role models. This could lead to heightened impulsivity and a stronger drive for immediate gratification.

Meanwhile, the twin raised in a stable environment would see stress-related genes deactivated and those supporting emotional regulation and psychological well-being activated. Growing up in a healthy context, this twin would be less prone to impulsive behavior and the pursuit of immediate gratification, remaining protected from addiction risks even if exposed to substances later in life.

In both scenarios, genetic plasticity provides additional support. In the dysfunctional context, the twin develops behaviors associated with impulsivity and craving, reinforced by exposure to addiction models. In contrast, the other twin, benefiting from a healthy environment, strengthens skills that promote resilience and emotional regulation, reducing their risk of addiction.

Ultimately, epigenetics and genetic plasticity work together to modulate addiction risk. Epigenetics switches genetic traits on or off based on external conditions, while genetic plasticity allows individuals to adapt to circumstances, generating responses and behaviors that over time may solidify into a path of addiction or resilience.

TOWARDS PERSONALIZED THERAPIES

Recent research on epigenetics and genetic plasticity is opening new therapeutic possibilities for addiction. The goal is to modify or "erase" the epigenetic marks left by addiction on genes, restoring balance to the brain's reward system. Certain medications, for example, work by inhibiting the acetylation of specific genes, thereby reducing craving.

By integrating genetic and epigenetic testing, it becomes possible to develop personalized treatments, tailoring therapies to each individual's genetic and epigenetic characteristics to enhance effectiveness.

Epigenetics and genetic plasticity teach us that it is not just DNA but also the environment and experiences that influence addiction vulnerability. Epigenetic modifications, such as methylation and histone alterations, regulate gene expression and open new pathways for tailored treatments. The hope is to develop epigenetic therapies capable of restoring balanced gene expression, addressing addiction at its root without invasive side effects, and improving recovery outcomes for millions of people.

EXPLORING ADDICTION THROUGH BRAIN IMAGING TECHNIQUES

Neuroscience has made significant strides in understanding addiction, thanks to brain imaging techniques such as functional magnetic resonance imaging (fMRI) and positron emission tomography (PET). These tools allow scientists to observe brain activity in real-time and map the regions involved in addictive behaviors, revealing how addiction profoundly impacts the brain.

fMRI measures brain activity by detecting changes in blood flow, highlighting active areas during specific moments. In addiction studies, this technique has revealed significant alterations in the **reward circuit**, which, as previously noted, includes the nucleus accumbens, the ventral tegmental area, and the prefrontal cortex.

In individuals with addiction, these areas exhibit heightened activity when exposed to stimuli associated with the addictive substance or behavior. This heightened activity reflects the brain's tendency to seek gratification. Simultaneously, fMRI studies have shown reduced activity in the **prefrontal cortex**, the brain region responsible for impulse control and emotional regulation. This diminished function may explain why individuals with addiction struggle to resist compulsive behaviors, as the part of the brain involved in rational decision-making becomes less effective.

PET, on the other hand, uses radioactive tracers to measure the brain's metabolic activity, providing insights into variations in neurotransmitter availability, such as dopamine and serotonin—key components in understanding addiction mechanisms.

PET studies have demonstrated a reduction in dopamine receptor availability in the nucleus accumbens and prefrontal cortex of addicted individuals. This phenomenon reflects dopamine desensitization, meaning the brain adapts to high levels of stimulation and reduces its response to dopamine. As a result, everyday activities lose their capacity to bring pleasure, pushing individuals to seek increasingly intense stimuli for compensation.

Additionally, PET imaging has revealed how substance use disrupts glucose metabolism in the brain, reducing the energy available for cognitive functions and contributing to cognitive deficits.

These imaging techniques have uncovered other structural and functional changes in the brains of individuals with addiction. These include **hyperactivation of the reward circuit**, **reduced prefrontal cortex activity** impairing decision-making abilities, and **hyperactivation of the amygdala**, which intensifies emotional responses like fear and anxiety, further increasing the risk of relapse.

A study by Goldstein and Volkow (2002) utilized fMRI to examine brain activity in individuals addicted to cocaine. The findings revealed **hyperactivation of the reward circuit** in response to drug-related stimuli. This hyperactivation was linked to an intense craving for the substance and compulsive drug-seeking behavior.

Simultaneously, the study identified a **reduction in activity within the dorsolateral prefrontal cortex**, a region critical for impulse control and decision-making. This diminished activity impaired the ability to resist the urge to consume the substance, contributing to the compulsive behaviors characteristic of addiction.

Additionally, the researchers observed **hyperactivation of the amygdala**, a structure involved in regulating emotions such as fear and anxiety. This heightened activity can intensify negative emotional responses, increasing the risk of relapse as individuals may use substances as a coping mechanism to manage such emotions.

These findings have been corroborated by subsequent studies on other substances. For instance, a 2018 investigation by Zilverstand et al. used fMRI to analyze brain activity in individuals with alcohol dependence. The results showed **hyperactivation of the reward circuit** in response to alcohol-related images, a reduction in prefrontal cortex activity, and increased amygdala reactivity—similar patterns to those observed in cocaine addiction.

In summary, neuroimaging techniques have highlighted that substance addiction is associated with:

- **Hyperactivation of the reward circuit**,
- **Reduced activity in the prefrontal cortex**, and
- **Increased amygdala reactivity**.

These neurobiological changes contribute to compulsive behaviors, impaired decision-making, and heightened relapse risks—hallmarks of addiction.

Advancing treatment with brain imaging

Brain imaging has revolutionized not only the understanding of addiction but also how treatment efficacy is monitored. Studies have demonstrated that certain therapies, such as **transcranial magnetic stimulation (TMS)** and **cognitive-behavioral therapy (CBT)**, can reduce abnormal activity in the reward circuit and help restore self-control.

Thanks to these imaging techniques, treatments can be personalized and tailored to the individual responses of patients, making therapy more targeted and effective.

THE USE OF BRAIN IMAGING IN PREVENTION

Brain scans also offer new possibilities for prevention. Identifying individuals with atypical reward circuits or prefrontal cortex activity could help pinpoint those at risk of developing addictions, enabling targeted preventive interventions.

In summary, tools like fMRI and PET have revolutionized the understanding of addiction, revealing its profound impact on the brain, particularly on the reward circuit and cognitive control areas. These discoveries are helping shift addiction from a stigmatized problem to a treatable neurological condition.

LOOKING TO THE FUTURE

Looking ahead, advanced neuroimaging technologies are further enhancing the ability to map the brain areas involved in addiction. Scans are becoming increasingly precise, allowing for the creation of personalized brain maps for each patient.

This development paves the way for the design of tailored therapies aimed at rebalancing the specific abnormalities in each patient's reward circuit, taking addiction treatment to an increasingly advanced and personalized level.

PHARMACOLOGICAL THERAPIES: **BENEFITS AND DRAWBACKS**

Addictions, whether related to substances or behaviors, often require targeted interventions to break the compulsive cycle and facilitate recovery. Among various therapeutic strategies, pharmacological treatments are primarily used for substance addictions and include agonist medications, antagonists, and maintenance therapies. Each has distinct objectives and mechanisms to reduce craving, alleviate withdrawal symptoms, and prevent relapse.

Agonists activate brain receptors in a manner similar to the addictive substance but in a controlled way. For example, methadone is commonly used in opioid addiction therapy; it reduces cravings and withdrawal symptoms without producing the intense euphoria of heroin, enabling patients to lead more stable lives during the early stages of treatment.

Similarly, nicotine is administered through patches, gums, and nasal sprays to ease tobacco dependency. However, it is crucial to consider that prolonged use of opioid agonists or nicotine replacement therapies can result in secondary dependency, as these substances may lead to habituation and tolerance.

Antagonists, on the other hand, block the brain's receptors for addictive substances, reducing the sensation of pleasure and, consequently, the motivation to consume.

For instance, **naltrexone** is used to curb alcohol and opioid consumption by blocking opioid receptors and lowering the risk of relapse. In emergency situations, such as an overdose, **naloxone** acts as a fast-acting antagonist, reversing the substance's effects and saving lives.

MAINTENANCE THERAPIES: A NUANCED APPROACH

Maintenance therapies, which combine agonists and antagonists, are widely used but often raise questions and concerns.

For instance, **buprenorphine**, a partial agonist, reduces cravings without inducing intense euphoria and carries a lower risk of accidental overdose. However, it is crucial that opioid agonist-based therapies are carefully monitored and limited in duration.

As we've seen, while effective in the early stages of recovery, these therapies can easily lead to a new dependency if not properly supervised, complicating the rehabilitation process.

Pharmacological treatments are not a standalone solution but a support system requiring continuous and personalized medical oversight. Each patient has specific needs, and the medication must be selected and dosed based on the type and duration of the addiction, as well as the individual's physical and mental health.

While some individuals respond better to agonists, others benefit more from antagonists or combined therapies.

Pharmacological treatment should be integrated with psychotherapeutic interventions, such as **cognitive-behavioral therapy (CBT)** and support programs, to address the psychological aspects of addiction. Personalization and constant supervision are essential to ensure safety and efficacy, paving the way for a focused and sustainable recovery journey.

LOOKING TO THE FUTURE

Neuropharmacological research is exploring new molecules capable of precisely targeting the key neurotransmitters involved in addiction, such as dopamine, serotonin, glutamate, and GABA.

Sophisticated agonists and antagonists are being developed to modulate these systems with greater accuracy, aiming to control cravings and withdrawal symptoms.

One of the most promising areas is the development of medications that selectively target dopamine receptors within the reward circuit. These drugs aim to reduce cravings without compromising other cognitive and emotional functions.

Other medications that act on the glutamatergic system, which influences learning and memory associated with addiction, could prove useful in reducing relapse rates.

EVIDENCE-BASED PSYCHOTHERAPIES: CBT, DBT, AND MOTIVATIONAL INTERVIEWING

Evidence-based psychotherapies, such as Cognitive Behavioral Therapy (CBT), Dialectical Behavior Therapy (DBT), and Motivational Interviewing (MI), are scientifically validated approaches for treating addiction and other psychological disorders. Each method specifically addresses the thoughts, emotions, and behaviors that fuel addiction, equipping patients with tools to support change and promote well-being.

Cognitive Behavioral Therapy (CBT) is one of the most widely used interventions. It is based on the premise that dysfunctional thoughts can lead to negative emotions and behaviors, working to disrupt this cycle.

For instance, someone struggling with addiction might think, "I can’t handle stress without drinking." CBT helps individuals recognize these thoughts and replace them with more positive and realistic beliefs, such as, "I can learn effective strategies to manage stress without relying on alcohol."

CBT also addresses avoidance habits and fosters coping strategies for managing stress, teaching individuals how to navigate challenging situations without resorting to substances or compulsive behaviors. Through CBT, patients develop greater self-awareness and learn to identify and manage triggers with increased effectiveness.

Dialectical Behavior Therapy (DBT) evolved from CBT and was originally designed to treat borderline personality disorder. Today, it is widely used to address addiction. DBT focuses on emotional regulation, distress tolerance, and mindfulness—teaching individuals to remain fully present and aware of their internal and external experiences without judgment or automatic reactions.

This approach equips patients with strategies to manage intense emotions without resorting to harmful solutions. For individuals with addiction, emotions like shame, anger, or sadness often serve as powerful triggers for substance use. DBT helps patients develop techniques to face these emotions without avoiding them or seeking quick fixes like substance use.

Through mindfulness practices, patients learn to observe their emotions and thoughts without becoming overwhelmed, fostering emotional resilience and enabling them to handle stressful situations in a more balanced and adaptive manner.

Motivational Interviewing (MI) is an empathetic, nondirective method designed to help patients explore and resolve ambivalence about change.

Many individuals struggling with addiction are aware of the harm caused by their behavior but find it difficult to take the first steps toward change. Instead of imposing external goals, MI helps patients discover their own reasons for change. Through exploratory questions and attentive listening, therapists guide patients in weighing the pros and cons of change, encouraging them to take steps to improve their lives.

This approach is particularly effective in the early stages of treatment when motivation is low and can be combined with CBT and DBT to reinforce progress and sustain motivation over the long term.

In conclusion, CBT, DBT, and Motivational Interviewing are powerful, complementary tools for treating addiction. While CBT focuses on dysfunctional thoughts and behaviors, DBT addresses emotional regulation and distress tolerance, and MI strengthens the motivation for change.

By integrating these approaches, patients can build a solid foundation for recovery, learning to navigate emotional challenges, sustain intrinsic motivation, and develop skills to support a life free from addiction.

INNOVATIVE APPROACHES: PSYCHOTHERAPY INTEGRATED WITH PSYCHEDELICS AND TMS

Transcranial Magnetic Stimulation (TMS) and the clinical use of psychedelics represent promising new frontiers in addiction treatment. These approaches aim to reduce cravings, enhance self-control, and address the emotional and cognitive roots of addiction, offering particularly effective solutions for patients who do not respond to conventional treatments while providing safe and personalized alternatives.

Psychedelic-assisted psychotherapy, using substances like psilocybin, MDMA, and ketamine, is opening new and exciting pathways in addiction research. Clinical studies suggest that, when administered in a therapeutic setting under careful supervision, these psychedelics can profoundly affect patients' consciousness, enabling them to reprocess traumatic experiences and behaviors linked to addiction.

The controlled clinical use of psychedelics such as psilocybin, ketamine, and MDMA offers significant possibilities for addiction treatment. These substances alter perception and awareness, allowing patients to explore their consciousness on a deeper level. Combined with psychotherapy, these treatments have shown effectiveness in reducing cravings and breaking thought and behavior patterns that sustain addiction.

For example, **psilocybin**, the active compound in so-called "magic mushrooms," is currently being studied for treating alcohol and tobacco addictions. The transformative experiences it induces appear to help patients reevaluate their relationship with these substances, fostering a new perspective. **Ketamine**, initially used as a dissociative anesthetic, has shown positive results in reducing cravings and managing anxiety and depression—conditions often linked to addiction. Similarly, **MDMA**, commonly known as ecstasy, is being researched for treating addiction, particularly in patients with unresolved trauma.

MDMA facilitates emotional processing, enabling patients to confront the traumas that fuel their addiction. Although these therapies remain experimental, preliminary results highlight their significant potential, especially when integrated with psychotherapy. Combining psychedelics with psychotherapeutic support can promote profound introspection, helping patients develop a more conscious and positive outlook on their lives, guiding them toward recovery through transformation and stability.

TMS AND TDCS

Transcranial Magnetic Stimulation (TMS) is a non-invasive technique that uses magnetic pulses to stimulate specific areas of the brain, such as the dorsolateral prefrontal cortex, which plays a crucial role in self-control and decision-making. In individuals with addictions, this region is often underactive, impairing impulse resistance and leading to compulsive behaviors.
TMS employs a magnetic coil placed on the scalp to deliver targeted pulses that reactivate neuronal activity in this area. Numerous studies have demonstrated that TMS can help reduce cravings and improve impulse control in people with addictions to alcohol, nicotine, and stimulants. Treatment typically involves daily sessions lasting about 30 minutes over several weeks. It requires no anesthesia and allows patients to resume daily activities immediately, making it an ideal option for those who have not benefited from traditional therapies.
In addition to TMS, other non-invasive brain stimulation techniques, such as **transcranial direct current stimulation (tDCS)**, are gaining traction in addiction research. tDCS uses low-intensity electrical currents to stimulate specific brain regions, often focusing on the prefrontal cortex. This technique has shown promise in enhancing self-control and reducing cravings without pharmacological interventions, offering an innovative potential for addiction treatment.
These non-invasive brain stimulation methods represent a new frontier in addiction treatment, providing a safe and effective pathway to recovery through targeted techniques that reactivate and rebalance compromised brain areas.

INNOVATIVE TECHNOLOGIES AND ARTIFICIAL INTELLIGENCE

Artificial intelligence (AI) and digital technologies are paving new pathways in addiction treatment, offering personalized and accessible approaches tailored to the unique needs of each individual. Digital therapies, such as smartphone apps, virtual reality (VR), and online platforms, provide modern and customized support for recovery journeys, transforming assistance into a constant and individualized presence.

APPS FOR CRAVING MANAGEMENT

Among the most widely used tools are apps for craving management and cognitive-behavioral therapy (CBT), which have proven particularly effective. These apps guide users through mindfulness exercises, coping techniques, and progress tracking, encouraging the adoption of healthier habits.
Developed in collaboration with research institutions and validated through rigorous studies, these apps are used both in clinical programs and as recommended support by healthcare organizations.

VIRTUAL REALITY (VR)

Virtual reality is another groundbreaking technology that allows patients to simulate high-risk situations in a safe environment, enabling them to practice impulse control without real-world exposure to danger.
This technique is especially beneficial for behavioral addictions, such as gambling, and in situations involving social anxiety. Patients can train to handle challenging scenarios with the support of therapists, who monitor reactions and provide immediate feedback.
In parallel, online therapies make support accessible from anywhere, enabling the creation of flexible therapeutic pathways.

ARTIFICIAL INTELLIGENCE IN THERAPEUTIC SUPPORT

Artificial intelligence (AI) is revolutionizing the field of therapeutic support with its ability to analyze user behavior and emotions in real time. This enables the prediction of moments of vulnerability and the delivery of timely, targeted interventions. Through personalized programs, AI makes therapy dynamic and tailored, constantly adapting to individual progress.

An exciting frontier in this field is the integration of AI with neuroimaging techniques, which could lead to increasingly accurate diagnoses and ultra-personalized treatments.

Data analysis and interpretation

One of AI's primary advantages lies in its ability to collect and analyze vast amounts of clinical, genetic, and behavioral data. This process identifies patterns that can influence treatment response. For example, using biometric data such as heart rate variability, AI can predict critical moments of relapse risk, suggesting proactive interventions to help patients stay on a stable path.

Apps and machine learning

AI-powered apps play a crucial role in monitoring cravings and tracking therapeutic progress. Equipped with machine learning algorithms, these applications adjust support based on real-time data.

Some apps send motivational messages or recommend coping techniques when they detect a risk of relapse. For instance, if the app identifies that the patient is in a location associated with past substance use, it might send a reminder to help maintain impulse control.

Predicting and preventing relapses

Machine learning enables AI to analyze complex behaviors and identify risk factors, allowing for timely interventions. This ability to predict critical moments, such as specific days or situations, provides extra support or encouraging messages during periods of heightened vulnerability, creating a safety net that reinforces the recovery process.

VIRTUAL REALITY AND CHATBOTS FOR COMPREHENSIVE SUPPORT

Virtual reality (VR) and therapeutic chatbots represent additional frontiers in addiction treatment. VR allows patients to simulate high-risk situations in a safe environment, where they can practice managing impulses without fear of real consequences. In the future, VR could automatically adapt to patients' progress, increasing scenario difficulty and making therapy even more effective.

Therapeutic chatbots, available 24/7, are designed to simulate conversations with patients, offering both emotional and technical support. These chatbots not only answer questions but also guide users through relaxation exercises and stress management techniques.

Thanks to AI algorithms, these virtual assistants learn from interactions and adapt to the patient's emotional needs, providing immediate support during moments of heightened vulnerability.

However, it is essential to note that, as of today, the only support system available 24/7 and 365 days a year to individuals in recovery—outside of communities, clinics, and treatment centers—remains the **12-Step mutual aid groups**, which are explored in the second part of this book.

Interviews conducted for this study revealed that many patients have rebuilt their identities through the human connections formed in these groups. Genuine human relationships—complete with imperfections—help restore trust, empathy, and compassion, essential traits for establishing authentic bonds with oneself and others.

These elements, which are difficult to replicate with artificial intelligence, underscore the unique value of human interactions.

AI AND LONG-TERM TREATMENT PROGRAMS

AI enables the creation of long-term treatment programs tailored to the patient's needs, monitoring the effectiveness of interventions and optimizing support in real time. Thanks to its dynamic nature, AI ensures that treatment evolves alongside the patient, continually improving the quality of care.

Conclusions

Artificial intelligence and advanced technologies are revolutionizing addiction treatment, providing continuous and personalized support with unprecedented precision. Through biometric data, machine learning, and virtual reality, AI offers a glimpse into a future where treatments will be increasingly customized, adaptive, and preventive, enhancing recovery outcomes and improving the quality of life for those battling addiction.

SUMMARY OF PROGRESS AND FUTURE CHALLENGES

In recent decades, the understanding and treatment of addiction have undergone remarkable advancements. Science has progressively moved beyond the moralistic view of addiction, demonstrating that it is a complex condition involving neurological, psychological, and social mechanisms.

The introduction of technologies such as neuroimaging and genetics, alongside evidence-based therapies, has marked a turning point. Approaches like Cognitive Behavioral Therapy (CBT) and Dialectical Behavior Therapy (DBT) have become pillars of treatment, while new strategies—including Transcranial Magnetic Stimulation (TMS), personalized digital treatments, and the controlled use of psychedelics—are opening promising avenues in addiction care.

One of the most significant advancements has been the recognition of addiction as a chronic condition that alters the brain's reward circuits, self-control mechanisms, and emotional regulation.

This understanding has shifted addiction treatment toward approaches that increasingly incorporate personalized interventions, including the use of artificial intelligence to adapt to each patient's specific needs and provide continuous support. Already, digital therapies and therapeutic chatbots offer accessible and immediate assistance, essential for helping patients maintain motivation and manage relapse risks.

Research into psychedelic treatments in controlled therapeutic settings has also shown significant potential, helping patients process emotions and overcome rigid thought patterns.

RESEARCH AND PERSONALIZED MEDICINE

Addiction research is evolving toward increasingly personalized and preventive medicine. This approach, combining genetics, neuroimaging, and artificial intelligence, allows for the early identification of at-risk individuals, enabling targeted preventive interventions.

With the ability to intervene in the early stages of a person's life by offering strategies tailored to their genetic predisposition or other individual characteristics, preventive research has the potential to significantly reduce the prevalence of addiction in the population.

CHALLENGES FOR ACCESSIBLE AND ETHICAL THERAPY

Despite the progress made, many challenges remain. One of the main obstacles is the need to make innovative treatments more accessible. Currently, therapies like Transcranial Magnetic Stimulation (TMS) and AI-assisted treatment programs are available to only a limited number of individuals, as high costs and limited availability restrict access.

Addressing these issues will require concrete efforts in health policy, investment in infrastructure, and enhanced training for professionals.

The multidisciplinary nature of addiction also demands close collaboration among scientists, clinicians, and technologists to develop integrated treatments that address all facets of this complex condition.
The future of addiction treatment must include ongoing dialogue between genetics, epigenetics, psychology, and technology to offer increasingly effective and tailored care pathways.
Finally, advancements in addiction treatment raise critical ethical questions, particularly regarding safety, data privacy, and patient protection.
Treatments involving AI or psychedelics require clear and transparent guidelines to ensure the privacy and safety of patients are upheld.

A VISION ROOTED IN SCIENCE AND EMPATHY

Adopting a scientific and compassionate approach can foster a profound cultural shift in how addiction is perceived. Recognizing addiction as a condition involving neurological and chemical changes, rather than a lack of willpower, shifts the focus from blame to treatment.
Neuroscientific studies demonstrate that addiction involves alterations in the brain circuits responsible for reward, emotional regulation, and impulse control, steering attention away from judgment and toward support.
Compassion plays a crucial role in creating a healing environment, reducing the stigma that often prevents individuals from seeking help. Viewing addiction as a response to trauma and adverse environmental conditions enables us to approach people with empathy, supporting their recovery with interventions that take into account their histories and vulnerabilities.

EDUCATION AND PREVENTION: THE KEY TO A FUTURE FREE FROM ADDICTION

An integrated approach that combines science and compassion places prevention at the heart of the fight against addiction. Educating young people on managing emotions, building resilience, and coping with stress can significantly reduce the risk of addiction, particularly among those with genetic or environmental predispositions. Prevention means providing tangible tools for emotional management and psychological well-being, helping individuals avoid substances or compulsive behaviors as automatic responses to life's challenges.

In summary, a treatment model that blends science and compassion not only improves therapeutic outcomes but also fosters an environment of acceptance and support, offering individuals concrete tools for a life free from addiction. Science provides advanced solutions and technologies, while compassion builds the essential human bridge to encourage those struggling with addiction to take the first step toward a healthier, more fulfilling life.

This integrated approach represents a tangible hope for the future of addiction treatment, reducing the risk of isolation and offering recovery pathways that address the emotional and psychological needs of each individual.

BILL WAS RIGHT…

Bill was right: that dark force pulling individuals toward self-destruction, consuming every aspect of their lives, is now finally recognized as an illness. This understanding acknowledges that addictions—whether substance-related or behavioral—do not stem from moral failings but rather from complex interactions between biology, psychology, and environment.

It also encompasses a spiritual dimension, understood as the deep need for a more connected and meaningful sense of existence.

PART II

FINDING THE WAY OUT: 12 STEPS TOWARD THE LIGHT

The second part of this book delves into the pivotal role of Twelve-Step Fellowships in addiction recovery.

It is worth emphasizing that this work is entirely independent of these fellowships and is not formally endorsed or affiliated with them.

Twelve-Step Fellowships have profoundly reshaped the understanding of addiction as a disease, lifting millions of individuals and their families from the burden of stigma rooted in notions of vice and moral failing.

The tireless, freely given, and far-reaching efforts of these groups provide unwavering support to anyone battling addiction, in every corner of the world.

Including the history and influence of these fellowships was essential to this book, as their work has transformed—and continues to transform—the lives of countless people.

Nevertheless, it must be reiterated that all opinions expressed herein are those of the author alone and do not reflect the official views of Twelve-Step Fellowships.

THE TWELVE STEPS

Twelve-Step program is much more than a simple list of good intentions—it is a transformative journey that has helped millions worldwide escape the darkness of addiction.

Born in the 1930s in the United States within a small fellowship known as Alcoholics Anonymous (AA), the Twelve-Step program has become a beacon of hope for anyone battling alcoholism, drug dependency, or other forms of addiction.

The core idea behind the Twelve Steps is as simple as it is powerful: acknowledging one's powerlessness over addiction, turning to a Higher Power—whether that's God, the universe, or simply the community itself—and embarking on a path of personal growth grounded in honesty and humility. This program doesn't stop at simply saying, "Stop drinking" or "Quit using drugs." It represents a profound revolution in the way one lives and thinks. The first step is often the hardest but also the most liberating: admitting you have a problem. This act of acknowledgment opens the door to healing. Subsequent steps, such as conducting a moral inventory, taking responsibility, and making amends, represent further rungs on a ladder leading to renewal.

The Twelve Steps are not merely an individual endeavor; they are, above all, a collective experience. Those who undertake this journey are never alone—they find steadfast support in a community that deeply understands their struggles. Each meeting and every shared story strengthen the determination and courage to keep moving forward. This journey toward awareness goes far beyond recovery from addiction.

Many who complete the Twelve Steps describe a transformation that surpasses sobriety or abstinence—a new way of living that is more mindful, peaceful, and empathetic. The twelfth step, in fact, calls for sharing one's journey with others still trapped in addiction, spreading the message of hope. The Twelve Steps have been adapted to address a wide range of addictions and compulsive behaviors—from gambling to food dependency, anger management, and codependency. Each adaptation retains the program's structure and spirit, as its essence is universal: accept, act, and transform.

THE CONCEPT OF ADDICTION AS A DISEASE

At the heart of the Twelve-Step Program lies a groundbreaking idea that has revolutionized how we perceive addiction: the inability to control the use of a substance or a behavior is not a vice or a weakness of willpower but a disease in every sense of the word. This shift in perspective, as we have extensively discussed, has profoundly transformed the way we approach individuals battling alcoholism, drug dependency, or other addictions. It has replaced judgment with understanding and paved the way for a more empathetic and scientific approach.

When we accept addiction as a disease, our relationship with those who suffer from it changes: judgment and blame give way to compassion and support. This transformative idea was embraced by the Twelve-Step Program long before it became widely recognized. Addiction, as a chronic illness, requires ongoing treatment and sustained effort, much like other chronic conditions such as diabetes or hypertension.

But what does it mean to consider addiction a disease? As explored in depth in the chapter on the science of addiction, it means acknowledging that it operates on three main levels: physical, mental, and emotional. The Twelve-Step Program adds a fourth dimension to this framework: the spiritual level. While this aspect cannot currently be scientifically measured, it remains a vital part of the program, addressing a profound need for meaning and connection that many find essential on their path to recovery.

On a physical level, addiction may stem from an underlying chemical imbalance in the brain and undoubtedly creates a chemical response that fuels a compulsive need for a substance or behavior. Mentally, it dominates thoughts, driving individuals to relentlessly pursue the substance or behavior tied to their addiction. Emotionally, addiction often becomes a refuge—a way to escape pain, stress, or feelings of inadequacy. As we progress through this chapter, we will also explore how addiction is intertwined with the spiritual dimension of those affected by it.

The Twelve-Step Program approaches addiction in the way any complex illness should be addressed: with a tailored strategy. There are no quick fixes or miraculous cures. Recovery is a long journey requiring a combination of accepting one's condition, seeking community support, and engaging in continuous self-work. This is why the first step is so vital: admitting one's powerlessness over addiction. This acknowledgment is not a defeat but a pivotal act of surrender. Accepting the existence of a problem unlocks the door to addressing the problem itself.

Viewing addiction as a disease not only clarifies the behavior of those affected but also helps break the cycle of shame and guilt. Understanding that an addicted person is neither "bad" nor "weak" but instead battling an illness creates space for offering the right kind of help. The Twelve-Step Program does not stop at identifying addiction as a disease; it provides a concrete path to recovery. It is a program of action and reflection that encourages individuals to confront their illness, work on themselves, and build healthier and more fulfilling lives.

Each step represents a milestone on this journey, a rung on the ladder toward deeper self-awareness and renewed inner strength. Just like other chronic illnesses, addiction can be managed with the right treatment and a healthy dose of hope, enabling those affected to live fulfilling and rewarding lives.

HOW IT WORKS

The 12-Step groups are a powerful example of how unity and mutual support can make a difference in the fight against addiction.

But how do these groups actually work? What enables them to transform the lives of millions of people, regardless of cultural, social, or other differences? Let's take a closer look.

THE MEETINGS

Imagine walking into a room that could be a church hall, a community center, or even someone's living room. The chairs are arranged in a circle, with no hierarchies or distinctions. In this space, there are no judges—only individuals, like each of us, striving to overcome an internal battle.

This is where the 12 Steps come to life.

The meetings of 12-Step groups are the beating heart of this program. These regular gatherings, often held weekly, bring members together to share experiences, strength, and hope. Attendance isn't mandatory, but many find that consistency helps maintain focus on their recovery.

During these meetings, participants sit in a circle and take turns speaking.

This safe space, where confidentiality is sacred, allows each person to share their story, talk about their struggles, progress, and even relapses.

Relapses, in particular, are finally addressed as part of the illness rather than something to be ashamed of.

What is said within that circle stays within that circle. Each person has their time to speak without interruptions, and no one passes judgment. It is a moment to be heard, to feel understood, and to discover that no one is alone in their fight.

SERVING OTHERS

Another essential aspect is service.

Once a member achieves a certain level of stability, they are encouraged to "give back" by helping others on their journey. This act not only strengthens the person receiving help but also the one offering it. Supporting others in overcoming their challenges becomes a powerful tool for maintaining one's own sobriety and well-being.

The Role of the Sponsor

A key figure in 12-Step groups is the sponsor. This is a more experienced member who has walked part of the path and offers to guide and support those just starting out. A sponsor isn't a therapist but a fellow traveller—someone who helps navigate the rough patches, listens when times get tough, and encourages perseverance when hope seems lost.

The sponsor's support is, and must always be, entirely free. Sponsors freely give what they have freely received. It is with the sponsor that members work through the 12 Steps.

As we've seen, each step is a milestone in the healing process: beginning with admitting powerlessness over addiction, moving toward relying on something greater (whether it's a religion, the community, or inner strength), conducting a moral inventory, making amends, and ultimately living with newfound awareness. It's a deeply personal journey, but one always supported by the community.

Anonymity

One of the fundamental principles is anonymity. It not only protects the privacy of members but also serves as a reminder that who you are or where you come from doesn't matter in this journey. Anonymity preserves humility and equality among all participants. There are no titles, statuses, or distinctions—just individuals supporting one another.

HOW LONG DOES THE "TREATMENT" LAST?

There's no end to the journey. Life is a continuous process of self-improvement, and the same applies to the 12 Steps. Even after years of sobriety, members continue to attend meetings, work on the Steps, and support others.
It's a process of ongoing growth, where every day offers a chance to learn something new about oneself and others.

"LET'S KEEP IT SIMPLE"

The 12-Step program is rich with anecdotes and slogans designed to emphasize its core principles. One of these is: *"Take it easy"* or *"Let's keep it simple."*
This phrase is deeply rooted in the history of Alcoholics Anonymous and is attributed to Dr. Bob Smith, one of the movement's founders.
The story goes that Dr. Bob, ill and hospitalized, said these words to Bill Wilson, the other co-founder, to stress the importance of keeping the recovery program accessible and straightforward. Bill W. was worried that the program might become too complicated, losing its effectiveness. With his pragmatic approach, Dr. Bob urged Bill to focus on the essentials of the journey, ensuring that anyone, even in the toughest circumstances, could follow it.
This advice profoundly shaped the philosophy of the 12-Step groups, helping to keep the program grounded in simple, universal principles that continue to guide millions on their path to sobriety.

THE IMPORTANCE OF SPIRITUALITY

Spirituality in 12-Step groups serves as a compass: it's not a prescribed destination, but a guiding force that can provide direction on the journey toward a life free from addiction.
Here, spirituality isn't synonymous with religion. In fact, one of the most remarkable aspects of these groups is their

openness to diverse interpretations: whether you believe in God, the energy of the universe, or simply the collective strength of the group itself, every belief is valued and respected.

The essence of this spirituality lies in acknowledging that there is something greater than oneself that can inspire and support the recovery process.

For some, this "something" is God; for others, it may be a deeper sense of human connection, inner awareness, or a bond with nature.

There are no predefined answers, and everyone is free to create their own version of the "Higher Power" mentioned in the program—a force that helps find balance and hope without imposing any doctrines.

In the early steps, participants are encouraged to let go of the illusion of complete control and open themselves to the possibility of external help.

This “surrender” isn’t passive; it’s a conscious choice to welcome the support of something larger.

Recognizing that one isn’t omnipotent can be liberating; it creates space for growth and transformation.

Spirituality in the 12 Steps is also a powerful tool for personal transformation. It helps individuals shift their focus from self-destruction to self-care and respect for others. It’s an invitation to cultivate values such as humility, gratitude, and acceptance—qualities that might seem secondary but become the foundation of a healthy life in the context of recovery.

This spirituality is free of dogmas or hierarchies, accessible to everyone, and inclusive of all faiths (or none at all). The 12-Step program is built on an inclusive idea: no matter who you are, where you come from, or what you believe, you have a place in this journey.

For many, the program’s spirituality becomes a way to face life with a sense of purpose and peace, all while retaining the freedom to discover and live out their own inner truth.

In essence, the spirituality of the 12 Steps is an invitation to rediscover inner strength and to connect with what surrounds us, be it faith, community, or deep self-awareness. It's a simple, powerful, and open resource that anyone can shape to their own image, to find themselves and build a new and fulfilling life.

SPIRITUS CONTRA SPIRITUM: C.G. JUNG'S CONTRIBUTION

In Latin, alcohol and soul share the same term: *"Spiritus."* In the texts of the Twelve-Step programs, a fascinating observation often appears: how can the harm caused by alcohol (or other addictive substances) be countered? By nourishing the soul!

Spiritus contra Spiritum...

Some attribute this phrase to Carl Gustav Jung, although no official documents confirm it.

What is certain, however, is that Bill Wilson, co-founder of Alcoholics Anonymous, and the renowned psychiatrist—one of the fathers of psychoanalysis—discussed this idea, ultimately concluding that only a spiritual awakening could counteract the destructive power of alcohol.

The correspondence between Jung and Bill Wilson in 1961 was pivotal in shaping the concept of spirituality as applied to the Twelve-Step Program. This exchange represents a bridge between the psychological and spiritual understanding of alcoholism.

Bill wrote to Jung to thank him for the indirect role he had played in founding AA, crediting Jung with helping to lay the foundation for a spiritual understanding of addiction through his work with a former alcoholic patient, Rowland H.

To grasp the connection between the Twelve Steps and Jung, we must step back and trace this extraordinary chain of events.

Rowland Hazard III, known simply as Rowland H., was a wealthy American businessman from Rhode Island, born into a family of influential industrialists and politicians. Despite his privileged position, Rowland struggled with a serious problem: alcoholism.

Determined to overcome his addiction, Rowland sought help from various doctors and specialists, but to no avail. Desperate, he eventually turned to Carl Gustav Jung, the famous Swiss psychiatrist.

During their sessions, Jung gave him a stark diagnosis: his case was practically incurable using the traditional medical methods of the time. Only a profound spiritual experience, Jung told him, could free him from alcoholism. This statement left a deep impression on Rowland.

Back in the United States, Rowland found spiritual refuge in the Oxford Group, a Christian organization promoting personal transformation through sharing, confession, amends, and spreading these principles. Rowland passed on his spiritual experiences to another alcoholic, Edwin "Ebby" Thacher, who, in turn, shared them with Bill Wilson.

The emphasis on spiritual awakening thus became a cornerstone of the Twelve-Step program.

In the famous correspondence between Bill and Jung, Bill thanked the psychoanalyst for directing Rowland H. toward a spiritual path, noting that this message was one of the sparks that inspired the creation of AA.

In his reply, Jung acknowledged his meeting with Rowland and reiterated his belief that some cases of alcoholism were untreatable with rational or medical methods and that only a spiritual transformation could offer a way out. He also expressed admiration for AA's success and its ability to transform the destructive energy of alcoholism into a quest for spirituality and meaning.

Below, we present the two letters, allowing you to read this illuminating exchange for yourselves.[1]

---

[1] Here is a bibliography that includes relevant sources on the letters between Bill Wilson and Carl Gustav Jung, the history of Alcoholics Anonymous, and Jung's influence:

Wilson, Bill. *Alcoholics Anonymous Comes of Age: A Brief History of A.A.* New York: Alcoholics Anonymous World Services, 1957.

Bill Wilson's Letter to Jung

My dear Dr. Jung,
This letter of great appreciation has been very long overdue. May I first introduce myself as Bill W., a co-founder of the Society of Alcoholics Anonymous. Though you have surely heard of us, I doubt if you are aware that a certain conversation you once had with one of your patients, a Mr. Roland H., back in the early 1930's, did play a critical role in the founding of our Fellowship.

Though Roland H. has long since passed away, the recollection of his remarkable experience while under treatment by you has definitely become part of A.A. history. Our remembrance of Roland H.'s statements about his experience with you is as follows:

Having exhausted other means of recovery from his alcoholism, it was about 1931 that he became your patient. I believe he remained under your care for perhaps a year. His admiration for you was boundless, and he left you with a feeling of much confidence.

To his great consternation, he soon relapsed into intoxication. Certain that you were his "court of last resort," he

---

Wilson, Bill. *The Language of the Heart: Bill W.'s Grapevine Writings.* New York: The AA Grapevine, Inc., 1988.
Jung, Carl Gustav. *Letters of C.G. Jung: Volume 2, 1951–1961.* Edited by Gerhard Adler and Aniela Jaffé. Princeton: Princeton University Press, 1975.
Kurtz, Ernest. *Not-God: A History of Alcoholics Anonymous.* Center City, MN: Hazelden, 1991.
Miller, William R., and Janet C'de Baca. *Quantum Change: When Epiphanies and Sudden Insights Transform Ordinary Lives.* New York: The Guilford Press, 2001.
Dick B. *The Good Book and The Big Book: A.A.'s Roots in the Bible.* Kihei, HI: Paradise Research Publications, Inc., 1997.
These works provide a comprehensive overview of the psychological, spiritual, and historical influences that contributed to the founding and development of Alcoholics Anonymous, with a particular focus on the interactions between Bill Wilson and Carl Jung.

again returned to your care. Then followed the conversation between you that was to become the first link in the chain of events that led to the founding of Alcoholics Anonymous.

My recollection of his account of that conversation is this: First of all, you frankly told him of his hopelessness, so far as any further medical or psychiatric treatment might be concerned. This candid and humble statement of yours was beyond doubt the first foundation stone upon which our Society has since been built.

Coming from you, one he so trusted and admired, the impact upon him was immense. When he then asked you if there was any other hope, you told him that there might be, provided he could become the subject of a spiritual or religious experience—in short, a genuine conversion. You pointed out how such an experience, if brought about, might re-motivate him when nothing else could. But you did caution, though, that while such experiences had sometimes brought recovery to alcoholics, they were, nevertheless, comparatively rare. You recommended that he place himself in a religious atmosphere and hope for the best. This I believe was the substance of your advice.

Shortly thereafter, Mr. H. joined the Oxford Group, an evangelical movement then at the height of its success in Europe, and one with which you are doubtless familiar. You will remember their large emphasis upon the principles of self-survey, confession, restitution, and the giving of oneself in service to others. They strongly stressed meditation and prayer. In these surroundings, Roland H. did find a conversion experience that released him for the time being from his compulsion to drink.

Returning to New York, he became very active with the "O.G." here, then led by an Episcopal clergyman, Dr. Samuel Shoemaker. Dr. Shoemaker had been one of the founders of that movement, and his was a powerful personality that carried immense sincerity and conviction.

At this time (1932-34), the Oxford Group had already sobered a number of alcoholics, and Roland, feeling that he could especially identify with these sufferers, addressed himself to the help of still others. One of these chanced to be an old schoolmate of mine, named Edwin T. ["Ebby"]. He had been threatened with commitment to an institution, but Mr. H. and another ex-alcoholic, a member of the Oxford Group, procured his parole and brought him to Brooklyn. I, too, was threatened with commitment, and Ebby, who became my sponsor, visited me and brought me the message that release from alcoholism was possible through the Oxford Group. He cited his own case and that of Roland H., both of whom had been set free.

Here was my golden opportunity. Something had to be done at once. My alcoholic deterioration was rapid and near fatal. Following my release from the hospital, I contacted the Oxford Group and became an active member.

As you will perceive, this astonishing chain of events actually started long ago in your consulting room, and it was directly founded upon your own conviction that alcoholism, in hopeless cases, could be cured only by an experience of conversion. So, to you, Dr. Jung, we of A.A. owe an immense debt of gratitude.

Yours most sincerely,

William G. Wilson
Co-founder of Alcoholics Anonymous

Jung's Letter to Bill

Dear Mr. Wilson,

Your letter has been very welcome indeed. I had no news from Roland H. anymore and often wondered what has been his fate. Our conversation which he had adequately reported to you had an aspect of which he did not know. The reason, that I could not tell him everything, was that those days I had to be exceedingly careful of what I said. I had found out that I was misunderstood in every possible way. Thus I was very careful when I talked to Roland H. But what I really thought about, was the result of many experiences with men of his kind.

His craving for alcohol was the equivalent on a low level of the spiritual thirst of our being for wholeness, expressed in medieval language: the union with God. How could one formulate such an insight in a language that is not misunderstood in our days? The only right and legitimate way to such an experience is, that it happens to you in reality and it can only happen to you when you walk on a path, which leads you to a higher understanding. You might be led to that goal by an act of grace or through a personal and honest contact with friends, or through a higher education of the mind beyond the confines of mere rationalism.

I am strongly convinced that the evil principle prevailing in this world, leads the unrecognized spiritual need into perdition, if it is not counteracted either by a real religious insight or by the protective wall of human community. An ordinary man, not protected by higher action and isolated in society cannot resist the power of evil, which is called very aptly the Devil. But the use of such words arouse so many mistakes that one can only keep aloof from them as much as possible.

These are the reasons why I could not give a full and sufficient explanation to Roland H., but I am risking it with you because I conclude from your very decent and honest letter, that you have acquired a point of view above the misleading platitudes, one usually hears about alcoholism.

You see, Alcohol in Latin is "spiritus" and you use the same word for the highest religious experience as well as for the most depraving poison. The helpful formula therefore is: spiritus contra spiritum.

Thanking you again for your kind letter.

I remain yours sincerely,
C.G. Jung

***

In summary, Rowland H. wasn't just someone trying to overcome alcoholism but also a catalyst who, through his personal journey and search for spiritual solutions, helped ignite the chain of events that led to the founding of Alcoholics Anonymous and, later, the other 12-Step groups.

HOW THE GROUPS SUSTAIN THEMSELVES

Twelve-Step groups, such as Alcoholics Anonymous (AA) and Narcotics Anonymous (NA), are financially self-sustaining, relying on the fundamental principle of financial independence.
This means that their activities are funded solely through voluntary contributions from members, avoiding any external funding.
This principle is enshrined in the Traditions, the non-negotiable guidelines that every group and the fellowship must follow.

The Seventh Tradition clearly states: *"Every group ought to be fully self-supporting, declining outside contributions."* This principle, established at AA's founding in 1935, preserves the group's independence and integrity.
During meetings, members contribute anonymously and voluntarily through a collection: a basket is passed around, allowing participants to give what they can or abstain entirely, without pressure. The funds are used to cover basic expenses, such as rent for meeting spaces, informational materials, and occasionally small refreshments. This straightforward funding mechanism ensures that group activities remain free from external influence.
A portion of the funds may also be allocated to central or regional service bodies that support local groups. These organizations produce informational materials, manage emergency helplines, and organize conferences to spread the Twelve-Step message. Even in these cases, all resources come exclusively from voluntary contributions by members and affiliated groups, avoiding any ties to foundations or government entities.
Twelve-Step groups also maintain strict oversight of their finances to prevent the accumulation of excessive reserves.
This approach to financial simplicity reflects the values of humility and anonymity upon which the groups are founded, ensuring that the focus remains on mutual support and the recovery of their members.
Thanks to this model, the groups remain free from external pressures and can fully dedicate themselves to their primary mission: helping those struggling with addiction find serenity and stability.

THE RELATIONSHIP WITH ROCKEFELLER: BETWEEN MYTH AND HISTORY

The extraordinary spread of Alcoholics Anonymous (A.A.) and, later, other Twelve-Step associations has given rise to a range of stories, some true and others less so, about the organization's origins and funding. It seemed almost inconceivable that, in a world dominated by money, an association could grow globally without substantial financial backing.

There is, however, a grain of truth to these narratives: in 1937, Bill Wilson, one of A.A.'s co-founders, sought support from John D. Rockefeller Jr. At the time, neither Wilson nor the early members had yet established the principles that now define the organization. The pioneers of A.A. dreamed of creating treatment centers and recovery facilities in addition to self-help groups—an ambitious idea that never materialized.

In 1938, Bill met with Rockefeller Jr., hoping for financial support to launch these centers and hire professional staff. While Rockefeller Jr. recognized the importance of A.A., he also saw the risk that external funding might compromise the organization's integrity or distract members from their primary mission. Appreciating A.A.'s focus on mutual help and self-sufficiency, he famously remarked that "money would ruin" the association.

Nonetheless, Rockefeller offered a modest personal contribution of $5,000 to cover some initial expenses, while insisting that A.A. remain financially independent. This small financial boost, combined with the visibility and credibility derived from Rockefeller's involvement, helped bring attention to the movement and supported its early growth.

Thus, while Rockefeller Jr. did not directly fund A.A.'s large-scale expansion, his moral support and modest initial contribution played a crucial role in reinforcing the principle of financial self-sufficiency. This principle allowed the organization to expand without external ties.

Ironically, Bill approached Rockefeller seeking money but instead received a foundational principle: self-sufficiency. Today, this remains the cornerstone of the Twelve-Step groups' freedom and independence from any external influence, whether governmental or private.

OTHER EARLY EXTERNAL "SUPPORTERS"

In addition to John D. Rockefeller Jr., several other influential figures contributed to the early success and growth of Alcoholics Anonymous (A.A.).

A pivotal role in helping Bill Wilson understand addiction as a disease was played by Dr. William D. Silkworth, a physician at New York's Towns Hospital specializing in the treatment of alcoholism. Bill had been hospitalized there multiple times.

Silkworth's theories on alcoholism treatment and his medical endorsement of A.A.'s program provided the fledgling organization with crucial legitimacy during its formative years.

Another key supporter was Charles B. Towns, an influential entrepreneur in the field of addiction treatment and owner of a detox clinic in New York. Towns not only offered financial assistance to Bill and his early companions but also provided him with a place to stay at his clinic, giving him the space needed to focus on spreading A.A.'s message.

Another noteworthy figure is Henry Ford.

Although his involvement is not as well-documented as Rockefeller's, Ford is believed to have been a supporter of self-help initiatives for alcoholics and to have offered both moral and financial support to ideas that later influenced A.A.

Rounding out this brief overview of A.A.'s early supporters, we must mention Morris Markey and Bernard Smith. Markey, a journalist, published one of the first articles about A.A., titled *Alcoholics and God*, in the *Saturday Evening Post* in 1941. This article had an extraordinary impact, significantly contributing to the movement's growth across the United States.

Bernard Smith, a successful lawyer, became A.A.'s legal advisor and helped structure the organization, ensuring legal and financial stability. His influence was instrumental in creating A.A.'s administrative framework, enabling the movement to grow sustainably.

EFFECTIVENESS OF THE PROGRAM

The Twelve-Step Program has been the subject of numerous scientific studies.

While its effectiveness may vary from person to person, countless individuals attest that the program has transformed their lives, offering not only sobriety and freedom from substances or destructive behaviors but also a renewed sense of purpose and connection.

The program's success seems to lie in its unique combination of community support, self-examination, and spiritual growth.

In fact, the Twelve-Step Program represents a time-tested path to recovery for those struggling with addiction and compulsive behaviors.

With its emphasis on personal growth, accountability, and mutual support, the program provides a pathway to a healthier, more fulfilling life, helping millions of people worldwide break free from the chains of addiction.

SCIENTIFIC EVIDENCE IN SUPPORT

The Twelve-Step Program has been extensively studied to assess its effectiveness in treating addiction.

Research has often confirmed the therapeutic value of this model, demonstrating how peer support and a structured recovery path can aid those struggling with addiction. Here are some key findings from scientific studies conducted in this field.

COCHRANE COLLABORATION REVIEW

A review conducted by the Cochrane Collaboration[2] evaluated the effects of Twelve-Step Facilitation Therapy

---

[2] The Cochrane Collaboration is an independent, non-profit international organization dedicated to producing high-quality systematic reviews and meta-analyses to evaluate the effectiveness of healthcare interventions. Founded in 1993, it is named after British physician and researcher Archie Cochrane, who championed the importance of basing medicine on solid and accessible scientific evidence.

(TSF) compared to other treatment methods for alcohol addiction. This study concluded that TSF, inspired by the Twelve Steps, demonstrates positive long-term effects, particularly when integrated with traditional treatments. The Cochrane review highlighted that consistent participation in Twelve-Step-based support groups increases the likelihood of maintaining sobriety, showing better long-term outcomes compared to other therapies.

MOOS AND MOOS STUDY (2006)

One of the most frequently cited longitudinal studies is that of Moos and Moos, which tracked a group of individuals with alcoholism over a 16-year period. The findings revealed that participants who regularly attended Twelve-Step groups had significantly higher recovery rates and more stable sobriety compared to those who did not attend such groups. The study emphasized that frequent and consistent engagement in Twelve-Step programs is closely linked to long-term success, demonstrating that stability in participation is a critical factor.

BENEFITS FOR PATIENTS WITH DUAL DIAGNOSIS

Research published in the *Journal of Studies on Alcohol and Drugs* has examined the impact of the Twelve-Step program on patients with dual diagnosis—those with both addiction and psychiatric disorders. Studies have found that the program not only improves addiction symptoms but also helps reduce those of co-occurring mental health conditions, thanks to its supportive environment and principles of personal accountability. This suggests that the program can be particularly beneficial for individuals facing complex challenges, offering a stable foundation for recovery and emotional well-being.

AMERICAN PSYCHIATRIC ASSOCIATION REVIEW

In 2020, the American Psychiatric Association (APA) published a review endorsing the Twelve-Step program as a treatment option. The APA noted that, in addition to facilitating recovery from alcoholism and other addictions, the program enhances overall quality of life, a benefit attributed to continuous peer support and the program's community-oriented approach. This review confirms the program's effectiveness as a long-term intervention, providing not only sobriety and freedom from substances but also a supportive social network and a sense of belonging.

EFFECTIVENESS AMONG YOUNG ADULTS AND ADOLESCENTS

Studies conducted at the University of California, including those led by Dr. Lee Ann Kaskutas, have explored the program's effectiveness for young adults and adolescents. The findings revealed that, while originally designed for adults, the program is also effective for younger participants. It provides critical support and a sense of belonging that help this age group navigate the challenges of addiction. The program's emphasis on personal responsibility has proven beneficial even for younger individuals, making it an adaptable option across different age groups.

CONCLUSIONS

The studies mentioned above reinforce the evidence supporting the effectiveness of the Twelve-Step Program. They demonstrate that the combined approach of community support, self-examination, and spiritual growth has a positive impact on the lives of participants. These findings support the notion that the program not only fosters sobriety but also cultivates a renewed sense of purpose, connection, and resilience.

Today, the Twelve-Step Program stands as one of the most validated and widely applied recovery paths in the world, providing a foundation of support for millions of people[3].

Summary of Key Studies on the Effectiveness of Twelve-Step Groups
The Cochrane Review (2020):

A systematic review concluded that AA and Twelve-Step-based programs significantly increase the likelihood of long-term abstinence compared to other treatments for alcohol use disorders.

Source: Kelly, J. F., Humphreys, K., & Ferri, M. (2020), Cochrane Database of Systematic Reviews.

Project MATCH (1997):

A randomized clinical trial found the Twelve-Step approach particularly effective for specific subgroups of alcoholics.

Source: Project MATCH Research Group (1997), Journal of Studies on Alcohol.

Harvard Medical School Study (2001):

This study linked active and consistent participation in AA groups to a higher likelihood of maintaining abstinence.

Source: Kelly et al. (2011), Addiction.

Follow-Up Studies and Meta-Analyses:

Numerous studies have confirmed that Twelve-Step groups improve abstinence rates and quality of life, highlighting the role of social support. *Source: Moos, R. H., & Moos, B. S. (2006), Journal of Clinical Psychology.*

Comparative Effectiveness Research (2012):

This research found that Twelve-Step groups are particularly effective in reducing substance use and improving psychosocial functioning. *Source: Kelly, J. F., & Yeterian, J. D. (2012), Alcohol Research: Current Reviews.*

Other Studies:

The literature also includes research on the role of Twelve-Step programs for individuals with dual diagnoses, young adults, and the official recognition by the American Psychiatric Association (APA) of the program's effectiveness for substance use disorders.

These studies provide robust evidence supporting the effectiveness of the Twelve-Step Program.

ALCOHOLISM
ALCOHOLICS ANONYMOUS – 1935

It was a December evening in 1934 in New York City. The metropolis, wrapped in a blanket of snow, was illuminated by Christmas lights reflecting off the sidewalks. In a small apartment, Bill Wilson, a former World War I officer and brilliant stockbroker, sat alone, consumed by a sense of defeat. The gin bottle on the table was nearly empty, as was his hope of escaping alcohol. His marriage was in shambles, his career destroyed, and his friends lost. Alcohol had devoured everything.

Yet that night, a thought stirred him from his stupor: the memory of an old friend, Ebby Thacher. He too had been an alcoholic like Bill but, to everyone's surprise, had recently found stability. Ebby spoke of an extraordinary change, a spiritual awakening brought about by the Oxford Group, a Christian organization promoting practices like confession, restitution, and surrendering to God—a group encouraging members to lead honest lives, free from "vices," and focused on values of solidarity and moral growth.

For someone like Bill, who had witnessed the devastation of alcoholism, Ebby's sobriety seemed almost miraculous. Driven by curiosity and a glimmer of hope, Bill decided to attend an Oxford Group meeting. However, despite the prayers and sermons, he couldn't feel the inner strength his friend described. Serenity eluded him, like a mirage in the desert. It seemed there was an invisible barrier between him and the peace he so desperately sought.

In the days that followed, Bill continued to wrestle with his demons. One afternoon, he was admitted once again to Manhattan's Towns Hospital, under the care of Dr. William Silkworth, a compassionate physician determined to understand alcoholism.

Silkworth was among the first to view alcoholism as a disease rather than simply a vice—a condition affecting the body, mind, and spirit and thus requiring a deeper approach. "Medicine alone isn't enough," he had told Bill many times. "You need a spiritual force, something greater."

During one of his worst withdrawal episodes, Bill had a startling experience. Lying in his hospital bed, tormented by hallucinations, he saw a blinding light flood the room. In that moment, a sensation of peace and well-being enveloped him. Later, he would describe the event as a genuine spiritual ecstasy, an encounter with a higher power that freed him from the chains of alcohol. When he regained full consciousness, his desire to drink had vanished. He felt liberated. At last, he understood what Ebby meant by "spiritual connection."

After leaving the hospital, Bill began attending the Oxford Group regularly but still sensed something was missing. He realized that not everyone could or would have a mystical experience; a practical path was needed—a structure that could help anyone.

During a business trip to Akron, Ohio, a chance meeting changed the course of his life—and the lives of millions. He met Dr. Bob Smith, a physician tormented by the same addiction. Thanks to the insight of a mutual clerical friend, the two found themselves talking in the dining room of an old Akron house. Bill shared his experience and his belief that only a spiritual awakening could save an alcoholic. Bob was skeptical but found Bill's account sincere and passionate. He felt that perhaps, together, they could find a solution.

That first conversation lasted hours, during which they shared their struggles and hopes. For the first time, neither felt alone in their battles. The secret to recovery seemed to lie in mutual support and a shared path.

That conversation marked the beginning of a fellowship that would fight alcoholism—not just to escape addiction but to build a new life.

Alcoholics Anonymous (A.A.) was formally born from that meeting. Bill and Bob adopted some principles of the Oxford Group and transformed them into a 12-step program—a recovery path that aimed not only to maintain sobriety but to foster spiritual healing and inner renewal. The program became a comprehensive system, accessible to anyone, centered on sharing, mutual support, and the pursuit of a higher power, however individuals chose to define it.

Meetings quickly spread, along with the message of hope. A.A. soon became a refuge for those seeking a way out of alcoholism—a global community that now includes over 123,000 groups in 180 countries and more than two million members.

Alcoholics Anonymous not only offered a way out of alcoholism but also introduced a new way of living, centered on personal and spiritual growth. Thanks to this fellowship, anyone struggling with addiction can find genuine support in the group, rediscovering the strength to face even the most challenging storms—together[4].

***

Alcoholism, scientifically defined as alcohol use disorder, is a chronic illness characterized by an inability to control the consumption of alcoholic beverages despite negative consequences on health, social relationships, and professional life.

According to the *Diagnostic and Statistical Manual of Mental Disorders (DSM-5)*, this disorder manifests through symptoms such as an intense craving for alcohol, a loss of control over its use, increased tolerance requiring larger quantities to achieve the same effects, and physical and psychological withdrawal symptoms when consumption is reduced or stopped.

---

[4] For further information, you can visit the official websites:

- International A.A. Website: www.aa.org

Alcoholism is considered a multifactorial condition, influenced by genetic, psychological, and environmental components. Effective treatment often combines medical interventions, psychotherapy, and social support, such as self-help groups. Early recognition and intervention are crucial to preventing severe physical and psychological complications.

DRUG AND OTHER PSYCHOTROPIC SUBSTANCES ADDICTION
NARCOTICS ANONYMOUS – 1953

United States of America, 1950s. There are no New York skyscrapers or snowy scenes to set the stage—just the desert and the scorching sun.

We are in Sun Valley, part of the San Fernando Valley, northwest of Los Angeles. Here, low hills and arid lands alternate with residential, commercial, and industrial areas. Wide streets lined with palm trees and drought-resistant plants reflect the essence of the Californian landscape. The Verdugo and Santa Susana Mountains frame this sun-drenched corner, where heat reigns supreme for much of the year.

While the world is recovering from the ashes of World War II, America finds itself in a period of contradictions. On one hand, the post-war economic boom ignites hopes and dreams; on the other, the ominous shadow of the Cold War and nuclear fear weigh heavily on society. It is a climate of uncertainty, where substance addictions begin to emerge as an issue, though society either ignores or misunderstands them.

Let's focus on one particular scene: an unassuming window in Sun Valley. Behind the curtains, a modest but tidy room hosts a few chairs arranged in a circle. A symbol—a triangle within a circle—hangs on the wall. A man speaks while the others listen silently. Their eyes reveal suffering but also a glimmer of light emerging from deep within.

This is not a casual evening among friends—there are no beers or games. It's an Alcoholics Anonymous (A.A.) meeting.

A man of average height takes the floor. His light, deep-set eyes bear the scars of life, yet they exude undeniable strength. His smile is bittersweet but reassuring. "My name is Jimmy, and I am an alcoholic." His voice cracks, and his gaze drops to the floor. After a moment, he continues: "My name is Jimmy K., and I am an alcoholic. But alcohol isn't the only monster I have to fight. Staying away from that first drink isn't enough for me to find serenity..."

Jimmy K., born James Patrick Kinnon in Philadelphia in 1911, is in his early 40s, and his life has been a rollercoaster of challenges. Raised during the Great Depression, he knows poverty and economic hardship firsthand. He is neither a businessman nor a natural leader but a man who knows how to listen, hiding a troubled past behind his smile. To support his wife, Sylvia, and their eight children, he works countless jobs. He builds, but when the "monster" takes over, he destroys everything.

In the 1930s and 1940s, like many others, he found solace in alcohol and drugs, falling into the trap of addiction. Then, in the 1940s, he discovered Alcoholics Anonymous (A.A.), founded by Bill W. and Dr. Bob, which treated alcoholism as a disease rather than a moral failing. A.A. became his lifeline, but he felt it wasn't enough. A.A. worked for those battling alcoholism, but not for those facing other addictions. "Stay away from the first drink, and you'll be fine," they told him. But Jimmy felt something was missing.

One evening, after a meeting, he pondered: "What if there were something like A.A., but for those fighting all kinds of addictions?"

Drugs were becoming an increasingly visible problem, especially among young people, yet society struggled to acknowledge it. "What if we created a group of our own?" he suggested. "A place where anyone, regardless of their addiction, could come for support and understanding."

Initially met with scepticism, his idea gradually won over those who listened. Step by step, the project began to take shape. In 1953, together with others like him, Jimmy founded Narcotics Anonymous (N.A.). The first official meeting was held in a small room loaned by a church in

Sun Valley. There were no red carpets, just people determined to change their lives, one day at a time.

N.A. was based on A.A.'s Twelve Steps but adapted to be inclusive of all forms of addiction. For the first time, the focus was not on powerlessness over a single substance but on the disease of addiction—a ravenous monster that consumed everything. The core philosophy remained unchanged: no one could do it alone. The strength of the group, fueled by sharing and listening, was the key to success.

The first N.A. meetings were held in church basements or small rooms. There were no comfortable chairs or coffee breaks, but there was a profound sense of belonging. Each participant became part of a family offering support with patience and humor.

N.A. grew slowly but steadily. Success stories spread, bringing more participants. Some arrived in despair, others with a sliver of hope, but all found the strength to face a new day.

Jimmy K. didn't live to see N.A.'s global reach; he passed away on July 9, 1985, at peace, leaving behind an immortal legacy. Today, Narcotics Anonymous boasts over 76,000 groups worldwide, with more than 500,000 active members. Jimmy, despite his imperfections, understood two profound truths: addiction goes beyond substances, and the power of mutual support can overcome any obstacle. Thanks to him, millions of people find a way out of this illness every day, writing new chapters in the story of Narcotics Anonymous[5].

***

Today, science also acknowledges it: addiction to psychotropic substances is a chronic and complex condition characterized by the compulsive use of drugs, medications, or

[5] Regarding official websites, the international Narcotics Anonymous website is www.na.org, where you can find resources, information, and links to global events.

other mind-altering substances, despite severe negative consequences for physical, mental, and social health.
This condition manifests with an intense need to consume the substance (craving), difficulty in controlling its use, the development of tolerance (requiring higher doses to achieve the same effects), and withdrawal symptoms when consumption is reduced or stopped.
Psychotropic substances can include illegal drugs (such as cocaine, heroin, and amphetamines), prescription medications (such as opioids and benzodiazepines), and legal substances that are abused (such as alcohol).
Addiction causes severe health damage, including cardiovascular, liver, and brain diseases, as well as mental health disorders like depression and anxiety. Additionally, it has a significant impact on the individual's social and professional life, leading to isolation, legal problems, and financial difficulties.
Managing addiction requires an integrated treatment approach that may include behavioral therapy, pharmacotherapy, and psychosocial support to help individuals achieve sobriety and improve their quality of life.

GAMBLING ADDICTION
GAMBLERS ANONYMOUS – 1957

Once upon a time, in a world where cards, chips, and lotteries seemed like harmless pastimes, a silent army of men and women fought against an invisible enemy. Not a flesh-and-blood adversary, but a seductive force—a downward spiral that dragged them deeper and deeper: gambling.

Amid despair and hope, a light emerged—a guide for those seeking to reclaim their lives: Gamblers Anonymous.

We are in Los Angeles, California, in the 1950s, a time of contrasts and relentless dynamism. The city, sprawling along the Pacific coast, is a crossroads of the film industry and dreams—a melting pot of cultures interwoven into a vibrant, pulsating tapestry. Streets glimmer under the warm sun, and the roar of cars mingles with lively conversations in crowded cafés. Downtown buzzes with activity: modern skyscrapers rise as symbols of economic prosperity, while film studios teem with creativity, attracting artists and dreamers from far and wide.

In residential neighborhoods, children play on the streets with a timeless innocence. Bungalow-style homes, with manicured gardens and towering palm trees, tell the stories of families striving to build better futures. By night, restaurants and dance halls sparkle with lights and colors, while jazz and rock 'n' roll fill the air, capturing the spirit of a nation in transformation.

But beneath the facade of prosperity and optimism, the Californian metropolis hides its shadows. Skyscrapers, symbols of progress, bring constant pressure and ruthless competition. Behind the glittering lights lurk economic and social challenges. Gambling halls, with their dazzling neon signs and green tables, become a temptation for those unable to bear the weight of daily life's frenetic pace.

The city's inhabitants navigate between prosperity and struggle, between security and uncertainty. It's a place where the future shines brightly for some but remains a turbulent journey for others, marked by the very shadows hidden among the lights.

In this mosaic of emotions and ambitions, we find the protagonists of our story: Jim W. and Harry B. In this vibrant and contradictory city, they found the strength and inspiration to create something unique: Gamblers Anonymous. Los Angeles, with all its dynamism and contradictions, became fertile ground for an organization destined to change lives and write new chapters of hope.

Let's take a closer look at their story.

James Willis, known as Jim W., was, like so many others, consumed by the world of gambling. Horse races, casinos, betting—all promised thrills and easy winnings but soon turned into a nightmare. A respected engineer with a stable career, he found himself alone and desperate. His gambling addiction began to interfere with his work and family life, bringing him to a point where he felt he had lost control.

Jim, with his easy smile and affable demeanor, was an ordinary man. Gambling had seduced him like a dangerous lover, promising fortune and happiness but leaving him in ruin. His life became a rollercoaster—one moment soaring with a win, the next plunging into the depths of despair. Behind his friendly smile was a tumultuous heart, a man increasingly burdened by debt and lies.

One day, while wandering aimlessly through the streets of Los Angeles, Jim met a man who would become not only a friend but also the co-founder of an organization that would change countless lives.

Harry B., born Harry B. Burke, was another survivor of addiction. A man of few words but great determination, he battled both gambling and alcoholism—a dual compulsion that made his life even more challenging.

He was also married, but, as often happens, addiction strained his marriage to its limits. Harry was a businessman, whose career required managerial and entrepreneurial skills. His professional experience helped him understand the importance of a structured recovery program.

Thanks to Alcoholics Anonymous, Harry managed to stay away from alcohol, learning to face reality without escapism. This allowed him to explore new ways to address his problem and support others who shared his addiction.

It was in a modest bar on the city's outskirts that Jim and Harry began talking about their experiences, sharing sleepless nights, debts, and lies. Jim spoke, and Harry nodded, understanding all too well. But Harry had an advantage: he knew the Twelve Steps program created by A.A. and adopted by Narcotics Anonymous. He wondered if that approach could work for gamblers, too.

Although alcoholics and drug addicts battle substances while gamblers face behaviors, Harry recognized a similar dynamic. If the root of the problem was the same, perhaps the solution could be as well.

What began as a conversation between two friends became the seed of something extraordinary. Jim and Harry decided to adapt the Twelve Steps to gambling, creating a program that would help not only to stop gambling but also to achieve inner rebirth. The Twelve Steps were not just a list of actions but a spiritual and practical journey—from admitting powerlessness over addiction to seeking help from a higher power, repairing damages, and sharing experiences.

The first Gamblers Anonymous meetings were held in a small parish hall, where a few brave individuals gathered to share their stories, struggles, and solace. Anonymity was sacred—no one wanted to be judged, and everyone could speak freely, knowing that what was said stayed in the room.

From those first steps, Gamblers Anonymous expanded rapidly. Word of mouth among those seeking help grew the group—first in other cities, then other states, and eventually, other countries. It wasn't just about quitting gambling; it was about healing internally and finding purpose again. The Twelve Steps became a beacon, a guide to staying on track.

Today, Gamblers Anonymous is a global organization with over 1,500 groups in more than 50 countries. Thousands of members share the same struggle and the same hope for recovery. The simple yet powerful idea of Jim and Harry has come to life, becoming a movement that has restored hope to countless people.

It's not just about breaking the chains of gambling addiction but embarking on a journey that begins with one simple admission: "I am a gambler." From that moment, with the Twelve Steps, a new future begins—one that is free and full of hope.

Even today, whenever someone steps into a GA group for the first time, scared and lost, there's always someone ready to say: "Welcome. You're in the right place. You're no longer alone."[6].

***

Gambling addiction, or pathological gambling, is a disorder characterized by the compulsive and uncontrollable urge to gamble despite severe negative consequences for health, finances, and social life.

This addiction manifests as a strong desire to gamble, an inability to limit or stop gambling behavior, and the continued investment of time and money, even in the face of significant losses.

Symptoms include an obsession with gambling, the need to bet increasingly larger amounts to achieve the same level of excitement (tolerance), and irritability or anxiety when unable to gamble. Gambling addiction can lead to serious financial consequences, such as debt and bankruptcy, and has a devastating impact on personal and family relationships, often resulting in social isolation, conflicts, and legal problems. Treating gambling addiction requires an integrated approach that may include cognitive-behavioral therapy, psychological support, and, in some cases, pharmacological treatment. The goal is to help individuals regain control over their behavior and improve their quality of life.

---

[6]The official websites of Gamblers Anonymous are as follows: www.gamblersanonymous.org

COMPULSIVE EATING
OVEREATERS ANONYMOUS – 1960

In the tumultuous post-war years, while the spotlight was on great heroes, industrial successes, and the American dream, a silent battle was being fought.

A struggle waged in kitchens, living rooms, and solitary nights in front of the refrigerator. It was the fight against food—not just for survival but for comfort, escape, and that elusive peace missing from daily life.

At the time—and sadly, even today—the inability to regulate eating was often seen as a character flaw. It was within this context that one of the world's most widespread self-help groups was born: Overeaters Anonymous, or OA.

In the 1960s, body image was heavily influenced by beauty standards promoted by the media and popular culture. During an era when the ideal feminine figure was epitomized by slender icons like Twiggy, even slight fullness carried intense stigma. Being overweight, or simply curvy, wasn't just considered an aesthetic flaw but came with moral and character judgments: laziness, lack of self-control, disorderliness.

These prejudices permeated every aspect of daily life. Overweight people were often ridiculed, marginalized, and discriminated against—both at work and in personal relationships. Meanwhile, the dieting culture was gaining momentum, pushing the belief that the ideal body could—and should—be achieved at any cost. This fostered shame and guilt in those who didn't fit the standards.

The lack of awareness about the complex factors contributing to obesity—such as genetics, environment, and mental health—led to a reductive and stigmatizing perspective. In the 1960s, the overweight body was seen as a "problem" to be fixed, not as part of human diversity.

It was in this climate that our story begins.

We are in Pacific Palisades, a charming and serene neighborhood in Los Angeles overlooking the Pacific Ocean. Amid coastal hills and expansive beaches, shaded streets, and elegant homes lived Rozanne Sanders, born in 1929.

Rozanne S. was a woman of average height with a neat, understated style, brown hair, and an intense gaze. Growing up in an era of transition between generations, she had experienced both the hardships of the Great Depression and the post-war economic boom. She was married, with a supportive family, yet her life hid a silent battle: a complicated relationship with food.

On a bright morning, Rozanne woke early, tidied the house, served breakfast to her family, and then found herself alone. The Californian sun sparkled on the ocean waves, and a light breeze carried the scent of salt and wildflowers. Gazing out the window at well-kept gardens and towering palm trees, Rozanne realized she had everything, and yet inside, a storm raged.

The beauty of Pacific Palisades, with its breathtaking views and tranquility, contrasted sharply with her inner turmoil. For Rozanne, food had become both refuge and torment, a cycle of binge eating and regret that isolated her more and more. Her inner conflict was an invisible secret, hidden from those who saw only her seemingly perfect life.

She was a woman capable of sacrifice, respected for her dedication. Yet when it came to food, despite her best intentions, she found herself succumbing to a force that seemed to possess her, driving her to eat until exhaustion. After every binge, her body felt drained, and her heart weighed down with shame. She knew something was wrong, and with her practical and determined nature, she resolved to seek answers.

Her search for help was desperate. But in the 1960s, doctors, psychiatrists, and clergy had no answers for her. She wasn't crazy or physically ill; her mind and body appeared healthy, but her suffering remained undiagnosed.

The turning point came when she discovered Alcoholics Anonymous. Rozanne found inspiration in the movement, seeing in it a glimmer of hope. A.A. provided a recovery path for those battling alcohol addiction, and its Twelve Steps seemed applicable to her struggle with compulsive eating. She began attending A.A. meetings, where she learned the principles of the program and the power of shared experiences.

With this inspiration, she founded Overeaters Anonymous in 1960. On a warm August day, she opened the doors of her home and gathered a small group of friends and acquaintances who shared similar struggles. It was a simple meeting but full of hope. In the cozy and bright living room of her home in Pacific Palisades, amid laughter, tears, and shared stories, something special was born: the realization that no one was alone.

Over time, Overeaters Anonymous began to take shape. Like their "siblings" in A.A., OA members adopted the Twelve Steps, adapting them to food addiction. These steps were not just rules but a spiritual journey of rebirth and healing. OA was not merely a support group; it became a movement for rediscovering oneself, reconnecting with inner strength, and finding a life beyond binge eating. The movement grew quickly. From its small group in California, OA expanded across the United States and then worldwide. People of all ages, genders, and cultures joined, finding solace in a program that didn't judge but welcomed with compassion. The connection with Alcoholics Anonymous provided a solid foundation, demonstrating how a Twelve-Step program could help overcome addictions and compulsive behaviors.

Today, Overeaters Anonymous has thousands of groups in over 80 countries. The success stories are countless: people who found peace with food, learned to nourish their bodies and souls healthily, and rediscovered the joy of living. But the heart of OA remains the same as that first meeting: community, sharing, and the belief that together, it is possible to find a way out of the darkness.

OA 90—or "Overeaters Anonymous 90 Day"—is a sub-community of Overeaters Anonymous that follows a rigorous 90-day food plan, with total abstinence from certain foods and behaviors, still based on the Twelve Steps.
The story of Overeaters Anonymous is not just about recovery from food addiction but about hope, resilience, and the extraordinary strength that emerges when we unite to overcome the most challenging struggles. It is the story of people who, guided by a vision powerful in its simplicity, have changed the course of their lives—and countless others—one day at a time, one step at a time[7].

***

Compulsive eating, or binge eating disorder (BED), is a condition characterized by recurrent episodes of consuming excessive amounts of food in a short period of time, accompanied by a sense of loss of control during the episode.
Individuals with this disorder often eat large quantities of food rapidly, even when they are not hungry, and may experience feelings of guilt, shame, or disgust afterward.
Unlike other eating disorders, such as bulimia, binge eating does not regularly involve compensatory behaviors like self-induced vomiting or excessive exercise. This disorder can lead to significant physical consequences, such as obesity, type 2 diabetes, hypertension, and other weight-related medical complications. Additionally, it is often associated with mental health issues, including depression, anxiety, and low self-esteem.
Treating binge eating disorder requires a multidisciplinary approach, which may include cognitive-behavioral therapy, nutritional interventions, and, in some cases, pharmacological treatment. The goal is to help individuals de-

[7] Here are the official websites of Overeaters Anonymous (OA):

- International: www.oa.org

velop a healthier relationship with food, improve emotional regulation, and prevent episodes of uncontrolled eating while promoting overall well-being.

Overeaters Anonymous (OA) can also support individuals suffering from bulimia and anorexia. Although the organization was initially established to support people with compulsive eating behaviors, the OA program has evolved to welcome all individuals struggling with eating disorders, including bulimia and anorexia. The focus is not solely on overeating but on any dysfunctional relationship with food.

OA follows the Twelve Steps program, adapting it to all forms of food addiction and encouraging members to address psychological, emotional, and spiritual aspects of their relationship with food. The group's support and the principle of anonymity provide a safe environment where individuals can share their experiences without fear of judgment. This is particularly valuable for those who have experienced the shame, guilt, and isolation often associated with eating disorders.

Naturally, OA can be integrated with other therapeutic pathways, especially in cases of medical conditions requiring specific management by specialists.

DYSFUNCTIONAL EMOTIONALITY
EMOTIONS ANONYMOUS – 1971

It was another cold and rainy evening in 1987, but… don't worry… we're not in New York this time. The story we're telling speaks Italian.

It was a cold and rainy evening in 1987, as we said, when Laura, a young woman from Milan, sat alone at a café table, absentmindedly gazing out of a foggy window. Her mind was filled with thoughts of insecurity, anxiety, and a constant sense of inadequacy that had tormented her for years. Every day was a battle against overwhelming emotions, exaggerated reactions to trivial situations, and an insatiable need for approval that never seemed to be fulfilled.

Laura felt alone, unique in her nameless suffering.

In reality, many people lived the same inner battles, especially during those years when the world seemed to demand more and more, leaving little room for human fragility. But while others managed to hide their insecurities behind a mask of apparent strength, Laura felt the weight of her emotions could no longer be ignored.

No one seemed to truly understand her, and no matter how much she sought comfort from those around her, no one could offer the support she desperately needed.

It was during one of those moments of despair that Laura stumbled upon an article about a recovery program called Narcotics Anonymous. Although she had never used drugs and only occasionally drank excessively, she found temporary solace in sleeping pills and anti-anxiety medications to numb her mind and heart. She didn't consider herself an addict, but she was drawn to the concept of these groups and decided to attend the meeting mentioned in the article.

The group was called "Living Free," and that was exactly what she desired above all else.

When she arrived at the meeting, the Twelve Steps framework, designed to help people recognize and overcome their addiction, immediately captured her attention. After the session, she spoke with some members: "My problem isn't drugs or alcohol… sure, I need 'help' to survive too, but what's killing me is something much more subtle, hidden in the folds of my mind, in how my emotions have completely taken over my life."

"And you think it's different for us?" a woman's voice called out from the back of the room. "Do you think the external substance is the only problem? At first, the substance was a 'help' for all of us, but then it became an even bigger problem than what it was supposed to 'fix.' So, you're in the right place here, but if you're looking for something more specific, you might want to try Emotions Anonymous!"

"There aren't any groups here in Milan yet… but I know someone who attends this fellowship in Turin. You might want to give it a try there!"

That night, Laura couldn't sleep. The thought of that group in Turin planted itself firmly in her mind, and the next day, she began searching for a contact. In a time without the internet, she found the number, written in small print, in the gray pages of the phone book. She made contact and finally set off for Turin—not exactly close to home, but to find a solution, she would have walked there… or even crawled!

The group, founded in 1985, met weekly in a small room—a modest but welcoming space where everyone could openly discuss their fears, anxieties, and struggles to manage their emotions. Through the Twelve Steps, members learned to recognize their emotions, not to be overwhelmed by them, and to find an inner balance that helped them lead more peaceful and fulfilling lives.

The group became a second family for Laura, a safe place to return to whenever the outside world became too difficult to face.

Laura, who had started her journey feeling so alone and incomplete, found not only the inner peace she had sought her entire life in Emotions Anonymous but also the joy of helping others find their own path to serenity.

It was there she also learned the story of the fellowship's origin.

In 1971, Marion Fleser, a middle-aged woman from Minnesota, was reflecting on her life as she sat quietly in her kitchen. For years, Marion had fought a silent battle—an invisible war against her emotions.

It wasn't a physical addiction that consumed her, but a constant sense of dissatisfaction, anxiety, and emotional burden that seemed to crush her day by day.

Marion wasn't an ordinary woman. She had lived through experiences that had profoundly marked her, and over time, she had learned to hide her inner turmoil behind a polite smile and an appearance of normality. But beneath that serene facade lay a stormy sea—a chaos of emotions that she couldn't fully understand.

One evening, after attending an Alcoholics Anonymous meeting to support someone she deeply cared about, Marion had a revelation. Looking at the determined faces sharing their stories of struggle and recovery, she wondered: what if there was a way to address invisible battles too? The ones that left no scars on the body but wounded the soul and kept people from living fully?

That's when Marion decided to act. She began talking to others who, like her, felt they had no place to freely express their emotions without being judged. People who, although they didn't have a physical addiction, felt imprisoned by their emotional states, unable to find inner peace.

With the support of friends and inspiration from Alcoholics Anonymous' Twelve Steps, Marion founded the first Emotions Anonymous (EA) group in 1971.

The group met weekly in a small community hall with the goal of creating a safe and welcoming space where people could talk openly about their emotions without fear of misunderstanding or judgment. The Twelve Steps program, adapted for EA, didn't promise easy solutions but offered a path to self-awareness and acceptance. Participants learned to recognize their emotions, not fear them, and, most importantly, manage them healthily and constructively.

Each meeting became a moment of sharing, personal growth, and discovery—a place where people found mutual support and new hope.

The movement quickly grew, spreading first across the United States and then to other countries. People were drawn to the idea of a space where they could open up completely, in front of a group of peers, without the fear of being seen as "weak" or "flawed."

Every new group that formed testified to the deep and universal need to connect with others on an emotional level, to find understanding, and to discover that no one is truly alone in their struggles.

Today, Emotions Anonymous is a global community, with thousands of members worldwide meeting regularly to share their experiences, strength, and hope. Currently, EA has hundreds of active groups in over 30 countries, including Italy. The small spark Marion lit in 1971 has become a beacon of hope for anyone navigating the turbulent waters of their emotions, proving that even in the darkest moments, there is always a way to serenity[8].

***

Dysfunctional emotionality refers to a way of experiencing emotions that creates difficulties in daily life.

People who struggle with this type of emotionality often react excessively or inappropriately to ordinary situations, feeling intense and prolonged anxiety, sadness, or anger. This can make it challenging to maintain healthy relationships and feel good about oneself.

Those living with dysfunctional emotionality may feel overwhelmed by their feelings, caught in a spiral of emotions that seems impossible to control.

The Twelve Steps program, though originally designed to address addictions, can also be a valuable tool for those facing these emotional challenges.

The first thing the program encourages is recognizing that there is a problem. This step is fundamental because, for many, it is difficult to admit that their emotions are causing distress in their lives. Accepting this reality is the first step toward change.

---

[8] Here the website addresses for Emotions Anonymous (EA): www.emotionsanonymous.org

Next, the program encourages deep reflection on how one feels and the reasons behind these emotions. Through this process, individuals begin to understand which emotions cause the most difficulties and how they manifest in their lives. It's a journey of self-discovery that helps identify dysfunctional patterns—behaviors and reactions that do not lead to positive outcomes.

Once the problem is recognized and greater awareness is achieved, the program invites individuals to accept their situation without self-judgment. Taking responsibility for one's emotions is essential to begin changing them. This step is crucial in moving from being victims of one's emotions to becoming active participants in one's transformation.

The support of a group is another key element of the program. Sharing experiences with others facing similar challenges provides a safe and understanding environment where individuals feel welcomed and understood. This sense of community helps reduce the isolation often associated with dysfunctional emotionality, showing that no one is alone in their struggles.

Finally, the program provides practical tools for managing emotions in healthier ways. Techniques such as meditation and reflection help to manage anxiety and sadness, offering constructive and positive ways to cope with emotional difficulties. Through this journey, individuals can learn to see their emotions as opportunities for growth rather than burdens to bear.

In this way, the Twelve Steps program proves to be not only a support for those dealing with addictions but also a valuable resource for anyone seeking to better understand and manage their emotions. With the right support and personal commitment, it is possible to transform dysfunctional emotionality into a journey of personal growth and self-discovery.

COMPULSIVE SHOPPING AND DEBTS
DEBTORS ANONYMOUS – 1976

We're back in New York, but nearly fifty years have passed since Bill W. walked these same streets, burdened by an unbearable weight. Amid the bustling avenues and dazzling lights of the Big Apple, a successful man roams. He is impeccably dressed in a charcoal gray wool-blend suit: tailored jacket, trousers, and vest with slightly padded shoulders and a moderately nipped-in waist to emphasize his frame. Naturally, he wears a crisp, freshly ironed shirt with a stiff collar, adorned with cufflinks featuring mother-of-pearl details. Completing the ensemble, a slim burgundy silk tie with diagonal stripes, paired with a matching pocket square. On his feet, glossy black leather Oxford shoes, topped off with a gray trench coat and a Fedora hat.

His attire strikes the perfect balance between elegance and professionalism, embodying the style of a successful businessman.

His name is John, around fifty years old, and he seems to have it all. Yet, beneath the polished surface lies a secret tearing him apart: his accounts are overdrawn, his pockets empty. He struggles to keep control of a life slipping through his fingers like sand, while his debts spiral out of control. The banks call, creditors knock on his door, and in his desperate attempt to maintain appearances, he sinks further into the darkness of financial despair.

On a cold, rainy night in 1976, our protagonist, teetering on the edge of emotional and financial bankruptcy, makes a decision that would change his life forever. Sitting in a small bar after hours of reflection and an embarrassing amount of black coffee, he realizes he needs help—not just financial aid but something deeper: psychological, spiritual support and, most importantly, a community that could understand him.

That night, John recalls a story told by his friend Gemma, who years earlier had found salvation from prescription drug addiction through a group called Narcotics Anonymous. That fellowship had offered thousands of people a way out of the chains of addiction through a simple, yet powerful program based on the Twelve Steps. Gemma had confided in him that, thanks to the program, she had made peace with her own struggles, including financial mismanagement, which had once been a nightmare for her.

Her confession had left John speechless. He had known her since childhood and had always thought of her as a kind of wonder woman—always in control, always smiling.

Gemma, a successful professional and mother of two, had lost her mother to an incurable illness when she was a child. Though she seemed to recover quickly, she carried the pain with her, pushing herself to live life to the fullest as if to ward off the same fate. "Never wait for tomorrow. If you want something, get it today," she would tell herself and anyone who dared suggest she might be overspending. "As long as I'm here, I want to give my daughters everything," she would justify.

Shopping became her refuge whenever life felt overwhelming. For a fleeting moment, purchasing something took away her fear. But this behavior led to unsustainable debt. Her financial instability strained her relationship with her daughters and turned her life into a cycle of dashed hopes and guilt. Sleep eluded her, and pills became her escape. Thankfully, Gemma eventually surrendered, stopped making excuses, and sought help. Initially, she reached out for the pills, but through the Twelve Steps program, she realized there was another compulsive behavior draining her life and wallet.

John called her, and face to face, they asked the same question that would change everything: "What if there was something similar for people crushed by debt?" That night, the dream of **Debtors Anonymous (DA)** was born.

The first DA meetings were humble, held in small apartments or church basements. Yet the simplicity of those initial gatherings masked a revolutionary power. Few, the

attendees shared similar stories—men and women overwhelmed by debt, burdened by the shame of admitting financial failure, but desperate for a fresh start.
Like all Twelve-Step groups, DA's magic lay in its approach: no judgment, no recrimination, only understanding and a path to recovery together. The DA program, modelled after the Twelve Steps, offered more than financial advice. It was an inner journey, a process enabling members to address not just material debts but also emotional and spiritual ones. Each step helped lighten the burdens of the past, teaching members to live mindfully in the present and build a financially secure future.
Over the years, DA expanded exponentially, reaching far beyond New York. Its growth responded to an increasingly consumerist world plagued by challenges like credit cards, easy loans, and the societal pressure to live beyond one's means. Yet, DA adapted, remaining a beacon of hope for those seeking a way out of the debt maze.
Today, Debtors Anonymous is an international organization with thousands of members regularly meeting to support each other in recovering from debt addiction. Its success stems from a simple yet powerful truth: debt is not just about numbers but a soul-deep ailment that can only be healed through mutual support, shared experiences, and a sincere desire to change.
The story of DA is one of collective redemption—a journey that begins with acknowledging the problem and ends with achieving financial freedom. It stands as proof that even from the darkest situations, one can emerge stronger, with a renewed understanding of oneself and the value of what truly matters. And so, while the figures of John and Gemma as DA founders are fictional, their tale represents countless lives transformed by mutual support and shared hope[9].

***

---

[9] Official site: [www.debtorsanonymous.org] (https://www.debtorsanonymous.org/)

Compulsive debt addiction, or compulsive shopping addiction, is a behavioral condition characterized by an uncontrollable urge to purchase goods or services, often beyond one's financial means, leading to the accumulation of significant debt. Those affected by this addiction feel a powerful need to buy, often as a response to emotional stress, anxiety, or depression. While the act of purchasing may bring temporary relief or pleasure, it is quickly followed by feelings of guilt, shame, and remorse.

This behavior can result in severe financial consequences, including debt, bankruptcy, and the loss of assets. Furthermore, it can harm personal and familial relationships, lead to social isolation, and, in some cases, cause legal troubles. Compulsive debt addiction is often linked to other psychological disorders, such as depression, anxiety, or additional compulsive behaviors.

Treating this addiction requires an integrated approach, which may include cognitive-behavioral therapy to address the underlying causes of the dysfunctional behavior, self-help groups, financial counseling to manage debt, and, if necessary, pharmacological support to treat any co-occurring psychological conditions.

The primary goal is to help individuals establish a healthy relationship with money, improve financial management skills, and foster emotional and relational well-being.

SEX ADDICTION
THE "S" GROUPS – 1977

It was the late 1970s, a time of significant social and cultural change. In the shadows of American cities, far from the limelight and glittering lights, a group of people gathered in quiet living rooms, parish halls, and church basements. They were not seeking redemption in the traditional sense but something deeper.

For them, one of the supreme joys of human existence—sexuality—had become a source of distress. They seemed incapable of experiencing this fundamental aspect of life in a healthy, serene, and joyful way. Instead, they were enslaved by it.

Sex and the ideas surrounding it had become demons, consuming their every thought and breath. They were prisoners of their compulsions, unable to break free from the destructive cycle that bound them to momentary, yet devastating, pleasure.

Like all members of Twelve-Step programs, they sought freedom, but in their case, it was from the invisible chains of sexual addiction.

Although the 1970s are often celebrated as the height of the sexual liberation movement, openly discussing sex was still taboo—let alone admitting to being obsessed with it!

It was in this context that Roy K., a man scarred by his own internal battles, decided to take action. He had found salvation from alcoholism through Alcoholics Anonymous and its Twelve-Step program, but his obsession with sex persisted. He had assumed and hoped that this fixation was a byproduct of his drinking. However, even after putting down the bottle, the problem of sexual addiction remained.

In 1979, Roy K. founded **Sexaholics Anonymous (SA)**, a program modeled on the principles of the Twelve Steps but applied to sexual addiction.

BEHAVIORAL ADDICTIONS: A UNIQUE CHALLENGE

Adapting the Twelve-Step program to behavioral addictions is no easy task. Substances like alcohol, drugs, psychotropics, and tobacco are external and can be entirely avoided. Compulsive behaviors, on the other hand, stem from fundamental human needs. Food is essential for survival, sexuality is vital for the continuation of the species, risk-taking is intrinsic to human evolution, and relationships are central to social life. When addiction takes root in these areas, distinguishing between what is healthy and what is destructive becomes challenging.

For those battling substance addiction, the first step is recognizing their inability to control it. The solution lies in total abstinence. As Narcotics Anonymous puts it: "One is too many, and a thousand is never enough."

Taking that first hit, drink, or cigarette triggers the cycle of obsession and compulsion. But how does one approach behaviors?

If someone is obsessed with food, they cannot stop eating altogether; if they are compulsive gamblers, they cannot avoid all risks, as these are integral to human nature.

Roy K., however, saw things differently. SA immediately set itself apart from other emerging sexual addiction groups with its stringent definition of "sexual sobriety": no sex outside of heterosexual marriage. This simple yet rigid rule would define SA's path for decades, bringing both clarity and controversy.

Roy K.'s vision recognized a fundamental characteristic of addiction: denial. To prevent the illness from taking hold, SA established very clear rules and boundaries: black or white, with no gray areas.

SAA AND THE CONCEPT OF THE THREE CIRCLES

Not everyone, however, agreed with the idea of rigid abstinence or the obligation of marriage. As SA grew, some members began to feel uneasy with its strict rules. They believed that sexual sobriety could not be defined by a single, universal standard.

In 1977, even before SA's official founding, a group of pioneers created **Sex Addicts Anonymous (SAA)**. SAA offered a more flexible approach: each member could define their own sexual sobriety based on personal experiences and needs.

The introduction of the "three circles" concept allowed members to craft a personalized recovery path.

The "three circles" framework is a tool used by SAA members to define and manage their sexual sobriety. This method organizes behaviors into three distinct categories, helping members identify which actions to avoid, monitor, and promote.

- **The Inner Circle** includes behaviors the member identifies as part of their sexual addiction, from which they must completely abstain to maintain sobriety. These might include activities like pornography use, anonymous sex, infidelity, or any other behavior deemed destructive to the member's well-being.
- **The Middle Circle** consists of behaviors that are not inherently addictive but could lead to relapse if left unchecked. These are "risky" behaviors that can act as a bridge to the inner circle. Examples might include excessive internet use or flirting.
- **The Outer Circle** comprises healthy and positive behaviors the member aims to encourage in their life. These activities help maintain balance and sobriety, such as exercising, spending time with family, pursuing hobbies, meditating, or attending support meetings.

Practical Applications

Take, for instance, someone struggling with pornography addiction.

- In the **inner circle**, they might place actions like watching pornography, participating in erotic chats, or visiting establishments with overt sexual content.

- In the **middle circle**, they might include behaviors like aimlessly browsing the internet, which could lead to exposure to explicit material.
- In the **outer circle**, they might include healthy activities like exercising or engaging in hobbies like reading or music.

For someone addicted to toxic relationships:

- The **inner circle** might include reaching out to an ex-partner from a toxic relationship.
- The **middle circle** could involve maintaining frequent contact with people who could trigger old patterns of dependence.
- The **outer circle** would promote fostering healthy, respectful relationships.

In the case of sexting or online encounters:

- The **inner circle** might include sending or receiving sexually explicit messages or joining chat rooms dedicated to such content.
- The **middle circle** could involve spending excessive time on social media without a clear purpose.
- The **outer circle** would encourage activities like setting clear boundaries with technology use.

In these examples, the "three circles" concept helps individuals clearly identify behaviors to avoid, those requiring vigilance, and those that support a balanced and healthy lifestyle.

DIVERGENT PATHS: SA AND SAA

This difference in approach marked the first major schism within the burgeoning "S" groups. While SA maintained a rigid vision of sexual sobriety, SAA embraced the complexity of addiction, acknowledging that the path to recovery is not linear but filled with nuances.

SEX AND LOVE ADDICTS ANONYMOUS (SLAA)

It soon became evident that, for some, addiction was not solely sexual but also tied to love and emotional relationships. These individuals often found themselves trapped in toxic dynamics, confusing passion with dependency and love with obsession. To address this need, **Sex and Love Addicts Anonymous (SLAA)** was founded in 1976, offering support to those struggling not only with sexual addiction but also with the destructive patterns of their relationships.

THE GREAT CONTROVERSY AND THE BIRTH OF SEXUAL RECOVERY ANONYMOUS (SRA)

In the heart of the 1990s, SA was shaken by a major controversy. Some members began to challenge SA's definition of sexual sobriety, considering it overly restrictive and exclusionary of homosexual relationships and unmarried couples. This tension reached its peak in 1991, when a group of dissenters, led by Murray R., broke away from SA to establish **Sexual Recovery Anonymous (SRA)** as a more inclusive alternative. In 1999, SA's General Assembly of Delegates clarified its stance: sexual sobriety could only be achieved within a marriage between a man and a woman. This decision, known as the **Cleveland Statement of Principle**, became a defining moment in SA's history.

Despite the tensions and divisions, the "S" groups continued to grow, offering a safe haven for thousands of individuals worldwide. Today, they remain a beacon of hope for anyone battling sexual addiction[10].

***

Sexual addiction is a complex condition characterized by a compulsive need for sexual behaviors, often accompanied by obsessive thoughts. This addiction can manifest

---

[10] Official sites:
- Sexaholics Anonymous (SA): https://www.sa.org] (https://www.sa.org)
- Sex Addicts Anonymous (SAA):
[https://saa-recovery.org] (https://saa-recovery.org)
- Sex and Love Addicts Anonymous (SLAA): [https://www.slaafws.org] (https://www.slaafws.org)
- Sexual Compulsives Anonymous (SCA):
[https://sca-recovery.org] (https://sca-recovery.org)
- Sexual Recovery Anonymous (SRA): [https://sexualrecovery.org] (https://sexualrecovery.org)
- Sexaholics Anonymous (SA)
- Sex and Love Addicts Anonymous (SLAA)

through excessive use of pornography, compulsive masturbation, constant pursuit of relationships, or promiscuous sexual behaviors.

Individuals struggling with sexual addiction may feel an irresistible urge to seek sexual gratification, often as a means of escaping emotional or psychological stress. This cycle of obsession and gratification is typically followed by feelings of guilt or shame and can lead to a deterioration in personal, professional, and social relationships.

Effective treatment for sexual addiction often involves therapeutic interventions such as cognitive-behavioral therapy, support groups, and, in some cases, pharmacological treatment.

SMOKING ADDICTION
NICOTINE ANONYMOUS – 1982

On a cold January evening in 1982, the Atlantic wind swept fiercely over the shores of Marblehead, a small fishing village in Massachusetts. Inside a modest house, a group of individuals gathered around a table, their faces reflecting the kind of determination only those who have known true suffering can understand.

These were people for whom a single cigarette had become a prison. Society saw them as second-class addicts—the "real" junkies were the ones dying with needles in their arms.

"Everyone smokes, and everyone quits. All it takes is a little willpower," they had heard countless times. Yet they knew they were trapped in a slavery that gripped not just their bodies but their very souls.

Among them was Elena, a 45-year-old woman whose youthful face was etched with pain. Her battle with cigarettes—"the blondes," as she called them—had started at 18. The daughter of a smoker and alcoholic, she had witnessed firsthand the destructive power of addiction.

The first time she bought a pack of cigarettes, an old man approached her and said, "Throw them away. They'll bring you nothing but trouble." Frightened, she obeyed, but moments later, she retrieved the pack from the trash, as if reclaiming a part of herself.

Now, facing advanced cancer, Elena sat in the group's circle to share her story. Her illness hadn't been enough to give her the strength to quit, nor had the accusing eyes of the man she loved, who suffered each time he saw her light up.

"I don't know why I can't do it," she said, her voice trembling, tears threatening to fall. "I know I should stop, but the substance calls to me. It's like a demon whispering in my ear every time I think of letting go."

The group knew all too well how insidious and tenacious tobacco addiction could be. It wasn't just a habit; it was a form of slavery that mocked their willpower and every promise they made to themselves and others.

The substance wormed its way into their brains, stimulating dopamine release and creating a fleeting, devastating sensation of pleasure.

Each member bore invisible scars, marks of a daily battle. Fighting this addiction required more than individual effort; it demanded an alliance—a community of people ready to support one another on the journey to freedom.

Their model was clear: they would follow the path of the Twelve-Step Groups.

Thus, **Smokers Anonymous** was born. The name didn't last long, though. They soon realized the problem extended beyond cigarettes—the substance took many forms, from cigars to pipes to chewing tobacco. By 1986, they decided to rename the fellowship **Nicotine Anonymous**.

This new name was a declaration of intent. The mission was simple and clear: to offer support to anyone struggling with nicotine addiction, no matter how it manifested.

In the years that followed, the movement began to spread. The first Nic-Anonymous groups sprouted like seeds of hope across the United States and, over time, crossed the Atlantic to take root in Europe.

During the 1990s, the fellowship expanded exponentially, with groups forming in Canada, the United Kingdom, Australia, and eventually Italy. This growth was fueled by a growing awareness of smoking's dangers and people's determination to break free from nicotine for good.

Success, however, was not guaranteed. The road to freedom was long and fraught with challenges, but those who chose to embark on it knew they weren't alone.

Meetings grew in number and participation. Each gathering became an opportunity to share stories, fears, successes, and failures.

People sat in a circle, creating a safe space to open up without fear of judgment. It was a place where suffering found understanding and hope was renewed—a refuge where words became an anthem to resilience.

This was about more than just quitting smoking. It was about transforming one's life with the support of a group that truly understood the struggle against an inner demon. Each meeting brimmed with stories of challenge and victory, of setbacks and recoveries, but above all, of a steady journey toward freedom.

Over time, Nicotine Anonymous solidified itself as a beacon of hope for anyone seeking to break the chains of addiction. Its principles remained rooted in the Twelve Steps and Twelve Traditions that had guided generations toward sobriety from alcohol, drugs, and dysfunctional behaviors—now adapted for the fight against nicotine.

Today, Nicotine Anonymous is a global community, a network of support stretching across continents and cultures, uniting people of all ages and backgrounds in a common struggle.

Every day, somewhere in the world, a Nicotine Anonymous group meets—whether in person or online—to share experiences, strength, and hope. These meetings are the lifeblood of the fellowship.

And so, Nicotine Anonymous continues its journey, offering a safe haven to anyone choosing to walk the challenging path toward freedom and self-care[11].

***

Tobacco addiction is a chronic dependence characterized by the compulsive use of tobacco, often in the form of cigarettes, cigars, or chewing tobacco. Nicotine, the primary active component in tobacco, acts on the central nervous system by stimulating the release of dopamine, a neurotransmitter associated with pleasure and reward.

---

[11] [Nicotine Anonymous] (https://nicotine-anonymous.org/)

This addiction involves not only a strong physical and psychological compulsion but also serious health risks, including heart disease, respiratory disorders, and various forms of cancer.

Tobacco addiction is classified as a chronic, relapsing disease that requires an integrated and often multidisciplinary approach for effective treatment.

WORK ADDICTION
WORKAHOLICS ANONYMOUS – 1983

In 1983, in a city as iconic and dynamic as San Francisco, where winding streets reflect the constant motion and energy of urban life, a quiet revolution was about to take shape—not within the walls of a major corporation but deep in the minds of those exhausted by the weight of work, seeking a way out.

San Francisco, with its towering skyscrapers, bustling cafés, and breathtaking views of the bay, was a place where success seemed to be the only currency for happiness. It was the city of dreamers, innovators, and also workaholics—people for whom work was not just a means of survival but a refuge, an obsession.

Amid this energetic landscape, two individuals—whose identities remain private in accordance with the anonymity they would soon embrace—began to realize that their love for work had become something darker, a demon consuming them from within.

They could no longer enjoy life's simple pleasures; personal relationships, health, and even inner peace had been sacrificed at the altar of productivity. Yet, amid the whirlwind of deadlines and responsibilities, they knew they couldn't go on like this.

One quiet evening in June, as the city was slowly enveloped in fog, creating an almost mystical atmosphere, they sat together to discuss their condition. In a small apartment in the heart of San Francisco, with a window overlooking the city illuminated by streetlights, they spoke at length about their fears, their pain, and their desperate need to find balance.

It was in that moment, against the muffled sounds of passing cars and distant voices echoing through the night, that the idea of **Workaholics Anonymous** was born.

Both individuals were already involved in, or had friends participating in, other Twelve-Step Groups. They were convinced that the recovery model envisioned by Bill W. and Dr. Bob could also be applied to other forms of addiction, including work addiction.

Adapting the Twelve Steps to address work addiction wasn't unprecedented—and it had already proven successful in other contexts.

What was clear to these pioneers was that they wanted more than just freedom from work addiction. They wanted to learn how to live a true, liberated life.

Thus, 1983 became the year **Workaholics Anonymous (WA)** officially came into existence. The organization was founded to help those caught in the spiral of compulsive overworking, offering a program based on the Twelve Steps, similar to Alcoholics Anonymous but tailored to the specific challenges of excessive dedication to work.

The first meeting took place in a small living room, with just a handful of people sitting around a well-worn wooden table. A soft light created an intimate and welcoming atmosphere, and for the first time, these weary faces found the courage to speak openly about their struggles.

Some shared how they could no longer sleep peacefully; others admitted to growing distant from their loved ones. One person, tears streaming, confessed they had lost all interest in life outside of work.

But that evening wasn't just about problems—it was about hope. The air was charged with a new energy, a mix of relief and determination. Each word spoken seemed to resonate deeply with everyone in the room, like an echo carrying the promise of a different, healthier, more balanced future.

From those tentative first steps, Workaholics Anonymous began to expand—slowly at first, then more rapidly. Word of the new group spread quickly, like a fresh breeze sweeping through a room that had been closed for too long. The idea of finding help and support for an often-overlooked addiction—one even celebrated as a virtue—started to take root in the minds and hearts of many.

Workaholics Anonymous remains a beacon of hope for those seeking a balance between personal and professional life.
Today, the organization operates in numerous countries, with groups meeting regularly to share experiences, support one another, and walk together on a path toward a life where work is just one part of existence, no longer its all-consuming center. Globally, the movement includes approximately 175 active groups spread across various nations[12].

***

Work addiction (workaholism) is a psychological condition characterized by excessive and compulsive involvement in work activities, often at the expense of physical and mental health and social relationships. This addiction is driven by an internal need to achieve results, fueled by anxiety, perfectionism, or low self-esteem, and involves an inability to disconnect from work. Work addiction is associated with negative effects, including chronic stress, burnout, sleep disorders, and relational issues, and requires targeted therapeutic intervention for effective management.

[12] Official site [www.workaholics-anonymous.org] (https://www.workaholics-anonymous.org)

RELATIONAL ADDICTIONS
CODEPENDENTS ANONYMOUS – 1986

In 1986, amid a world shaken by Gorbachev's perestroika and the Chernobyl disaster, a movement was taking shape in the United States that would profoundly impact countless lives: **Co-Dependents Anonymous (Co-DA)**.

Ken and Mary Richardson, a couple deeply immersed in the Twelve-Step movements of Alcoholics Anonymous (A.A.) and Al-Anon, recognized an unaddressed need. Many people were struggling not only with substance addiction but also with relationships that seemed to consume them. They identified two interrelated forms of suffering: emotional dependency and "co-dependency."

Ken and Mary were not just advocates of the Twelve Steps; they embodied a genuine commitment to recovery and helping others. Mary, a spirited and warm woman with a fighting soul, and Ken, a thoughtful and reserved man, had both faced profound personal challenges and understood the pain of being trapped in toxic relational dynamics.

Moved by their own experiences and deep empathy for others' struggles, the Richardson duo decided to create a fellowship that could offer refuge and guidance for those feeling ensnared in painful relationships.

On October 22, 1986, in the warm city of Phoenix, Arizona, the first **Co-Dependents Anonymous** meeting was held—a milestone that marked the beginning of a transformative journey for many. Thirty people attended the initial meeting, but within weeks, the numbers grew rapidly, exceeding one hundred participants and leading to the formation of 120 groups nationwide by the end of the year.

In 1987, CoDA held its first National Service Conference, gathering representatives from seven states. This event marked the beginning of a movement that would eventually expand far beyond American borders.

The concept of co-dependency, already present in psychological discussions, gained widespread recognition with

the publication of Melody Beattie's **Codependent No More**, a book that provided a framework for understanding relational dynamics. Stories of those who found the courage to change, escape unhealthy relationships, and rediscover their self-worth inspired thousands to seek help.
Today, **Co-Dependents Anonymous** is active in over 60 countries, with thousands of groups offering support to individuals seeking healthier, more authentic relationships.
The story of Co-Dependents Anonymous, born from the courage and compassion of the Richardsons, stands as a testament to resilience and self-discovery. It has provided countless individuals with the tools to reclaim their lives and build healthier, more meaningful relationships[13].

***

Co-dependency and emotional dependence are two conditions often confused but distinct in their characteristics. Both manifest in dysfunctional relationships and can lead to significant suffering, yet co-dependency is a more complex and nuanced dynamic compared to emotional dependence.
The term **co-dependency** originally described individuals living alongside those with substance addictions, such as alcohol or drugs. In these contexts, the partner or family member of an addicted person often developed a form of "indirect" dependency, unconsciously adopting the role of "savior" or "martyr" within the relationship. A codependent person tends to prioritize the other's needs above their own, sacrificing themselves and deriving a sense of personal worth from helping or "saving" their loved one. This tendency can persist even in the absence of substance addiction, as those suffering from co-dependency are often drawn to individuals with problematic or destructive behaviors.
Emotional dependence, on the other hand, is a more straightforward form of excessive attachment. Here, the

---

13 CoDA, official site: [coda.org] (https://coda.org).

primary need is not to save or improve the other person but to feel loved in order to fill a personal void. In a symbiotic emotional relationship, the dependent individual obsessively seeks confirmation of the other's love, fearing abandonment and living in constant insecurity. Unlike codependency, emotional dependence focuses on the need to have the other person close as a source of reassurance and validation.

What distinguishes these conditions is their different orientation toward self and others: the codependent sacrifices themselves to help the other, while the emotionally dependent person is driven by the need to be loved, not necessarily to save.

Both conditions can arise from difficult relational contexts, but co-dependency often has roots in environments involving substance addiction or destructive behaviors. In either case, both co-dependency and emotional dependence involve placing excessive value on external approval, necessitating a journey of self-awareness and healing through self-help groups or specialized therapies.

INTERNET AND DEVICE ADDICTION
ITAA ANONYMOUS – 2017

In 2017, amid the towering skyscrapers of New York that rose toward the sky like antennas of an interconnected world, an unexpected realization was dawning. The world seemed wrapped in a web of invisible threads that, instead of uniting, began to suffocate. Every notification, every blue light from a screen, every like became a small seal of isolation. In this digital jungle, two faces stood out: Alex and Jamie. They were young, accomplished, and the epitome of a modern dream with dynamic careers and seemingly perfect social lives. Yet, behind the screen, this endless connectivity began to reveal a darker side: a sense of emptiness, sleepless nights, and relationships drained of meaning.

Alex, a programmer with unstoppable creative energy, found his days consumed by a whirlwind of notifications. Every break became an immersion in videos, and every real conversation turned into a quick exchange of soulless messages. Jamie, a freelance journalist, discovered the weight of "likes" as a measure of worth, with moods tied to the unstable carousel of virtual approval. Both felt an internal fracture, as if that digital web was separating them from their authentic selves.

One day, fate brought them together at a quiet Brooklyn café hosting a digital mindfulness workshop. The soft lighting and aroma of roasted coffee created an intimate setting, perfect for breaking the hyper-technological routine and reflecting deeply. There, sharing their stories, Alex and Jamie realized they were not alone in their struggle against the relentless pull of technology. Something new was beginning to take shape—something that could save them and others.

Inspired by the Twelve-Step programs that had freed millions from addiction, they envisioned a similar path for those suffering from technological dependence. They believed this structured and proven framework could be adapted to tackle the challenges of digital addiction, creating a journey of healing based on awareness, sharing, and mutual support.

On a crisp autumn evening in 2017, in a small room in the heart of Manhattan, the first meeting of what would become **Internet and Technology Addicts Anonymous (ITAA)** took place. Despite the light rain outside, a dozen people attended. The room, simple and welcoming with chairs arranged in a circle, soon filled with stories and confessions. Isolation, loss of real-life connections, neglect of responsibilities in favor of screen time—each person shared a complicated relationship with technology, all bound together by a thin thread of hope.

The Twelve Steps were adapted to address the risks of digital overuse, focusing on self-reflection, acceptance, and mindful action. Each member was encouraged to acknowledge their powerlessness over digital dependency and build a balanced, conscious relationship with technology through the supportive community.

The voice of ITAA began to spread, initially through word of mouth and later with a targeted online presence. Before long, other groups emerged, from Los Angeles to Chicago, eventually crossing U.S. borders to reach Europe, Asia, and beyond.

Today, ITAA boasts thousands of active groups worldwide and stands as a story of modern awareness—a testament to how, in a world connected to excess, true strength still lies in genuine human relationships and community support[14].

***

La dipendenza da internet e dispositivi digitali è una condizione psicologica caratterizzata da un uso eccessivo e

[14] Official website: [www.internetaddictsanonymous.org] (https://internetaddictsanonymous.org)

compulsivo di internet e dispositivi digitali, come smartphone, computer e tablet. Questo comportamento interferisce con la vita quotidiana, provocando un isolamento sociale, riduzione delle performance lavorative o scolastiche, e disturbi del sonno.
La dipendenza è spesso associata a un bisogno compulsivo di connettersi online, giocare, o utilizzare social media, e può portare a sintomi di astinenza quando l'accesso è limitato. La gestione della dipendenza può richiedere interventi psicologici e comportamentali specifici.

THE INTERTWINING CHAINS
POLYSUBSTANCE ADDICTION

In the hidden folds of the city, amidst dim lights and anonymous staircases, stories of invisible battles unfold. People fighting not just against one addiction but against an intricate web of ties and habits tightening around them.

It was from this urgent need for freedom that, in the late 1980s, a new necessity arose: to create space for those seeking to break not just one, but many chains. This is how the first groups for individuals facing **polyaddiction** came to be.

Within Twelve-Step associations, however, there is no official fellowship dedicated exclusively to those struggling with multiple addictions. Each group continues to focus on specific issues: alcohol for Alcoholics Anonymous, all mood- and mind-altering substances for Narcotics Anonymous, gambling for Gamblers Anonymous, and so on.

For those needing broader support, "mixed" meetings or specialized groups exist to welcome individuals facing **polyaddiction** simultaneously, adapting the Twelve Steps to address their complex needs.

In places without shared meeting locations, individual Twelve-Step groups welcome anyone seeking help, regardless of their addiction, often suggesting they substitute words like "alcohol," "drugs," or "gambling" with terms reflecting their specific struggle. From there, individuals can connect with the group best suited to their needs.

Globally, official mixed groups are not yet recognized, but the demand for support among those dealing with **polyaddiction** is increasingly evident.

Looking ahead, it's likely these communities will evolve and expand to address new challenges. Already, support groups and associations continue to grow, offering refuge to those who previously found no answers elsewhere. They demonstrate that, even when addictions multiply, a path to freedom always exists.

The Twelve-Step community and its program remain a safe harbor, a steadfast support for anyone ready to break even the deepest chains.

***

Polydisorder addiction is like a tangle of chains that envelops those who suffer from it, making every step toward freedom an arduous task. Imagine trying to break a single chain that's already strong; now multiply it by three, four, or even five. This is what living with multiple addictions feels like: each chain represents a substance or behavior, all interconnected in a complex knot that seems impossible to unravel.

Science recognizes that polysubstance addiction is neither an isolated case nor an exception—it is a common and well-documented reality. It's not just about alcohol, drugs, or nicotine but also compulsive behaviors like gambling or shopping. The **American Psychiatric Association (APA)**, in its DSM-5, classifies these conditions as substance use and behavioral disorders, and their co-occurrence makes treatment an even greater challenge.

On a neurobiological level, the brain of someone with polysubstance addiction is like an "addiction superhighway," where various substances and behaviors overlap, stimulating the pleasure and reward circuits. Dopamine release—the same chemical that makes us feel good after a run or a satisfying meal—becomes a chemical trap that is hard to escape. The combined effects of polysubstance addiction can be devastating: physical health problems, psychological disorders like anxiety and depression, and an increased risk of overdose.

However, not all is lost. Although treating polysubstance addiction requires an integrated approach that addresses all present addictions, the good news is that effective strategies exist. These include a combination of behavioral therapy, pharmacological interventions, and continuous social support.

Personalized treatment is essential because every individual presents unique addiction dynamics. Recent studies show that polyaddiction is common among those with severe dependencies. For example, someone addicted to alcohol can easily develop a dependence on nicotine or stimulant drugs, complicating the treatment further.
Research is exploring innovative solutions, such as medications that target multiple brain receptors involved in different addictions, and treatment models that integrate pharmacological and psychotherapeutic aspects.
Polysubstance addiction represents one of the most complex challenges in the field of mental health and addiction. Yet, thanks to support groups and targeted therapeutic strategies, there is hope. Despite the long and difficult struggle, community and mutual support offer a path to recovery. In a world that often promotes excess, it is reassuring to know that, with the right help, even the most intricate chains can be broken, one step at a time.

THE SILENT STRUGGLE OF FAMILIES: **SUPPORT GROUPS FOR RELATIVES**

Addiction doesn't only affect those who suffer from it directly; its devastating effects also ripple through families, creating a whirlwind of pain, frustration, and helplessness. Families grappling with the addiction of a loved one face an immense challenge, often in silence, trying to maintain balance in a situation that seems on the verge of collapse. When a family member is addicted to alcohol, drugs, gambling, or other forms of dependency, the home can become a place of constant tension. Parents, spouses, children, and siblings must confront not only the destructive behaviors of their loved one but also their own fears, guilt, and anxieties.

It is common for family members to feel isolated, misunderstood, and unequipped to handle the situation, which deepens their sense of despair.

In this context, Twelve-Step self-help groups for the relatives and friends of people with addictions offer a vital lifeline.

AL-ANON AND LOIS WILSON'S INSIGHT: THE WIFE OF BILL WILSON

Among the most well-known and widespread international groups is **Al-Anon**, an association founded in 1951 in the United States to support the families of alcoholics. Al-Anon follows the principles of the Twelve Steps, similar to those adopted by Alcoholics Anonymous, but tailored to the specific needs of family members.

Al-Anon provides a safe space where relatives can share their experiences, learn to better manage their situations, and find mutual support.

The support program for family members and friends of alcoholics was founded by **Lois Wilson**, the wife of Bill Wilson, one of the co-founders of Alcoholics Anonymous

(AA). Lois Wilson established Al-Anon in 1951, recognizing that the families of alcoholics needed their own space to share experiences and find support. While alcoholics had AA, their families often struggled alone with the effects of the disease.
Together with **Anne Bingham** and other women with similar experiences, Lois created this group, which has since become an international point of reference.

FOR FAMILIES OF SUBSTANCE DEPENDENTS: NAR-ANON AND FAMILIES ANONYMOUS

In addition to Al-Anon, there is **Nar-Anon**, founded in 1968, which supports the families and friends of people addicted to drugs. Like Al-Anon, Nar-Anon provides support based on the Twelve Steps, offering a community that understands the challenges of living alongside someone with a substance dependency. These groups, present in many cities and online, make support accessible to anyone in need. Nar-Anon is also active in Italy, though it is less widespread than Al-Anon.
Families Anonymous (FA) is a self-help association established to support the families and friends of individuals with substance addictions or compulsive behaviors. Linked to the Twelve-Step program of Narcotics Anonymous (NA), FA is dedicated to those experiencing the indirect impact of others' addictions, creating a safe space for sharing experiences, discovering new strategies to navigate daily challenges, and finding the support of a compassionate community.
Through regular meetings, FA members can freely express their concerns and the challenges of living with a dependent loved one. The program helps participants develop resilience and practice "emotional detachment," learning to recognize their own needs and avoid sacrificing their wellbeing. FA offers a space for sharing and growth for anyone wishing to build a healthy balance and maintain serenity, even in the context of family addiction.

ALATEEN AND NARATEEN: SUPPORT FOR THE CHILDREN OF ADDICTS

For the children of alcoholics or drug addicts, groups like **Alateen** and **Narateen**—extensions of Al-Anon and Nar-Anon—provide a safe space to talk about their experiences and find support among peers facing similar situations.

ACA AND ACOA: WHEN WOUNDS DON'T HEAL

The groups **ACA (Adult Children of Alcoholics)** and **ACOA (Adult Children of Alcoholics and Dysfunctional Families)** focus on supporting adults who grew up in dysfunctional families or with addicted parents. They offer assistance to those who, as adults, struggle with emotional and relational difficulties stemming from problematic childhood environments. ACA has been active in Italy since the 1990s, with groups providing a space for sharing and addressing challenges linked to growing up in such contexts.

GAM-ANON: A LIGHT FOR FAMILIES IN THE GAMBLING SPIRAL

Gam-Anon is a self-help group for the families and friends of compulsive gamblers. Associated with **Gamblers Anonymous (GA)**, it follows the Twelve Steps and helps relatives recognize codependent behaviors and establish healthy boundaries.

FAMILIES OF THE "S" GROUPS

S-Anon, a mutual-help group for the families of individuals with sexual addiction, is affiliated with **Sexaholics Anonymous (SA)** and follows the Twelve Steps. **COSA (Codependents of Sex Addicts)** provides similar support for those in relationships with individuals suffering from sexual addiction, helping them set boundaries and rebuild their self-esteem. While **S-Anon** and **COSA** are not widely present in Italy, online meetings are available for those seeking support.

SUMMING UP

There are many Twelve-Step self-help groups designed for the families of individuals with addictions. In Italy, groups like **Al-Anon**, **Nar-Anon**, **Families Anonymous**, and **Alateen** are active in many cities, offering support to thousands of families.

Through mutual support, participants learn to care for themselves, set healthy boundaries, and find peace even amidst the storm of addiction. These groups are an essential resource for families, helping them break the cycle of co-dependency and develop strategies for managing the situation in a balanced way.

Sharing pain and solutions with people who truly understand what it means to live alongside someone with addiction can profoundly transform the lives of participants, allowing them to regain serenity and trust in the future[15].

---

[15] Web sites:

Al-Anon Family Groups: [www.al-anon.org] (https://al-anon.org/)
Nar-Anon Family Groups: [www.nar-anon.org]
Alateen [www.al-anon.org/for-members/group-resources/alateen]
[www.al-anon.it/alateen] (https://www.al-anon.it/alateen/)
ACA (Adult Children of Alcoholics) e **ACOA**
(Adult Children of Alcoholics and Dysfunctional Families)
[www.adultchildren.org] (https://adultchildren.org/)
Gam-Anon [www.gamanon.it] (http://www.gamanon.it/)
S-Anon e COSA (Codependents of Sex Addicts)
- Sito Internazionale di S-Anon: [www.sanon.org] (https://www.sanon.org/)
- Sito Internazionale di COSA:
[www.cosa-recovery.org] (https://www.cosa-recovery.org/)

ACKNOWLEDGMENTS

A heartfelt thank you to the Twelve-Step associations, tireless guardians of a message of hope that transforms fragility into strength. Thank you for your dedication, for shedding light on the disease of addiction, and for the courage to be witnesses to rebirth.
A collective thanks to everyone, and a special one to those who generously shared their experiences: your stories have been the beating heart of these pages, essential in bringing this book to life.
Equally heartfelt gratitude goes to the professionals and social workers who enriched this journey with their invaluable contributions and expertise. Your support has been fundamental and deserves deep recognition.
A special thanks to **Teodolinda Gasparrini** for shaping the beauty of the cover, turning an idea into something tangible and unique.
Finally, my deepest gratitude to my life partner, **Gaetano**, who patiently supported and endured me as I followed the sacred fire of writing, and to my family: my mother **Marisa**, my brother **Vittorio**, and my father **Donato**. Without you, none of this would have been possible.

Sommario

www.ingramcontent.com/pod-product-compliance
Lightning Source LLC
Chambersburg PA
CBHW051244250726
48656CB00004B/1122

* 9 7 9 8 3 0 2 0 3 2 6 5 2 *